Contents

List of Illustrations   vii

Acknowledgments   xi

Introduction   1

PART 1: YORKSHIRE SLAVE OWNERS

Chapter 1   Eighteenth-Century Yorkshire   7

Chapter 2   The Slave Trade   17

Chapter 3   Yorkshire and Slavery   25

Chapter 4   East Yorkshire Slave Owners and Traders   35

Chapter 5   West Yorkshire Slave Owners and Traders   39

Chapter 6   North Yorkshire Slave Owners and Traders   49

Chapter 7   Wakefield, Capital of Slavery   53

Chapter 8   Kith and Kin   69

Chapter 9   Island Governance   91

Chapter 10   Yorkshire and the Slave Trade   95

PART 2: AFRICANS IN YORKSHIRE

Chapter 11   Slaves in Yorkshire?   101

Chapter 12   Free Black People in Yorkshire   113

PART 3: ABOLITION

Chapter 13   The Road to Abolition   127

Chapter 14   Abolition Round 1   139

Chapter 15   Yorkshire for Abolition   149

Chapter 16   Abolition Round 2   173

Chapter 17   State-Sponsored Terror   191

Chapter 18   Abolition!   203

Chapter 19   Yorkshire and the Abolition of Slavery   211

Conclusion   223

Notes   229

Bibliography   255

Index   261

THE BATTLE AGAINST SLAVERY

THE BATTLE AGAINST SLAVERY

THE UNTOLD STORY OF HOW A GROUP OF YORKSHIRE RADICALS BEGAN THE WAR TO END THE SLAVE TRADE

Paul L. Dawson

FRONTLINE
BOOKS

THE BATTLE AGAINST SLAVERY
The Untold Story of How a Group of Yorkshire Radicals
Began the War to End the Slave Trade

First published in 2022 by Frontline Books,
an imprint of Pen & Sword Books Ltd, Yorkshire – Philadelphia

Copyright © Paul L. Dawson 2022
ISBN: 9781399018487

Printed and bound by CPI Group (UK) Ltd, Croydon CR0 4YY

Pen & Sword Books Ltd incorporates the imprints of Pen & Sword Archaeology,
Air World Books, Atlas, Aviation, Battleground, Discovery, Family History,
History, Maritime, Military, Naval, Politics, Social History, Transport,
True Crime, Claymore Press, Frontline Books, Praetorian Press, Seaforth
Publishing and White Owl

For a complete list of Pen & Sword titles please contact:

PEN & SWORD BOOKS LTD
47 Church Street, Barnsley, South Yorkshire, S70 2AS, UK.
E-mail: enquiries@pen-and-sword.co.uk
Website: www.pen-and-sword.co.uk

Or

PEN AND SWORD BOOKS,
1950 Lawrence Roadd, Havertown, PA 19083, USA
E-mail: Uspen-and-sword@casematepublishers.com
Website: www.penandswordbooks.com

List of Illustrations

1. David Hartley MP. The largely forgotten founder of Yorkshire abolitionism in 1776.
2. The Rev. William Turner, minister of Westgate Chapel 1761–94.
3. The Rev. Thomas Johnstone, assistant minister of Westgate Chapel 1792–4, and minister till 1834.
4. The gravestone of Thomas Lang, chairman of the Wakefield Committee for the Abolition of the Slave Trade in 1788. He was a lifelong Unitarian, attending Westgate Chapel, where he is buried.
5. Daniel Gaskell, first MP for the enfranchised town of Wakefield.
6. The Rev. Dr Joseph Priestley, Minister of Mill Hill Unitarian Chapel in Leeds.
7. Major John Cartwright, abolitionist and political reformer, founded the Society for Constitutional Information in 1780.
8. John Milnes aka 'Jack Milnes the Democrat'.
9. Richard Slater Milnes, Whig MP for York 1784–1802.
10. The interior of Westgate Chapel, Wakefield as it was when Rev. William Turner thundered his denunciation of slavery in December 1776.
11. Walter Ramsden Fawkes, MP for Yorkshire 1806–07, left-wing Whig and ardent abolitionist.
12. Robert Prescott, Deputy Governor General of Lower Canada.
13. The Rev. Dr Coulthurst, vicar of Halifax, founder of Halifax Dispensary, and slave owner.
14. Cobblers Hall, Heath, Wakefield.
15. Westgate Chapel, Wakefield.
16. The Wakefield headquarters of the Aire and Calder Navigation Company.
17. The Wakefield home of the hugely wealthy slave trader Francis Ingram.

18. The banking premises of Milnes & Heywood on Burton Street, Wakefield.
19. Wentworth House, Wakefield.
20. The Rev. Richard Munkhouse, vicar of the newly-built and fashionable St John's Church in Wakefield.
21. Burney Tops House, Wakefield, home of members of the slave-owning Charnock family.
22. South Parade, Wakefield.
23. Interior of Wakefield Parish Church, now the Cathedral, c.1870.
24. Normanton Parish Church.
25. Kirby Misperton Parish Church
26. Shibden Hall near Halifax.
27. George Kirlew.
28. The funerary monument to Ebenezer Robertson.
29. The grave of Margaret Boghurst.
30. Memorial to Betsy Sawyer, a freed slave who lived in Leeds.
31. Northgate End Unitarian Chapel, Halifax.
32. Mill Hill Unitarian Chapel, Leeds.
33. Nostell Priory, home of Sir Rowland Winn who endeavoured to exchange 'a black boy' for a loaf of bread.
34. Henry Redhead Yorke.
35. Holy Trinity Parish Church, Wentworth.
36. St Giles Parish Church, Pontefract.

To Kate and John

With this, my 40th book, I must mark a debt of gratitude to the support and encouragement of Kate Taylor MBE and John Goodchild M. Univ, without which I would not have been a historian. Kate's support in publishing my first essay in 1997 as well as teaching the rudiments of archive research, ably assisted by John, set me on my life course. I am indebted to you.

Acknowledgements

Having written half a dozen books on Wakefield, I was aware of Francis Ingram the slave trader. What came as a surprise was how integrated my home city was into the slave economy of the eighteenth and early nineteenth century.

Little did I realise, as the research of this story progressed, that I would be sitting at my desk in a house built on what was once the pleasure gardens for a slave-owning family, with the home of a daughter-in-law of a slave owner less than 50 yards away. The 'Grove' in Wakefield was built by 1750 on the profits from slavery and the wool trade. By 1786 its extensive gardens were opened up as a new Georgian housing development called 'West Burney Tops House'; today this is now South Parade. The 'Grove' was home to Richard Brown, a runaway slave and servant to the Charnock family – he would have known my home town intimately, no doubt whilst being promenaded around the town as a sign of the wealth and prestige of his master. The sad truth is, a slave would have served his master in my front garden.

The past is a foreign country and we cannot do anything to change the past. What we can do is shine a light of illumination on the darker corners of history, to bring out the forgotten story of slaves in Yorkshire and slave owners and traders from Yorkshire. As both a Yorkshireman and Unitarian, I am proud of what my forebears in faith achieved. Unitarians have long been overlooked for their contribution to abolition. This book seeks to tell the story of slaves in Yorkshire, and how a group of radical reformists sought to change the world.

I must thank Elizabeth Usher for her friendship, and critical comment on my thinking. I must also thank the Yorkshire Unitarian Engagement and Research Group for the support and interest from fellow Unitarians from Yorkshire and further field. My twin, Anthony, must also be thanked for his editorial input and oversight of this project.

This is a story I am passionate about, and one that I am hugely biased over. I first came into contact with Unitarians in 1997 thanks to Kate Taylor MBE and John Goodchild M Univ. These two friends, my twin Anthony will freely admit as well, were of the greatest influence on our lives in becoming historians with strings of published books to our names, but also in becoming Unitarian Lay Ministers. Without the support of John and Kate to continue our endeavours as historians, and to put into print our first essays when we were still teenagers with a glowing reference for our future endeavours in history, this book perhaps would not have been written, and no doubt we may never had heard of Unitarians. John always said that Westgate Chapel in Wakefield was one of the most important dissenting chapels in the country – this is a story that vindicates his statement. In researching the story, I have come to know many of the lead characters, none more so than Jack Milnes the Democrat, Tommy Johnstone and Goodwyn Barmby. I have told this story perhaps 200 times in person whilst conducting tours of the Milnes family vault beneath Westgate Chapel. I am proud and passionate of my ancestors in faith, their lives above all their legacy that they fought for that, in a small way, helped make the modern world which we enjoy.

Paul L. Dawson BSc Hons MRes MIFA FINS
Wakefield
1 December 2020

Introduction

1 3,813
13,813 men women and children.
Grandmothers, nursing mothers, aged grandfathers, young bucks.
People. Living breathing people.

All slaves. All owned by Yorkshire men and women in 1833.

Our horrific number is generated from work undertaken by University College London (UCL) and the Legacies of British Slave Ownership Database. To put thus ghastly figure into context, the North Yorkshire market town of Malton based on the 2011 Census has a population of 13,000. UCL records eighty-eight persons with interests in the slave trade or slave plantations, with thirty as actually owning slaves at abolition, receiving a total compensation sum of well over £300,000, equating in 2020 to roughly £39,000,000!

How was it possible that the population of a modern-day market town could be owned by just thirty Yorkshire men and women?

Simply put, because it was legal.

Yet another figure looms large in our story.

265,184

All men, women and children dragged from their homes in Africa and transported to the West Indies by just three men and their family from my home city of Wakefield which has in 2020 a population of around 100,000. How has the story of my home city ignored this act? As I researched the story of slavery in Yorkshire, little did I realise I would uncover this vast multitude of people stolen from their homes by Yorkshire folk or realise Wakefield was a regional centre for slavery in the eighteenth century!

How was this possible? Simply because it was legal.

This book sets out to tell the story of a group of men and women, who were slave owners and traders and 'theological negroes'[1] who fought to rid the country of slavery: these 'slaves to conscience' were a group of religious radicals, known today as Unitarians.

It is morally and intellectually supreme that in order to understand the past, we must encompass understandings based on the experiences of people from every social background and to exclude no one. Any approach to the past that neglects this fundamental truth is flawed. The human past is common to us all: it is not a fixed single narrative. It is multi-vocal. History changes, it is fluid and mobile. The past is not set in stone, and what is taught in schools or as accepted as 'set in stone', to quote Napoléon Bonaparte, 'is a set of lies we can all agree on'. Indeed, too often the story of the past is often told from a white background, largely from the government's/establishment's perspective. The story of Yorkshire, and the country as a whole, as has been neglectful of Black and Minority Ethnic (BAME) stories. The following few chapters I hope are a spring board for exploring black history in Yorkshire, as well as further afield. I also hope to spur interest into the direct legacy of the slave trade on real lives. The widest possible discussion and reflection are needed of our past to make it representative of the country as it was and is today: the past is easily used for social, ideological, religious and cultural memes both good and bad. To make our story inclusive, there has to be an acknowledgment, discussion and reflection of the past about those written out of history; only then will we achieve full inclusivity and understanding in history and heritage. To investigate the BAME community history around us and the impact of slavery on our communities is not 're-writing history'; it is presenting the stories from those around us who have been marginalised and forgotten with the homogenising of the past. The next few chapters are a glimpse into a forgotten part of Yorkshire's history and need to be seen as the springboard for more research into the diverse cultural history of the county. The diversity of culture, religion and ethnicity has been by and large edited from the past, along with the cultural legacies of the slave trade and slavery.

It is far too easy to forget that 200 years before the Windrush Generation arrived in the 1950s Africans already lived and loved in Yorkshire; they contributed to society at large and helped make the world a more equal and just place. Yorkshire has not been 'white Anglo-Saxon' as racists like to think. Two thousand years ago, the Roman city of Eboracum would have been home to black people: we know this as the skeletons of black people from the Roman city have been excavated, as well as skeletons of people from the Middle East at Driffield Terrace, where I was part of the excavation team. Indeed, black Vikings lived in Yorvik as their skeletal remains attest to; as a field archaeologist, I excavated the grave of a twelfth-century black person in the centre of York; people from Africa served on the *Mary Rose*. Our communities have been diverse for centuries.

These chapters are a starting point to reclaim the stories of these forgotten communities from the 'homogenised past' and recover African and Indian histories in Yorkshire: the further exploration of our diverse cultural heritage will add to the understanding of and respect for humanity and our communities as a whole. The widest possible terms of discussion are needed in order to achieve full inclusivity in understanding our past, as is practical action to follow up this research and to learn more about our diverse communities across Yorkshire. Bringing the stories of African, Indian and woman back to life does not in any diminish the history of Yorkshire, it adds greatly to the whole. Yet we have selectively edited out from our museums and cultural conscience that Africans and Indians lived in Yorkshire for hundreds if not thousands of years, either through indifference, ignorance or, simply put, racism. Black history was central to the making of Yorkshire for 2,000 years. Wakefield in the 1880s was home to the Brown family, who lived in fashionable South Parade and ran a successful brass foundry. They were black.

Our story is split into three complementary parts: first, the place of the slave trade in eighteenth-century Yorkshire and those Yorkshire men and women who owned and traded slaves. In the second part we look at Africans and Indians in Yorkshire in the eighteenth and early nineteenth century. In our third part, we concentrate on those Yorkshire men and women who helped contribute to the abolition of the slave trade and slavery. The story of abolition concentrates on a core group of no more than half-a-dozen Unitarians: two were ministers of religion – Thomas Johnstone and William Turner – the others were firebrand radicals: John Milnes, Henry Redhead Yorke, Robert Bakewell and Joseph Gales. These men sought to change the world. On a personal note, researching this book has made me inordinately proud of my forebears: I feel privileged to have led divine service from the same pulpit at Westgate Chapel Wakefield, as used by the Revs William Turner, Thomas Johnstone and Goodwyn Barmby; to have read the lesson from Rev. Johnstone's translation of the Bible; and to have worshipped in the same space as Esther Milnes, Rachel Milnes, Richard Slater 'Dick' Milnes and all the Milnes family who did much to make the world a better place, as we shall see.

These men and women were Unitarians like myself: ours is an open-minded and individualistic approach to religion that gives scope for a very wide range of beliefs and doubts: it has no creed or formal

3

statement of belief. Unitarians deny the divinity of Jesus and the Trinity, hence Unitarian rather than Trinitarian. Religious freedom for each individual is at the heart of Unitarianism. Everyone is free to search for meaning in life in a responsible way and to reach their own conclusions. As Unitarians, we see diversity and pluralism as valuable rather than threatening. We see religion to be broad, inclusive and tolerant. The roots of the Unitarian movement lie mainly in the Reformation of the sixteenth century. At that time people in many countries across Europe began to claim the right to read and interpret the Bible for themselves, to have a direct relationship with God without the mediation of priest or church, and to set their own conscience against the claims of religious institutions. The earliest organised Unitarian movements were founded in the sixteenth century in Poland and Transylvania. In Britain, Unitarianism was damned as heresy and the death penalty imposed on anyone who denied the Trinity. With Unitarianism seen as heresy and specifically forbidden by Parliament's Toleration Act of 1689, and were blocked from civil office under the Test and Corporation Acts. Several early radical reformers who professed Unitarian beliefs in the sixteenth and seventeenth centuries, suffered imprisonment and martyrdom. The Unitarian faith was legalised in 1813, but it was not until 1828 that the Test and Corporation Acts that forbade non-Anglicans from holding civil offices were repealed, and not until 1837, with the Civil Registration Acts, could Unitarians marry in Unitarian chapels, which were only legal thanks to the 1844 Dissenting Chapels Acts. Unitarians were forbidden from attending – or at least graduating from – university till 1871.

But what has this to do with slavery? Being outside the law made Unitarians a hotbed of political dissent. They sought to overturn the law, ostensibly to make their faith legal and to gain the same rights and privileges as those who were communicants of the Church of England. In writing this book, I hope to bring to light the struggle of a minority faith group against all the odds to claim equal rights. It was Unitarians who led the way in recent years to get same-sex weddings onto the statute books. Two hundred years ago it was Unitarians that led the way to getting abolition of the slave trade onto the statute books. Richard Slater Milnes's words ring true today as they did in 1785: 'We are forbidden by the first principles of our dissent to deny to any of our Fellow subjects that Liberty which we claim for ourselves.'

PART 1: YORKSHIRE SLAVE OWNERS

Chapter 1

Eighteenth-Century Yorkshire

Yorkshire was the largest political constituency in England. Its wealth was based on the cloth trade centred in the West Riding towns of Leeds, Halifax, Huddersfield and Wakefield. Sheffield was emerging as an industrial centre for metal working. Coal would not eclipse cloth till the middle of the nineteenth century. The politics of the county were centred on 'rotten boroughs': Aldborough in North Yorkshire, or Richmond returned two MPs but the large industrialising West Riding towns of Leeds, Wakefield, Halifax or Sheffield none at all! This reflected the status of the rural gentry of the north of the county. North Yorkshire returned eighteen MPs, East Yorkshire six and the West Riding just two at Pontefract. The rapidly-expanding urban centres became a hub for merchants, bankers and slave traders. They also became centres for political and religious dissenters who fought for political representation and equality in civil liberties.

The economics of Georgian England were such that very few avenues in life were more than three steps away from slavery. The economy was largely based on slavery: slave plantations generated huge wealth – the trade in people to work on the plantations made merchants spectacularly wealthy in a crime on a par with the Holocaust. Indeed, it has been reckoned that between 1761 and 1808, British traders moved 1,428,000 African people across the Atlantic and pocketed £60 million – perhaps £8 billion in today's money – from the resulting sale of their fellow human beings. Far outstripping the importance of the slave trade and slave-produced merchandise in terms of raw economics was trade with the American colonies, which when coupled with growing internal markets to cater for a burgeoning middle class – which emerged on the back of the trade with America – allowed Great Britain to dominate world trade, finance the Napoleonic Wars and take over India in a war of rape and conquest, as well as to fund the beginnings of the Industrial Revolution at home. Slavery benefited England in various complimentary economic spheres.

Banking

A growth centre of the economy which emerged in the late eighteenth century, and which was almost exclusively financed on the profits from the slave trade, was banking. The trade in corn, cattle and wool, as well as other goods, resulted in the need for available funds in the form of hard cash by the merchants dealing with these products. For the cloth trade to function, the merchant needed cash payments to buy cloth and pay his journeymen's wages. Therefore, the need to transmute bills of exchange (for example from payments for cloth shipments) into regular supplies of cash resulted in the formation of banks in the major towns of the county from the 1780s. The use of bills of exchange made every businessman a banker of sorts, and the pressing need for circulating currency was an inducement for some merchants to enter into banking. Thus, the Heywoods, Ingrams and others shifted from the slave trade and slave plantations to banking: their banking houses investing their clients' money in slave ships and plantations to earn interest and capital to invest in more slave trading voyages. This money underpinned the economy.

Internal Markets

Liverpool merchant bankers were heavily involved in the slave trade and the sale of slave-produced goods. They advanced credit to prospective plantation owners for a handsome percentage interest on the loan; the banks owned plantations as they guaranteed a return – a dividend – every year These merchants extended vital credit to the early cotton manufacturers of Liverpool's Lancashire hinterland; Peter Drinkwater in Manchester built the first steam-powered cotton mill in Manchester on the back of such loans. His daughter married John Pemberton Heywood, son of a Liverpool slave trader Arthur Heywood.[1] The cotton Drinkwater processed was wholly slave derived: slave money built the mill; slaves produced the raw materials; slave ships brought the cotton to Liverpool; slave money paid for the Leeds-Liverpool Canal and later the Liverpool and Manchester Railway for Drinkwater to get his goods to market.[2] After abolition, railways were the primary beneficiary of the £20 million of compensation offered to slave owners; it is reckoned at least 50 per cent

8

of this money was invested in railways. Railways therefore have a dark history, as does the cotton industry: Drinkwater, like Arkwright, built his business empire on the back of slavery. They were not unique in extracting huge profits from cotton, sugar, tobacco and other luxury goods that became staple items of late eighteenth-century society.

As well as financing the birth of the cotton industry in Lancashire and the expansion of the railways, the slave trade provided thousands of indirect means of employment and markets. For example, thousands worked as sailors in the shipping industry importing slave-produced goods like sugar, tobacco, coffee, chocolate, rum, tobacco and mahogany; as workers in ports and warehouses unloading the cargo; as labourers in the various industries refining the products, or in the transportation and retailing of the final products. The ubiquitous coffee shop of Georgian England was totally reliant on slavery and the value-chain economy which brought the coffee to the drinkers. As shipping expanded, so too did docks, shipbuilding and the allied trades of copper mining and smithing: copper was used to sheath the hulls of the ships. The copper industry of Wales expanded exponentially to provide copper sheeting and ingots for trade. Ships needed millions of iron nails and roves. Rope production, like copper and iron working, expanded exponentially and became a boom industry. These tradesmen and merchants earned their livelihoods from the money working in these value-chains – money which was ultimately derived from slavery.

West Indian planters built stately homes – some ridiculously extravagant dwellings such as William Beckford's Fonthill – and furthered the modernisation of British agriculture by 'improving' their estates. Others invested in canals or turnpikes. These houses had the latest and newest furniture by Chippendale, fireplaces by Robert Adam, gardens by Humphry Repton and Capability Brown. Until 1790 nearly all the mahogany used in furniture production by men like Chippendale came from Jamaica, with over 30,000 tons imported into England in 1788 alone! This timber came from slave-worked timber plantations that were virtually exhausted by 1790. How many Georgian houses still retain their 'must-have fashion accessories' of mahogany doors? How many owners of Chippendale furniture pass a moment in thought for where the timber came from to make the antique they own?

On the back of the growth in mercantile activity across the country – a rich country became richer – a new 'middling sort' of merchants developed their own burgeoning middle class: these people now had the money to spend on luxuries. Josiah Wedgewood, the Unitarian potter, sold fine tableware to this market. The Milnes family of Wakefield made super-fine broadcloth, which was to be made in the finest suits of clothes for the middle and upper classes both at home and for plantation owners.

Export Markets

As well as making spectacular profits from dealing in human beings, and supplying the ever-expanding home market with chocolate, tobacco, cotton, sugar, rum and other goods, merchants made huge profits exporting goods with the North American colonies. The North American colonies grew rich on the back of supplying goods and services to the slave plantations in the West Indies: a new country became rich on the value-chains of slavery. The burgeoning American middle class had emerged as a political and economic force on the trade of goods and services to slave plantations. They desired European goods to grace their homes as a sign of status: fine china from Wedgewood, English woollen goods and other textiles.

The self-same ships and merchants who moved slaves, sugar, tobacco, rum and cotton, also took to the American colonies' woollen textiles on a level far higher than any other manufactured products. English merchants based in the American colonies, like Thomas Charnock of Wakefield, the Digges of Manchester and the Heywoods of Liverpool, became important providers of maritime services in the form of shipping and merchandising. The northern mainland colonies' economies evolved in such a way that the residents' purchases of European products were financed by the sale of services, timber and foodstuffs to the slave plantation. Wakefield was for a time at the start of the eighteenth century the regional centre of the wool trade in the North of England. The merchants here were some of the richest and most important in the land. The eighteenth-century diarist John Brearley reports:

> The names of blankit merchants. Mr Ridghall, Mr Mills, Mr Willis and Way, Mr Norton, Mr Charnock, Mr Daniel Maude, Mr Frank Maude, Mr Nevison, Mr Naylor, Mr Zouch, Mr Rickaby, Mr Anison, Mr Yeld. Hull is a great place for blankits.
>
> These above merchant's bye cloth both broods and narrows and some of them bys bokins and bases.
>
> These merchants some trades into . . . to Hull, Lincolnshire, Scotland, London, Ile of White and all country plases in England and Wales and over sea to Holland, Lisbon, Ireland, Port Rico to Brassil and maney places more in America.[3]

Brearley adds: 'Wakefield. Mr Mills Richard and John and Pemberton all 3 partners sends a deal of bale goods from Wakefield to Manchester so the take shipping and goes down to Liverpool, then they are boarded of a ship of theire own wich sayles into the East and West Indias and to Bristoll.'[4]

The wealth of Wakefield, like that of the West Riding, in the eighteenth century derived from the wool trade and its merchant community. This wealth was in part earned from slavery! American and Indian cotton came into Wakefield for finishing and export; broadcloth was made in Wakefield and sold to rich plantation owners and low-grade cloth shipped out to be worn by the slaves themselves. Indeed, we note that the Atkinsons of Huddersfield were shipping broadcloth to American slave plantations well into the 1850s until the American Civil War interrupted this profitable trade. The Wakefield men Brearley mentions were the 'merchant princes' of the town. The Milnes, Naylor, Banks, Charnock and Maude families built lavish mansions in the town, of which just a few remain. They subscribed to the Wakefield, Leeds, Halifax and Huddersfield cloth halls.[5] These families' dominance of the cloth trade prompted the expansion of the town, from 4,000 inhabitants in 1723 to 16,000 by 1801 to work in the various textile factories of the town. The Milnes family and others were an embedded part of the value-chains of slavery by exporting woollen goods to America and the slave plantations, as Brearley notes. From Wakefield J & J Naylor was trading broad and narrow cloth, fancy cloth, worsted, haberdashery and other goods with eleven firms in New York and Philadelphia – the second largest trading concern in Yorkshire with these American states! They were eclipsed only by Cookson's of Leeds.[6] Naylor had been a principal supplier to Samuel Fludyer the agent for supplying the British Army with cloth. Yorkshire cloth merchants made vast profits selling cloth to the slave plantations and to those made rich by slavery in America.[7]

It is impossible to deny that money derived from the 'triangular trade' did not flood into the town; most of the merchant houses did business with plantations in the West Indies as well as mainland America. As we noted earlier, Yorkshire merchants were the largest exporter of woollen goods into New York and neighbouring states. More archive research is required to identify Wakefield and Yorkshire merchants as a collective, with goods as part of slave-ship manifests. Huge profits were to made from exporting to the American colonies. The same story is true of Leeds and Halifax: Yorkshire was made rich on the American trade.

This is not surprising, however: the economic value of the trade to North America outstripped the value of trade in slave-produced goods.

It was this trade that made the country rich. Goods and services being supplied by American merchants to English slave masters made America rich; the Americans then bought English goods making English merchants richer. It was a win-win situation for the English merchants: opportunity for huge profits importing slave produced goods, huge profits off the back of exporting to America. This economic model was soon practised within America with the creation of huge cotton farms reliant on slave labour and the export to England of cotton.

Comment

Does the fact that the great merchant houses of Yorkshire participated in the slave trade economy, make them bad people? Does it make them racists? Many would say so, and say they put profit before people: that is what capitalism does! It is far too simplistic – a knee-jerk reaction – to brand eighteenth-century merchants as racist.

The woollen industry of the West Riding was particularly dependent on slave-produced goods. Richard Fennell, a London merchant and Unitarian, was in business with the Hainsworth family of Mill Hill Chapel Leeds as Fennel & Hainsworth. Their principal imports to Yorkshire were log wood dye, indigo dye, cochineal and Nicaragua wood: all slave-produced goods sourced from continental America or the West Indies. Fennel & Hainsworth were the primary dye supplier to Benjamin Gott of Leeds, as well as the Holdsworths, Lumbs and Milnes of Wakefield. By 1794 the Hainsworth family had left the concern and with two other Mill Hill families, founded Hainsworth, Thursby and Dunn, which today trades as Abimelech Hainsworth of Pudsey. Richard Fennell continued importing slave produced goods under the concern Fennell & Son into the early 1820s. The Fennell family grew incredibly rich on the back of slavery, allowing Richard's granddaughter Louisa Fennell to become a famous artist. Henry Peterson, born in Utrecht in Holland, grew rich from growing tobacco and exporting it to Europe and sending woollen goods to America as back cargo. He settled in Wakefield following American Independence and his son Andrew used the family's wealth to build Peterson Road in Wakefield. Anyone who wore a blue suit of clothes or smoked a pipe was contributing to slavery.

Any middle-class family who had sugar or chocolate through the purchase of those goods participated in the value-chains of the slave economy; gentlemen with fine cotton shirts contributed to the slave trade. It was a self-perpetuating cycle in a value-chain economy centred around the exploitation of human beings. Every man who smoked a pipe of tobacco, or anyone who 'popped in for a coffee' in a ubiquitous eighteenth-century coffee house participated in the value-chains of the slave economy. The merchant houses that shipped slaves and imported slave-produced goods were thriving businesses, and offered handsome profits for those who invested in them. It is doubtful if participation in slavery was solely due to the consistently high profits which were presumably at least as high as any alternative business that merchants could have engaged in. Many merchants took part as they could spread the financial risk with other investors and it was a fairly easy trade to enter. The archive of slave ship owners from Liverpool show that most slave voyages were funded by a collective of merchants and middle-class persons: they all put a percentage of money into the ship, sat in their large town houses and mansions and waited for the handsome profit to come back. Active participation in the slave trade was open to anyone who had the capital to invest: they could make good returns with little to no effort on their behalf: easy money. Who would not be attracted to such 'investment opportunities' to 'get rich quick'? Even when the opportunity of 'making a fast buck' off slave trading was ended in 1807, the system carried on: the trade in human beings was of minor importance to the issue of slavery. Slave plantations could be owned by, in modern terms, 'investment companies' or 'hedge funds'. Mount Charles Estate Jamaica was purchased in 1768 by the Rev. Augustin Gwyn. He was part of a co-operative almost, where working men and the lower middle class had the opportunity to pool their financial resources into a 'hedge fund'. Gwyn was financed by the fund which included:

Simon Fanshawe of Hanover Square, Middlesex, Esq., John Fanshawe of Chandois Street, Cavendish Square, Middlesex, Esq., Peregrine Furye, Upper Grosvenor Street, Middlesex, Esq., John Howard of Fish Street Hill, City of London, warehouseman, Lewis Vickers of Holy Head, Wales, Esq., Anthony Todd, General Post Office, London, Esq., Charles Jackson, General Post Office, London, Esq., Thomas Carter, Cork Street, Burlington Gardens, Middlesex, Esq., Robert Thorne, Enfield, Middlesex, Esq., Patty Parsons of St George Hanover Square, Middlesex, spinster, Philip Grafton, Stoke Newington, Middlesex, gentleman, Duncan Dallas, Noth End, Hampstead, Middlesex, gentleman, William Stonehewer, Cannon Street, London, gentleman, John Barnhard, Wandsworth, Surrey, Esq., Dorcas Ann Cartwright, Lad Lane, London, spinster, Richard Smith of Bury Street, London, peruke maker, Charles Lander of Bishopsgate Street, London, mariner,

Lawrence Laforest of Bishopsgate Street, London, vintner, Catherine Thompson, York, spinster, Thomas Ord, Esq., Colonel of His Majesty's Royal Regiment of Artillery now at Shooters Hill, Kent, John Lagier Lamotte, Wanstead, Essex, Esq., Watkin Jenkins, Grays Inn, Middlesex, Esq., Dorothy Askew, Wakefield, Yorkshire, widow [investors in plantation to generate annuities][8]

We see two Yorkshire ladies as members of the 'hedge fund': Catherine Thompson of York and Dorothy Askew of Wakefield. The 'hedge fund' provided £12,000 in a deed of 24 September 1768. The fund received 4 per cent interest on the loan: thus, our Yorkshire ladies owned a share in 247 slaves on Mount Charles and a further 150 slaves and a sugar works which was to be established with their investment. Henry Ibbetson of Leeds in 1784 paid into another scheme.[9] This allowed these men and women in Yorkshire and further afield to have a modest annual income for their 'old age' derived from the blood, sweat and tears of slaves. Did these people care they were bankrolling slavery? No, all they were concerned about was making a safe investment that offered good returns.

Contrary to popular myths, when compared to the North American trade and the investment market for banking, the slave trade itself was not as profitable. The real money was to be made in the trade in slave-produced goods and fortunes were made in the more important export trade to America. Ending the slave trade was replaced with 'captive breeding' of slaves on the plantations. The slave trade was disgusting but it was not indispensable: the slave trade was not a vital link in the chains of slavery: 'free labour' underpinned the economy, and until such a time as a new source of 'very cheap labour' could be found, slavery continued. The rape of India by the East India Company opened up new markets, and ultimately allowed the discontinuance of slavery, through the virtual enslavement of millions of others. We are horrified by slave plantations and the slave trade – indeed it was a great evil, a great crime – yet where is the horror of what the British did in Africa and India? Where is the horror at modern slavery?

The Atlantic economy provided the focus of an expanding trading network, that was increasingly diversifying by 1800. The expansion of the American market after 1783 contributed greatly to the expansion of manufacturing in England. The closure of American ports to British shipping and renewed hostilities in America with the 'War of 1812' which lasted till 1815 heralded an abrupt end to expansion, and witnessed the bankruptcy of major English manufacturers: Cookson's of Leeds, for example. Unfavourable trading conditions with the Napoleonic

Continental System, instability on slave plantations and economic depression in England from 1826 heralded the end of the profitability of plantations.

The golden age of the American trade was 1784 to 1812. The northern American states, as we said earlier, financed their imports from English manufacturers via largely English merchants by sales of agricultural and forestry commodities, and crucially, shipping and mercantile services to the slave plantations of the West Indies. The North American imports of timber, foodstuffs etc allowed for the production of slave-produced goods, which were shipped to England. The slave plantations of the West Indies were thus the focus of the Atlantic economy of England and America and were fuelled by the trade in African slaves. The model kept working as slaves were 'grown at home' far cheaper and at less risk after 1807. Abolition of the slave trade did not affect the economic status quo. The economic model underpinning the American and English economy was slavery or more accurately free labour. The issue of slavery would rip America apart as two economic models competed for supremacy. Without American imports, slavery and the whole economic model simply would not operate. After 1833, the model was massively expanded in continental America: cotton and not sugar now drove slavery and the English economy. In the 1830s and 1840s the English economy was still vested in, reliant upon, slavery.

No aspect of the eighteenth or early nineteenth century was more than two steps away from a slave. Failure to participate in the economic model would result in bankruptcy. Participating in the then-current economic model does not make those who participated racists: this is too simplistic and knee-jerk a reaction. Was any conscionable thought given to the slaves themselves? By and large no. Do we in the modern era give any thought to the terrible conditions that women and children work in in Thailand, Cambodia, China and Nigeria to bring us cheap clothing and batteries for electric cars? More often no. We are no different to the slave owners of the eighteenth century. We like making money and we like 'getting bargains' and have little regard to the ethics of our actions. On the one hand we condemn the past, call our ancestors racist, yet by and large we participate in the value-chain of modern-day slavery in the name of free-market liberal capitalism. I ask the reader: what is the difference between our modern-day economy based on cheap or slave labour and our ancestors participating in the same economic model? Before we condemn the past, we must look to ourselves.

Chapter 2

The Slave Trade

The sale of human beings was where huge profits could be made for those with the finance to buy ships, fit them out and gamble on the ship completing its voyage. It was literally a simple case of supply and demand. The plantations needed slaves; the traffickers used whatever means they could to supply them. Slave trading financed banking across the county; it was the acceptable face of capitalism. Supporters of slavery and the slave trade could call on friends in high places: slave trader and banker William Joseph Denison, High Sheriff of Yorkshire, being one! Thomas Clarkson (1760–1846) was the leading campaigner against the slave trade in Britain. He helped found 'The Society for Effecting the Abolition of the Slave Trade' (also known as the Society for the Abolition of the Slave Trade) and helped achieve passage of the Slave Trade Act of 1807, which ended British trade in slaves. Clarkson's task was to collect information for the committee to present to Parliament and the public. He devoted his time and energy to travelling around Britain, particularly to the ports of Liverpool and Bristol, gathering evidence about the slave trade from eyewitnesses, especially from sailors who had worked on slave ships. Furthermore, Clarkson also bought examples of equipment used aboard the ships, including handcuffs, shackles and branding irons, which were used as visual aids. He said this in 1786 about the conditions on slave ships:

> The vessels, in which they are transported, are of different dimensions, from eleven to eight hundred tons, and carry from thirty to fifteen hundred of them at a time ... It is clear that none of the unfortunate people, perhaps at this moment on board, can stand upright, but that they must sit down, and contract their limbs within the limits of little more than three square feet, during the whole of the middle passage. I cannot compare the scene on board this vessel, to any other than that of a pen of sheep;

with this difference only, that the one have the advantages of a wholesome air, while that, which the others breathe, is putrid . . . Being stowed then in the manner thus described, they soon begin to experience the effects, which might naturally be presumed to arise from their situation. In consequence of the pestilential breath of so many confined in so small a space, they become sickly, and from the vicissitude of heat and cold, of heat when confined below, and of cold when suddenly brought up for air, a flux is generated . . . Imagine only for a moment the gratings to be opened, but particularly after a rain, which has occasioned them to be covered for some time.

The first scene that presents itself, is a cluster of unhappy people, who, overcome by excessive heat and stench, have fainted away.

The next that occurs, is that of one of them endeavouring to press forward to the light, to catch a mouthful of wholesome air, but hindered by the partner of his chains, who is lying dead at his feet, and whom he has not sufficient strength to drag after him.

The third is conspicuous in the instance of those, who are just on the point of fainting, and who are wallowing in the blood and mucus of the intestines, with which the floor is covered.

Such are the scenes, that universally present themselves in the case supposed; and how agonizing and insufferable their situation must have been during this period of their confinement, none, I believe, can possibly conceive, unless they had been the partners of their chains.

The gratings then being opened as before described, the receivers, who see their situation, bring them instantly upon deck. They give them such medical assistance as their case requires. Those, that are most affected, are picked out, and are put into an hospital or sick berth (which is prepared against cases of this kind) as objects of more immediate attention. The rest, having experienced a little respite, are returned to the same dungeon of wretchedness and woe, that had been the occasion of their sufferings.

As to those, who are removed into their new apartments, some of them live only for a few hours. Others become daily more emaciated and weak: and to such a degree of emaciation have many of them arrived, that in consequence of this, and additionally the circumstances of lying upon the bare boards, and the friction arising from the motion of the vessel, the prominent parts of some of their bones have worked their way through the muscles and the skin. In this situation they have lingered for some time, both objects of commiseration and horror, when death has been kind enough to pity their sufferings, and to put a period to their pain.[1]

Clarkson notes about the slaves that:

The unhappy slaves, who are thus annually taken from their native land, may be divided into seven classes.

The most considerable, and that which contains at least half of the whole number transported, consists of kidnapped people. Many of the Africans, who have been enticed by the Europeans, and have come on board their vessels in confidence, have been detained and carried off. Others have been invited to a conference on the shore. A puncheon of spirits has been opened to entertain them, and as soon as they have drank to intoxication, they have been seized, and forced, in that helpless and unguarded situation, to the ships.

But the number of Africans, that are annually kidnapped by the Europeans, bears no sort of comparison with the number of those, that are kidnapped by their own countrymen.

The great taste, which the Africans have acquired for European commodities, particularly Spirits, and the ready sale, which is found for the human species through the whole of their extensive continent, have tempted the strong to seize upon the weak, the cunning to lay snares for the unwary, and the rich to circumvent the poor. Some of them conceal themselves in the forests, and near the roads, watching for the unguarded traveller as an huntsman for his game. Others lie in wait in the rice fields, to carry off all such, as may be stationed there for the purpose of driving the birds from the grain. Others conceal themselves at the springs of water, to which the natives resort to quench their thirst, or in thickets by the side of creeks, to fall upon those solitary beings . . . they usually assemble their guards, and visit the villages, which are to become the objects of their avarice, in the night. Having surrounded them, and set them on fire, they seize such of the inhabitants as are endeavouring to escape from the flames, and either send them to a neighbouring market to be sold, or sell them to the different black traders that are constantly travelling through their dominions . . . But this change, though it greatly increased the number of slaves, was found insufficient either to answer the demands of the Europeans, or the avarice of the African princes. They were reduced therefore to the difficulty of inventing new crimes, that a greater number of criminals might be made and sold . . . For though the Africans are supplied by the Europeans with arms and ammunition; though wars are repeatedly made for the purpose of procuring slaves, and their whole continent may be said to be continually in a blaze, yet the battles fought on these occasions are so obstinate, and so many are killed on both sides, that the surviving captives are few.[2]

Who were these slave traders? The men who thought transporting fellow human beings was a good thing because they could earn money from the slavery of their fellow men? These men, as we shall see, were predominantly bankers, clustered around Arthur Heywood, an Irishman, living in Liverpool and Wakefield. Others, saw the trade as the way of 'making a fast buck' to use modern parlance, as we shall see in a later chapter.

Plantations

Sugar or tobacco plantations were the ultimate destination of the slaves. The Rev. James Ramsay MA wrote thusly in 1784 about them:

The French, in the treatment of their slaves, regard the suggestions of humanity, and enforce its dictates by their laws. The English have not paid the least attention to enforce by a law, either humanity or justice, as these may respect their slaves. Many are the restrictions, and severe are the punishments, to which our slaves are subjected . . . Nay a horse, a cow, or a sheep is much better protected with us by the law, than a poor slave. For these, if found in a trespass, are not to be injured, but secured for their owners; while a half starved Negroe, may, for breaking a single cane, which probably he himself has planted, be hacked to pieces with a cutlass; even though, perhaps, he be incapable of resistance, or of running away from the watchman, who finds him in the face. Nay, we have men among us, who dare boast of their giving orders to their watchmen, not to bring home any slave that they find breaking of canes, but, as they call it, to hide them, that is to kill, and bury them. And, accordingly, every now and then, some poor wretch is missed, and some lacerated carcase is discovered . . . While we reflect on the state of slavery in our colonies, among the freest people in the world, and extend our views to the like instances in history, it becomes a mournful, an humiliating consideration in human nature, to find that those men and nations, whom liberty hath exalted, and who, therefore, ought to regard it tenderly in others, are constantly for restraining its blessings within their own little circle, and delight more in augmenting the train of their dependents, than in adding to the rank of fellow citizens, or in diffusing the benefits of freedom among their neighbours. Everywhere, in every age, the chain of slavery has been fashioned, and applied by the hand of liberty.[3]

He continued:

We cannot pass over in silence the usual treatment of pregnant women and nurses. In almost every plantation they are fond of placing every Negroe who can wield an hoe in the field gangs, so fond, that hardly any remonstrance from the surgeon can, in many cases, save a poor diseased wretch from the labour; though, if method prevailed, work may be found on the plantation equally necessary and proportioned to every various degree of ability; and though one or two days attempts in the field be sure to lay them up in the hospital for weeks.

At this work are pregnant women often kept during the last months of their pregnancy, and hence suffer many an abortion; which some managers are unfeeling enough to express their joy at, because the woman, on recovery, having no child to care for, will have no pretence for indulgence.

If, after all, she carries her burden the full time, she must be delivered in a dark, damp, smoky hut, perhaps without a rag in which to wrap her child, except the manager has a wife to sympathize with her wants. Hence the frequent loss of Negroe children by cramp and convulsions within the month. A lying-in woman is allowed three, in some plantations four weeks for recovery. She then takes the field with her child, and hoe or bill. The infant is placed in the furrow, near her, generally exposed naked, or almost naked, to the sun and rain, on a kid skin, or such

21

rags as she can procure. Some very few people give nurses an extra allowance.[4]

Working on sugar plantations was especially harsh labour. Overseers organised their slaves into a gang system. The most physically demanding work – planting, manuring and cane-cutting – fell to the strongest and healthiest, whilst less physically demanding tasks were handled by the less robust, younger or older slaves. No one was spared from working: the very young and the old were put to work: driving away birds, cleaning and guarding. From cradle to almost grave, sugar slaves had to work the land:

In crop-time, which may be when reckoned altogether on a plantation, from five to six months; the cane tops, by supplying the cattle with food, gives the slaves some little relaxation in picking grass. But some pretendedly industrious planters, men of much bustle, and no method, will, especially in moon-light, keep their people till ten o'clock at night, carrying wowra, the decayed leaves of the cane, to boil off the cane juice. A considerable number of slaves is kept to attend in turn the mill and boiling house all night. They sleep over their work; the sugar is ill tempered, burnt in the boiler, and improperly struck; while the mill every now-and-then grinds off an hand, or an arm, of those drowsy worn-down creatures that feed it. Still the process of making sugar is carried on in many plantations, for months, without any other interruption, than during some part of day light on Sundays. In some plantations it is the custom, during croptime, to keep the whole gang employed as above, from morning to night, and alternately one half throughout the night, to supply the mill with canes, and the boiling house with wowra.

This labour is more or less moderated, in proportion to the method and good sense of the manager. In some plantations the young children and worn out slaves are set apart to pick grass, and bring cane tops from the field for the cattle. . .[5]

Thomas Clarkson adds:

. . . drooping with sickness or fatigue, he appears to work unwillingly, or if the bundle of grass that he has been collecting, appears too small in the eye of the overseer, he is equally sure of experiencing the whip. This instrument erates the skin, and cuts out small portions of the flesh at almost every stroke; and is so frequently applied, that the smack of it is all day long in the ears of those who are in the vicinity of the plantations. This severity of masters, or managers, to their slaves, which is considered only as common discipline, is attended with bad effects. It enables them to behold instances of cruelty without commiseration, and to be guilty of them without remorse. Hence those many acts of deliberate mutilation, that have taken place on the slightest occasions: hence those many acts of inferior, though shocking, barbarity, that have taken place without any occasion at all: the very slitting of ears has been considered as an operation, so perfectly devoid of pain, as to have been performed for no other reason than that for which a brand is set upon cattle, as a mark of property.

But this is not the only effect, which this severity produces: for while it hardens their hearts, and makes them insensible of the misery of their fellow-creatures, it begets a turn for wanton cruelty. As a proof of this, I shall mention one, among the many instances that occur, where ingenuity has been exerted in contriving modes of torture. An iron coffin, with holes in it, was kept by a certain colonist, as an auxiliary to the lash. In this the poor victim of the master's resentment was enclosed, and placed sufficiently near a fire, to occasion extreme pain, and consequently shrieks and groans, until the revenge of the master was satiated, without any other inconvenience on his part, than a temporary suspension of the slave's labour, Had he been flogged to death, or his limbs mutilated, the interest of the brutal tyrant would have suffered a more irreparable loss . . . Such then is the general situation of the unfortunate Africans. They are beaten and tortured at discretion. They are badly clothed. They are miserably fed. Their drudgery is intense and incessant, and their rest short. For scarcely are their heads reclined, scarcely have their bodies a respite from the labour of the day, or the cruel hand of the overseer, but they are summoned to renew their sorrows. In this manner they go on from year to year, in a state of the lowest degradation, without a single law to protect them, without the possibility of redress, without a hope that their situation will be changed, unless death should terminate the scene.[6]

Tobacco plantations were smaller than sugar plantations, but just as profitable. Unlike on sugar plantations, the slaves did not work in gangs but often toiled side by side with free labour. Tobacco and smoking were, like sugar, a boom industry from the seventeenth century. Anyone who smoked a pipe contributed to slavery. The supply of slaves to tobacco plantations was far smaller than to sugar plantations. It was a niche market dominated by the Heywood and Digges families from c. 1700 to 1730; the plantations being owned by men like Thomas Charnock from Wakefield who emigrated to the Americas to make money. Yorkshire men and women, perhaps blinded by avarice, had no issue with slavery and owned plantations where exploitation of people was an everyday occurrence.

But what of other slave owners? As the biggest county in the country Yorkshire had its fair share of slave owners. The UCL Legacies of British Slave Ownership Database provides details for eighty-eight men and women slave owners in Yorkshire. The Trans-Atlantic Slave Trade Database adds details of slave traders: they ranked from earls, to MPs, vicars and the affluent middle classes. These people all had a vested interest in maintaining the status quo.

Chapter 3

Yorkshire and Slavery

In popular opinion the story of Yorkshire slavery is dominated by the Earls of Harewood. The family were slave traders from the late seventeenth century and built up a vast fortune. The Trans-Atlantic Slave Trade Database records that Edward Lascelles invested in four slaving voyages from 1702 to 1710, two of which were shipping slaves to tobacco plantations in Barbados, and his son Henry (1690–1753) in a further six from 1736 to 1743, in total transporting a minimum of 1,934 men, women and children into slavery. Henry Lascelles was a banker and sugar importer who held shares in twenty-one ships involved in the slave trade between Barbados and Africa. He bought land in Yorkshire with the fortune he amassed. The Lascelles family received compensation in 1834 for 1,277 slaves and received a £26,307 payment at the time, worth £2.52 million in 2020. The Lascelles family today acknowledge their part in this crime of the slave trade, have an exhibition at Harewood about the family's past and have made their vast archive available online.[1] The Lascelles were not the largest slave owners in the county; the story of Harewood House so dominates the narrative of slavery in Yorkshire that it superficially appears to many that it was solely the Lascelles and no one else involved. This is wrong: Yorkshire had slave traders across the county and from the ranks of gentry to the middle class. Slave traders and owners on the whole fell into two camps:

1. Merchants who were self-made men, out to increase their own wealth
2. Established gentry families, who were already rich and sought to consolidate their wealth

These two groups reflected the divergent nature of the economic realities of eighteenth-century Yorkshire. The economic base of Yorkshire was the wool trade: this was centred in the West Riding in Halifax, Huddersfield,

Leeds and Wakefield. In the late seventeenth century Wakefield was the centre of the textile trade. The first cloth hall was opened there in 1710. Leeds followed quickly thereafter, and Huddersfield and Halifax by mid-century. These four wealthy towns attracted merchants from across the north of England. In rural East and North Yorkshire, the economy was centred on large rural estates farmed for grain, cattle and sheep. The money and patronage were centred in a few, already very wealthy gentry and aristocratic families. Thus, the pattern of slave ownership was markedly different across the county.

So, we ask, who were they?

Members of Parliament

An incredible amount of work has been done by UCL on the legacy of British slave ownership, their results being accessible via an online database and excellent academic publications. The UCL database shows that Yorkshire MPs were slave owners – as wealthy merchants or landed gentry, it was normal for these men to own slaves for generations. The self-made men like Richard Milnes and Wilberforce dramatically bucked this trend. Amongst the MPs in the county we find:

- Samuel Moulton Barrett, Whig MP for Richmond 1820–7, brother of Edward Barrett Moulton Barrett and uncle of Elizabeth Barrett Browning the poet. Moulton Barrett, as a Whig – i.e. a supporter of free trade, the supremacy of Parliament, enfranchisement of Catholic and Unitarians, expansion of the electoral base and reform of Parliament, talent and merit over wealth and family – found himself between a rock and a hard place. As a Whig he opposed the slave trade and slavery, yet owned slaves. His grandfather Edward was both a slave trader and plantation owner. His father Charles Moulton was a naval captain who had served in the West Indies and his maternal grandfather Edward Barrett was the owner of extensive estates in Jamaica, including Cinnamon Hill, where he was born and spent his early years. Moulton made four slaving voyages, two with Edward Barrett, transporting in 1791 295 slaves and in 1805, some 332 human beings.[2] Samuel's brother Edward made a slaving voyage in 1792 disembarking 414 slaves, and a second in 1793 disembarking 569 slaves.[3] The brothers inherited the Jamaican estates from their uncle George Goodin Barrett, who stipulated that they should assume the name of Barrett. From about 1811 Samuel, being more a man of business than his brother, 'shuttled to and fro between England and Jamaica' and became 'the indispensable custodian of the Moulton Barrett interests'. The dilemma of being a slave-owning Whig never weighed lightly with him: politically and religiously opposed to slavery, financially he had, it seemed to him, no other option but to keep slaves. To try and better the lot of his slaves, he reformed the regime under which his estates were managed. He abolished whippings as punishment and an incentive to work, appointed a negro overseer, built decent houses, schools and churches for his 1,100 slaves, and encouraged Nonconformist missions. As a result, his property survived almost intact during the uprisings of 1831–2.[4] He received compensation in 1834 of £8,791 14s 8d for 477 slaves.

- Robert Chaloner, MP for Richmond 1810–18, and York 1820–6.[5] He was a wealthy banker in York and Wakefield, drawing on the London bank of Boldero. Appearing in various iterations, the bank was formed c. 1765 when the partnership of Boldero, Carter and Boldero split. One of the successors firms became Boldero, Kendall & Adey, then Boldero, Lushington, Boldero and variants. The firm of Boldero & Adey was shown as the owner of Greenwood estate in St Mary Jamaica from 1790 until 1815.[6] Stephen Thurston Adey was described by Edmund Burke in 1780 as a Whig 'of worth and honour', with 'nothing of the banker in him' and was the Fitzwilliam interest MP for Higham Ferrers 1798–1801.[7] Edward Gale Boldero was a plantation owner. Boldero Kendall & Adey failed in 1812 – the assets recorded in 1817 included enslaved people on St Cyr and Tivoli estates and were in the lawful possession of John Hayes and George Gun Munro, attorneys to Messrs Idle, Timson and Marryat, assignees of Messrs Boldero & Co.[8] Boldero and Adey were slave owners, and used their money to finance banking services, which was used to secure a Wakefield banking house. Despite Boldero's failure, Townend and Rishworth staggered on for two years but failed on 13 June 1814. It was asset-stripped by the York banking firm of Wentworth and Chaloner, which opened a branch styled Wentworth, Chaloner & Rishworth, Thomas Rishworth being a partner in the failed bank of Townend & Rishworth! Thomas Rishworth's banking activities made him an extremely wealthy man. In 1826, he estimated his worth at £100,000, a fortune in those days valued at over a million in today's money, stating that he had but £100 to begin with. The bank was said to have made profits of £249,000 in 12 years. The bank failed in 1826, all three partners being declared bankrupt.[9]

Senior partner Robert Chaloner had interests in slave plantations, but Godfrey Wentworth does not appear in any records as a slave owner. Wentworth (1773–1834) was MP for Tregony 1806–08, Sheriff of Yorkshire 1796–7, Sheriff of York in 1814, and sold the family estates of Hickleton and Woolley in 1826 when he was declared bankrupt.[10] Robert Chaloner, was Whig MP for Richmond 1810–18 and York 1820–6. The Chaloner family were neighbours of the Dundas family, whose principal residence was at Aske, but who had a second house at Upleatham, only two miles from Guisborough. Chaloner was related through marriage to the Dundas family, who we mention again shortly: Chaloner's cousin Harriot Hale married Lord Thomas Dundas's eldest son Lawrence Dundas in 1794. He himself married Frances Laura Dundas, sister of Lawrence in 1805, whose mother was Lady Charlotte Fitzwilliam daughter of William Fitzwilliam, father of Earl Fitzwilliam, leader of the Yorkshire Whigs on the death of the Marquis of Rockingham. He was bankrupted in the financial crisis of 1825–6, when Fitzwilliam helped to save his Yorkshire property and appointed him steward of his Irish estates.[11] Chaloner was a trustee of the marriage settlement of his sister Caroline for the Cleland and Farm estates in Barbados.[12] His sister Caroline married Abraham Parry Cumberbatch (1784–1840) who claimed compensation totalling £5,388 10s 2d for the enslaved people on the Cleland – receiving £5,348 1s 11d for 246 slaves – and Farm estates – receiving £1,015 12s 8d for 47 slaves – on Barbados, which was paid to his trustees, which included Robert Chaloner, from which £500 per annum was to be paid to his wife during her natural life.[13]

- William Joseph Denison, MP for Hull 1806–07, banker and slave trader.[14] Denison was High Sheriff of Yorkshire 1808–09, and had been MP for Kingston upon Hull 1806–07. Denison's famed wealth derived from the London bank founded by his father, Joseph Denison and Company (known as Denison, Heywood, Kennard and Company after 1837), of which he became senior partner. From his father, who appears to have remained a Dissenter, he also inherited the estates of Seamer near Scarborough in Yorkshire, and Denbies in Surrey, on the latter's death in 1806. William Joseph Denison co-owned a number of slaving ships, and undertook 29 slaving voyages between 1784 and 1794, transporting 11,267 people. Denison's father Joseph (1726–1806), was from Burmantofts Hall, Leeds, and was a leading cloth merchant. His father John Denison was likewise the son of a woollen cloth merchant and he too had attended Mill Hill Chapel. William Joseph had made his fortune in London as the London agent for Arthur Heywood, and for a time had remained a Unitarian before conforming to the Church or England.[15] Understandably, as his fortune was based on slavery, William Joseph Denison was opposed to abolition. Denison's bank acted as agent at the National Debt Office for T & W Earle and Joseph Brooks Yates (both of Liverpool) in the compensation process in the late 1830s. To date no mortgages or slave ownership have been discovered for the firm. At his death, 'Denison was probably among the eight or ten wealthiest British businessmen at the time of his death', leaving an estimated £2.3 million.[16]

- Charles Duncombe, Baron Feversham, son of Charles Slingsby Duncombe of Duncombe Park, was MP for Aldborough 1796–1806 for the Tories.[17] At abolition he made a claim for slaves on Nevis amounting to £1,844 2s 3d.[18] Frances Rose, the daughter of Thomas Duncombe, was niece of Francis Jennings, and inherited from her Coley in St Thomas-in-the-East plantation. She married Sir George Henry Rose, MP for Launceston 1784–8, Lymington 1788–90 and Christ Church 1790–1818.[19] Between them, they received compensation for three plantations of £889 10s 1d, £3,306 6s 9d and £2,342 14s 0d respectively at abolition.[20]
- Sambroooke Freeman (1721–82) MP for Pontefract 1754–61, son and heir of John Cooke, who inherited his uncle William Freeman's estates on St Kitts.[21]
- The Hon. George Heneage Lawrence Dundas (1778–1834), the brother of Lord Lawrence Dundas, was the owner until his death of two estates, one in Grenada and one in Dominica. At abolition he owned 189 slaves and received £4,818 0s 6d.[22] He was MP for Richmond from 1802–06 and again in 1812.[23]
- William Needham (1740–1806), MP for Pontefract 1780–4. He inherited from his father, Robert Needham, the Water Valley Plantation in St Mary Jamaica. His mother was Catherine Pitt, sister to William Pitt the Elder. He was an attorney on the island before embarking on a political career.[24]
- Nathanial Smith, MP for Pontefract 1783. He was party to a mortgage deed of 1776/7 with Charles Payne Sharpe to secure his lending of £6,000 on 'slave-property' in St Vincent, and another of the same date to the Friths of St Vincent for £4,000.[25]
- James Wilson, MP for York 1826–30 who was according to George Strickland of Boynton Hall 'a man risen from nothing, partly by a relation leaving him a West India property',[26] who in 1817 had 340 slaves on his estate at Demerara.[27]

The Aristocracy

Already alluded to, the county gentry – many of whom were MPs – were slave owners. Amongst the so-called 'great and good' of the county the UCL database records:

- Sir William Payne Gallwey (1807–81), formerly a major in the 7th Fusiliers, was JP for the North Riding, the third generation of a wealthy West Indian slave plantation-owning family. He was Tory MP for Thirsk in the mid-nineteenth century. At abolition he received £2,400 14s 9d for 137 slaves. His father Sir William Payne (1759–1831) had added the name Gallwey in 1814 in accordance with the will of his maternal uncle, Tobias Wall Gallwe, of St Kitts. In his own right he owned Pond & Fancy estates, which was offered for sale in 1792 for £19,740, which was never completed. William's father, Ralph Payne (?–1763) was chief justice of St Kitts and owned two estates in the southern part of the island, at Majors Bay and White House Bay, both adjacent to the Great Salt Pond.[28] The Payne Gallwey family-built Thirsk Mechanics Institute. The family lived close by at the now-demolished eighteenth-century Neo-Palladian Thirkleby Park. The stable block and home farm remain. Thirkleby Park had been built in 1790 by Sir Thomas Frankland, 6th Baronet.
- Sir John Peniston Milbanke, 7th Baronet (1775–1850), of Halnaby Hall, received £1,079 13s 4d for sixty-one slaves in 1833.[29]
- Sir James Maxwell Wallace (1785–1867) was the son of the West India merchant John Wallace, and half owner of the Biscany estate in St Elizabeth, Jamaica, with Hugh Ritchie Wallace. His father, John Wallace, and uncle Hugh Wallace had purchased the plantation in 1762. Sir John at abolition owned 210 fellow human beings and was paid £4,363 4s 8d compensation for them. He lived at Ainderby Hall.[30]

Parsons

Remarkably, given the Anglican Church's opposition to slavery, the UCL database reveals several parsons in Yorkshire who owned or profited from slavery. Indeed, where religion of claimant is notes at abolition 57 'Anglicans' made 104 claims for compensation, and 232 persons listed as 'Church of England'. Of these claimants, we note 184 men listed as vicars, including the Dean of Bristol, the Right Rev. Henry Beeke, and the Right Rev. Henry Phillpotts, Bishop of Exeter, as being slave owners or having interests in slave plantations. Members of the Church of England were the largest faith group owning slaves or with interests in slave plantations. The UCL database records twenty-one Unitarians with interest in plantations and just nine owned slaves at abolition; in comparison three Methodists, one of whom was the Rev. Thomas Harrison, had slaves at abolition. No Roman Catholics are recorded as slave owners. It was a distinctly Protestant phenomenon in England.

Anglican vicars in Yorkshire who owned slaves or with interests in plantations were:

- Rev. Benjamin Fuller Tuckniss, vicar of Raskelf, via his wife Mary Jane Austin, was part owner of 250 slaves in Barbados at abolition.[31] Under the terms of his father-in-law Rev. Richard Austin's will, he was named a co-executor of Austin's plantations at Kleinhoop, L'Assistance and a third estate which appears to be Appecappe, which were left to his three children William Paul Austin, Charles Adye Austin and Mary Jane Austin and a legacy of £1,000 to the Rev. Wilshire Stanton Austin, his son by a former marriage and the transfer of specified enslaved people who had belonged to Sarah Stanton his first wife: Sam, Walker, Jos, Tom and a woman named Rose.[32]
- Rev. Richard Munkhouse of St John the Baptist Wakefield, a Tory, loyalist and reactionary who opposed the repeal of the Test and Corporation Acts, as well as political reform of any kind. Because of anti-establishment publications from mostly Unitarian writers in the library, he actually proposed closing down the library and burning its books, as they propagated the rights of man and condemned in no uncertain words all those who stood against church and king:

Boldly dare to oppose yourselves to this torrent of iniquity and licentiousness, and narrow the circulation of those noxious Publications so notoriously hostile to the Cause, - which such numbers of you are ready to maintain at the hazard of your lives. They have too long been the successful vehicles of Sedition; and, with unmerited impunity, have insulted your attachment to the Religion of your Ancestors, (all heavenly as it is) your Patriotism, and your Loyalty, by their avowed contempt of whatever bears the name of Truth, Honour, Honesty, and Decorum . . . As Subscribing Members of News-Rooms, and Public Libraries, exclude or expel them. To Provincial Booksellers—to such more especially as I know to rank with the most Virtuous And Patriotic of their fellow-citizens, who (many of them) whilst they hold themselves in readiness to repel, by Dint of Arms, any open attack upon the Rights and

Liberties, would shrink with horror from the bare idea of becoming accessory in corrupting, to any degree, the Morals of the People—to these I most earnestly address myself, and presume to suggest the Expediency of their exercising their own Private Judgment, in every possible instance, on the Contents of all those Volumes, which are unceasingly poured from certain Marked Metropolitan Presses, previous to the giving any order to have them transmitted to them, and for the honest and conscientious purpose of obviating by this precaution the evils, which must otherwise inevitably result from the wider dissemination of the most pernicious opinions through the Medium of their Circulating Libraries. They are of a nature, the tendency and design of which cannot be misunderstood. They are 'a scandal to any Christian Country;' and having once unhappily been permitted 'to pass through the Press,' ought instantaneously to be made 'to pass through the Fire.' [33]

Munkhouse's rant clearly exposed the views of the Tory mob. He preached no sermon against the slave trade and little wonder: Munkhouse personally benefited from slavery upon his marriage: his dowry of £1,000 was without a shadow of a doubt derived from slavery. Munkhouse had been instituted in the recently completed St John's Church on 25 July 1795, and was promoted to Vicar of Wakefield 20 September 1805. He died of a paralytic stroke on 20 January 1810. The Rev. Munkhouse had married Faith Savage, the daughter of Arthur Savage I (?–1801) an American Loyalist, and was a merchant based on Boston who traded slaves and slave produced goods. Under the terms of his will of April 1801, the Rev. Dr Munkhouse and his two sons received shares in the plantation.[34] Faith's brother Arthur Savage II (1766–1815) owned Strawberry Hill plantation in Port Royal. Arthur Savage II was a partner in Arthur Savage & Co. of Kingston Jamaica, a merchant and coffee planter of Strawberry Hill died c. 1815 and after specific bequests to among others his nieces, and left his residual estate to his sister Faith.[35] Arthur fathered numerous children Arthur Savage III, born 29 January 1804 and Richard, born 5 May 1806: they are recorded as the children of Jane Bowie, 'a free mestee by Arthur Savage', and were baptised in Kingston, Jamaica, on 14 June 1806. Jane is likely to be his mistress and no doubt a former slave. Arthur had two daughters as well: Eliza Sturgess, born 25 January 799 and baptised 8 January 1800; and Jane, born 15 July 1801 and baptised on

23 July 1802. Arthur Savage III went on to be a naval surgeon, who as surgeon-intendent sailed with three convict ships to Australia between 1833 and 1836 and with an emigrant ship on which he and his family sailed in 1838. He had acted as an immigration agent in the UK before his departure. He served as health officer for Sydney from November 1839 until his death in New South Wales on 19 July 1852. The London merchant firm of Bird, Savage & Bird was clearly connected to the family given the evidence of naming practices including 'Bird' among the children of Arthur's sister Faith.[36] Faith Munkhouse passed the estates to her children Fidella, Lucy and Anna Sophia.[37] No mention is made of Dolly Munkhouse, the eldest daughter, who married William Steer.[38] Maybe provision had been made for her in her marriage settlement. The Steer family were slave traders and owners in Liverpool. A John Steer, likely father of Edward and William Steer of Wakefield, was owner of Bradfield Pen in St Ann Jamaica.[39] The family had been cloth merchants in Wakefield in the mid-eighteenth century. More research is needed to establish the family's involvement with slavery and the textile trade in Yorkshire. At abolition, the Rev. Munkhouse's daughters Fidella, Lucy and Anna Sophia, received a share of £2,040 1s 1d compensation for the 109 slaves they jointly owned.[40] Fidella went onto become the first woman to have a book of poems published in Australia.

- Dorothy Mansfield, whose brother was the Rev. John Mansfield, rector of Patrington 1803–7, married Thomas Hibbert. The good reverend was named a devisee of Thomas Hibbert's will – Hibbert was a major slave owner. Rev. Mansfield endeavoured to claim £3,817 6s 11d at abolition from slaves at Agualta Vale Plantation but ultimately failed.[41]

- Rev. Charles John Sympson was Rector of Kirby Misperton in 1851. His father Robert Sympson received one of the largest single compensation awards at abolition for 704 slaves. He lived at Kirkby Misperton near Pickering. The good reverend's father received compensation for 94 slaves on St Ann at Phoenix Park, 64 at Angels Pen, 179 at New Hall, 244 at Georges Valley, 244 at Money Musk and 174 at Riverside. In total he owned 1,703 people and received almost £70,000 compensation. He was one of the largest slave owners in the county. He willed 'whatever sum can be afforded' from his estate of Monymusk in Jamaica to his three daughters, Harriet Fowler (to receive one-third more than the other two), Emma Charlotte O'Neill and Isabella Theophania Weguelin, but left the amount to the discretion of his son-in-law William John Law, 'who most kindly and nobly took up the heavy mortgage' on the estate. He also left

£2,000 each to his sons Charles John Sympson and George Frederick Sympson.[42]

- Rev. William Coulthurst, vicar of Halifax owned part of 'Grove Slave Plantation'– we will come back to him later on in our story.
- Rev. William Mason, vicar of Normanton, was paid compensation for eleven slaves at Port Royal on the Eden Estate St George, and a further twenty-four slaves at St George, all in Jamaica. He received just shy of £4,000 compensation. According to the 1851 Census he was living at 'The Vicarage' which records the household as follows: William, aged 48, Vicar of Normanton, born Lancaster, Lancashire, wife Margaret, aged 46, born Westmorland, son Edward, aged 13, Scholar at home, and daughter Mary Ann, aged 8, also Scholar at home. Living with the family are a governess and three female house servants. We know from other census records that his son Jackson was studying under George A. Butterton DD, Headmaster of King Edward VI School, Giggleswick. In the 1851 Census Jackson is given as aged 17, Scholar, born Normanton. The Rev. Mason subsequently lived in Pickhill, Thirsk, Yorkshire, and died aged 69 in 1873.[43] He had inherited the plantations from his mother Eleanor: she was the sister of John Thompson of Liverpool, who in his will made in 1824 delineated his Jamaican property: the sugar estate called Eden in the parish of St George with the 'negroes' on it, which had been in co-partnership with Daniel Steele but which he then owned outright; a coffee estate called Lancaster in St George; and a building on Port Royal Street in Kingston, which he put in trust for his minor son John Thompson, with remainder to his nephew and niece William and Mary Ann Mason. His executors were his sister Eleanor Blewart, his nephew William Mason of Milnthorpe and Charles Horsfall of Liverpool.[44]

These men of the cloth owned slaves and profited handsomely from them – profits before people?

Chapter 4

East Yorkshire Slave Owners and Traders

The UCL database records bourgeois men and women as slave holders across Yorkshire. What follows is a brief study of these people. Not all the records list exact places of habitation. For example, living somewhere in Yorkshire was Jane Sarah Burdekin. In 1832 she owned three slaves: Ann aged 31, Mary aged 5 and Jane aged 2 – presumably Ann's children.[1] She received £50 for four slaves in 1833, and her husband (?) had been a partner in Burdekin & Holdsworth of Kingston, Jamaica. She died in Islington in 1837.[2]

Slave owners in East Yorkshire included the following men and women.

- James Bean, who died sometime after 1767, had extensive land holdings in Jamaica and was listed in the Jamaican Quit Rent books for 1754 as the owner of 873 acres of land in Hanover. In his will he left 'dwelling house that I have lately built' – Wentworth House Aldbrough in Holderness – to his brother David Bean. He turned to 'all my real and personal estate near Lucea in the parish of Hanover in the island of Jamaica' towards the end of his will. First, he said 'whereas I am possessed of and entitled to a mulatto girl named . . . Nancie begotten on the body of a negro woman of mine named . . . Cuba residing upon my plantation estate in the parish of Hanover', he freed Nancie and provided for 'a very genteel maintenance' for her. Clearly, he had had sexual relationships with his slaves.[3] A 'mulatto' had a white parent and a black parent.
- Simon Taylor of Kingston, Jamaica lived in Yorkshire at the end of his life, at Etton Hall near Beverley. He was the richest man on the island. He was awarded compensation for Pleasant Hill in Port

Royal, Constant Spring, Ramble Pen and New York in St Ann, and two awards in Kingston, all as owner-in-fee, plus the compensation for an estate in St David as trustee. At abolition he owned 1,057 slaves and received over £20,000 in compensation.[4] In his will of 1839 he left £1,000 to his reputed daughter Letitia Taylor of Kingston – fathered with a slave – then a minor, and £1,000 each to his two sisters, Christiana Taylor and Catherine Taylor of Edinburgh, and £3,000 to his nephew Robert Taylor, son of his eldest brother Robert Taylor of Kirktonhill. He left his residuary estate, including the services of his apprenticed labourers i.e. his slaves that were freed in 1832 – for whom he had taken a hefty amount of compensation from the British government for and still employed them as free labour on his plantations – to his brother and sole executor George Taylor of Kingston.[5] He was known to several Yorkshire slaving families.

- Nearby at Beverley Park lived Stephen Denton. He had left Jamaica in April 1820 having been a resident for many years and appears to have sold off most of his estates and the enslaved people on them before his return to Britain. He was awarded the compensation both as owner-in-fee of enslaved people and as trustee on John's Hall & Somerset estate, as trustee of the same plantations and as mortgagee of the Devon and Green Vale & Norway estates, all in Manchester Jamaica. In total he was awarded in excess of £12,000 for the 637 slaves that he either owned outright or was mortgagee for between 1835 and 1836.[6] The Dentons went on to become one of the largest landowners in the Beverley area in the 1800s, acquiring an area that included Hampston Hill Farm and Old Hall Farm, which is located in the Woodmansey area on the outskirts of the town. His will of 1840 is silent on any Jamaican property.[7]

- Samuel Walter of Holmpton left in his will of 1810, his Yorkshire property, his houses in the 'back ropery' of Kingston upon Hull, and the plantation formerly known as Clarke's but known as Chancery Hall at the time of his death, and the enslaved people on it, to his only daughter Mary Ann Walter for life and then to his great-grandson Richard Lacy.[8] Chancery Hall had been owned by Maynard Clarke since 1720 and passed to Samuel Walter senior in the 1780s. In 1790 the plantation was supplying sugar, molasses, rum, lime, bricks and cattle. By 1809 the plantation had 86 slaves and was dealing solely in sugar and rum and by abolition it housed 164 slaves.[9]

- Thomas Ellinor Junior of Beverley, in his will dated 12 October 1726, notes that he lived in Jamaica and is described as a bricklayer. We find that under a codicil he gave 'negro boy slave called Beverley and £40 to Edward Johnson of Kingston, Jamaica, barber in whose house I now dwell in' on 19 March 1728 or 1729 (the date is unclear).[10]

Hull, we are traditionally told, played no part in slavery, yet records reveal that Elizabeth Haworth inherited a share of the Lancaster estate in St Elizabeth, Jamaica, from her father Samuel Warren Foster. She was living in Hull at the time of abolition and received £3,127 3s 1d.[11] Another Hull slave owner was Thomas Holt, living at 63 Great Thornton Street according to the 1851 Census. He had been awarded the compensation for eight enslaved people at Falmouth, Jamaica as owner-in-fee, a total of £198 11s 4d.[12]

Chapter 5

West Yorkshire Slave Owners and Traders

In West Yorkshire, slave owners and traders were concentrated around the major towns of Huddersfield, Leeds, Halifax and Wakefield. Leeds was a notable centre of slavery in the county: as it was the richest town in the county by 1800 this is not surprising.

Albertine Bird of Pudsey had 146 slaves; the widow of Thomas Bird, she had inherited Content estate in St Andrew, Jamaica, from David Haase. The plantation in 1832 was 400 acres and had 144 slaves. She received £2,714 5s 8d compensation. The 1841 Census shows she was aged 60 living at Chapel Row, Calverley, Pudsey, Yorkshire with her daughters Juliana 25 and Augusta 20.[1]

Anthony Wilkinson (1770–1842), the son of Robert Wilkinson and Mary Wilson, was born on 2 May 1770 in Sedbergh, then in the West Riding. According to family sources, he moved to Jamaica as a young man and lived there for 20 years before returning to Sedbergh where he married Jane Sedgwick in 1809. In 1824 he bought Brosdale Beck in Howgill, Yorkshire, for £1,164. The second of three brothers, he inherited the Kendal and Sedbergh estates in the West Indies from his younger brother William Robinson Wilkinson (1776–1831). At abolition he received £2,855 0s 11 for 139 slaves and in 1838 he sold Kendal, Friendship and Sedbergh estates to John Clark for £3,500.[2]

Barnaby Maddan was living in Huddersfield in the 1830s. He had been a plantation manager of an estate called Enfield in Jamaica. He had been a local partner of a Liverpool merchant firm until 1812, James Willasey & Co. The business was carried on in Liverpool by James Willasey and Abraham Garnett, with Maddan as the West Indian side of the concern. Maddan had numerous sexual relationships with the slaves under his supervision:

- Mary Elizabeth Marjean, 'quadroon woman',[3] bore him a daughter Sarah Ann Jane Maddan on 28 October 1802.
- Fanny Breandeau, 'free mulatto', gave birth to his daughter Elizabeth Grace Maddan on 29 November 1806. Grace married William Radley Townley in St Mary, Islington in 1831. In 1841 they were living in Huddersfield, Yorkshire, with two young sons. William Radley Townley died in 1860 in Ralph's Bay, Tasmania, aged 57. He had been a teacher at the Port Arthur penal colony and later at another penal colony on Norfolk Island. By 1871 Elizabeth had returned to England and was a lodger on Castle Street, Canterbury and died a year later aged 72.

Barnaby Maddan was the object of comment by *The Anti-slavery Monthly Reporter* in 1830 for standing by while three enslaved men were imprisoned for preaching on Mount Industry. He had married Caroline Strange in 1811. At abolition he received compensation for 1,155 slaves totalling well over £12,000, making him a very wealthy man during his residence in Huddersfield! He died in 1861 aged 83.[4]

Samuel Barrett (1788–1824) of Park Hill, Doncaster in his will of 9 December 1824 left his widow Margaret Gillies 'his carriage, horses etc. and £1000' from his personal estate. In his will he reported that from his sugar works called the Spring, his executors were to draw £1,200 per annum to his wife and £6,000 to be raised as portions for his daughter and younger sons. Likewise, his pen called Thatchfield was to be placed in trust to pay his wife an annuity of £300 per annum, over and above the amount already settled upon her. From the trust was also come an annuity of £200 per annum to his mother Elizabeth Barrett Williams – she never married Samuel Barrett (?–1794) by whom she had four children – and an annuity 'to his aunt Mary Barrett Lockhead [?] wife of John Lockhead'. He further commented in his will that there was '£22,535 4s 4d standing in the name of trustees for his children'.[5] In a codicil made in 1823 in Boulogne, he scaled back some of his monetary legacies because of the state of the West India colonies and appointed Laurence Oliphant of Conday – who later married his widow – as an additional trustee and executor. His son, Samuel Goodin Barrett, died in 1876 leaving under £8,000.[6] Samuel II's father, Samuel Barrett I (?–1794) was a slave owner on Jamaica, owning 140 acres in 1754. Samuel II's mother owned slaves in her own right from her first marriage to Martin Williams, and his brother Richard Barrett (1789–1839) was a major slave owner. The family owned Barrett Hall Estate, and Barrett Hall Pen amongst a dozen or so plantations.[7]

Mary Skelton, a widow of Little Horton Bradford, in her will of 1822 she left her 'three fourth part share' of the Yorkshire Hall plantation in Demerara to her three sons including 'all the negroes and slaves which may, at the time of my decease, be resident or belong to the said plantation'. She had forty-seven slaves, twenty-five of them being men and boys. By 1826 the estate was owned by Thomas Skelton, her eldest son.[8] She died on 18 January 1823.[9] Family member Ralph – husband? – was a planter on Demerara and owner of Yorkshire Hall from 1775. He died in 1801 after returning to England, his will being proved in Bradford on 12 January 1802.[10] We note he emigrated to Richmond, Jamaica in 1775, sailing from Portsmouth.

Thomas Staniforth (1735–1803) was baptised in Sheffield on 24 April 1735. He became a merchant and along with the Denisons, Ingrams and Heywoods financed slaving voyages. Staniforth found his own banking concern in Liverpool, his agent being Francis Ingram. Thomas was educated at Heath Academy, Wakefield, and upon completion of his schooling John Trevers Younge, his brother-in-law, arranged for him an apprenticeship to an 'old family friend' – Charles Goore, merchant of Liverpool. Goore had built up a shipping empire in 'oil, whales, seals, ivory, iron and slaves'.[11] The Trans-Atlantic Slave Trade Database records Goore participated in five slaving voyages. Staniforth married Goore's daughter, and inherited the business, trafficking some 7,000 slaves in the 1770s alone. The Trans-Atlantic Slave Trade Database records that between 1765 and 1795 he funded 79 slaving voyages and transported 24,621 slaves, of whom over 3,000 died on the journey. He invested his fortune in banking and was Mayor of Liverpool 1797–8. He died in 1803 leaving £15,000: £500 to his brother Samuel, £500 to his widow Mary, £100 to Liverpool Infirmary, £100 to the Blue Coat School Liverpool (founded by the slave-owning Blundell family), £50 to 'Lady Charity', and the same sum each to the 'Blind Asylum' and 'Liverpool Dispensary'. The residue, over £13,000, passed to his son Thomas.[12] Four Liverpool institutions benefited directly from slave money. A portrait of Goore by Joseph Wright of Derby exists in the Tate Gallery. Of his sons:

- Thomas Staniforth (?–1826) was in partnership with his brother Samuel, and participated in thirteen slave-trading voyages between 1795 and 1804.[13]
- Samuel Staniforth (1769–1851). Samuel lived in Liverpool for most of his life, where he was Lord Mayor 1812–13. Samuel's son, Rev. Thomas Staniforth was rector of Bolton-By-Bolland 1831–59. From his father-in-law, John Bolton, he inherited £180,000 derived from

the slave economy in 1837. The Trans-Atlantic Slave Trade Database shows him as participating in sixty-nine slave voyages between 1788 and 1807. Initially (1788–91) Bolton was one of a dozen or so partners in the voyages but subsequently he appears as the sole owner in the vast majority of them. His activity peaked between 1798 and 1805, in each year of which he sent at least five ships from Liverpool. Samuel Staniforth left £150,492 16s 8d (re-sworn from £149,667 16s 8d at probate). His executors were his great-nephews, Charles Staniforth Greenwood and Edwin Wilfrid [sic] Greenwood.[14]

As a regional centre for the cloth trade with its cloth hall opening in 1766, by the end of the eighteenth century Halifax had attracted slave owners and slave traders as its wealth and middle class grew. Made famous by the TV series *Gentleman Jack*, the Lister family, who would own Shibden Hall estate, received £3,500 a year in rents from the Adelphi plantation. Louisa Grant, the daughter of Major Charles Grant, a slave owner, married Dr John Lister. He had inherited the estate from his sister Ann in 1840, whose uncle James had inherited the estate in 1826. The income from the slave plantation was the sole income of the doctor, along with his small army pension, for the maintenance of the estate. At abolition Louisa Grant received £12,765 13s 8d for her 485 slaves![15]

Another Halifax slave owner was Joseph Crabtree. He was born c. 1791 – he may have been the Joseph Crabtree baptised at Northgate End on 5 December 1790[16] – and died it seems in Liverpool in January 1865 leaving £80,000. He was a Liverpool merchant, who traded as Crabtree, Scott and Co. He made six compensation claims and received over £5,000 for his slaves.[17]

Also making his home in Halifax was William Ingram, brother of Francis Ingram of Wakefield. Initially he was a merchant in Liverpool, setting himself up after a brief career in the army, and began slave trading in 1759 in partnership with his brother. History tells us that Ingram shipped slaves to sugar plantations as well as into the Americas to tobacco plantations. His ship *Hare* docked in in the Rappahannock in 1761 discharging 258 people as slaves. William became a banker in Halifax by 1785, where he was a stalwart member of the parish church. He used slave voyages as means of financing his bank – slave voyages were a sound investment and offered excellent returns. According to the Trans-Atlantic Slave Trade Database, William conducted twenty-one slaving voyages. He transported 6,900 slaves, 6,100 going to West Indies, some two-thirds being delivered to Jamaica. His voyages went to West Central Africa and the Congo Basin, thence to the West Indies and brought back rum, tobacco, dye stuff, spices and sugar. As a prominent member of Halifax society, William was made captain of the Halifax Volunteer Troop of Cavalry. A man with few morals when it concerned personal gain, he was caught in 1805 embezzling the men's pay. The bank experienced financial difficulties in 1808, when it was discovered that the Halifax co-partnership was in debt to the Wakefield co-partnership as William had been syphoning off the profits! The bank failed, but William's sons, William and Henry, Abraham Richard Ingram and Robert Witham continued the business becoming the 'Halifax Bank' by a deed of 1 July 1812. The bank failed in 1816.[18]

Stapleton Park, Pontefract and later Snydale Hall, was home to Ellis Leckenby Hodgson (1763–1831). He was baptised a Unitarian by Rev. Nicolas Clayton (1733–97) minister at the Octagon Chapel Liverpool. Clayton went onto become divinity tutor to Warrington Academy in 1781, succeeding John Aikin, and from 1785 to 1795 he ministered at the High Pavement Chapel, Nottingham as the colleague of George Walker. Hodgson attended Warrington Academy from 1776, along with members of the Gildart and Ogden families. Hodgson married a sister of the Whig Colonel John Dixon of Gledhow. He stood in 1812 as Whig MP in Pontefract, against Robert Pemberton Milnes.[19] His father, Thomas Hodgson (1729–1803), was a slave trader conducting 138 slaving voyages between 1751 and 1799. Between 1786 and 1799 Ellis undertook fifty-four voyages. He used his vast wealth to buy Stapleton Park. His daughter Mary Helen Hodgson married Henry Torre (1780–1866), the son of Esther and James Torre of Snydale Hall. Thomas Hodgson and his brother John were in partnership with the notorious James Penny and Moses Benson. The Hodgson family, according to the Trans-Atlantic Slave Trade Database, invested in 183 slaving voyages, transporting 55,010 human beings and disembarking 48,014 in mainland America and the West Indies. Some 7,000 people lost their lives because of their actions. Stapleton Park was built around 1762–4. The architect was John Carr (1723–1807) and it had been built for Edward Lascelles MP, who had become rich on slave plantations. Upon Lascelles inheriting Harewood in 1796, Stapleton Park was sold to Hodgson. By the 1820s it was home to the Hon. Robert Petre, a radical orator, MP and racehorse owner. The house has since been demolished. Snydale Hall still stands and the considerable dowry allowed the Georgian mansion to enlarged and updated.

Baptised at Royston Parish Church on 5 February 1742 was Benjamin Hammond, son of Benjamin Hammond. His brother Peter remained in Tankersley, so too brother Thomas where his son Benjamin was born in 1766 and he died in the same year as his uncle.[20] This may be the slave ship captain Benjamin Hammond. According to the Trans-Atlantic Slave Trade Database, Benjamin Hammond, now of Liverpool, undertook 35 slaving voyages, some in partnership with Ellis Leckenby Hodgson, and transported a minimum of 10,277 slaves. Between 1798 and 1799 he transported 1,257 people from Upper Guinea, working in partnership with William Begg, John Rackham, John Mill, Robert Sellar, Charles Shan and Robert Buddicam. As well as trading in people, Hammond also traded as a merchant: in 1795 he imported six pipes of wine from Portugal,[21] and trading as Briggs, Hammond & Co imported linen from Prussia[22] and Ireland.[23] Hammond died in 1803 leaving an estate of roughly £20,000, his executors being his wife, Benjamin Heywood of Stanley Hall, Arthur Heywood of Liverpool (Benjamin's younger brother), Dr James Currie and the Rev. John Yates of Liverpool:[24] we can only assume Hammond was a Unitarian as his executors were all Unitarians. He married Elizabeth Shaw at Darfield Parish Church on 11 November 1760. They had three sons, Joseph, Peter and George, and a daughter Ann. His widow died in 1814 and gave away over £15,000 in bequests.[25] George was also a slave trader, the Trans-Atlantic Slave Trade Database showing he undertook seven voyages between 1803 and 1807, transporting 2,316 slaves. We have been unable to find a will for George.

Living in Haymarket, Sheffield according to the 1841 Census was Robert Haynes (1795–1873), son of Lieutenant General Robert Haynes. His estate was worth £40,000 under the terms of his will. The Haynes family, originally of Reading, Berkshire, had originally settled in Barbados 'in the time of Cromwell' and are purported to have been Royalist emigres. Robert Jnr received £4,775s 4s 4d for 230 slaves at Pilgrims Place, Barbados, £4,064 9s 5d for 139 slaves listed 'on Barbados', £6,080 4s 4d for 260 slaves at Clifton Hall Plantation, £1,879 16s 1d for 81 slaves at Exchange Plantation, £2,415 15s 5d for 113 slaves at Clifden and £5,023 15s 8d for 247 slaves at Guinea Plantation. He used this money to buy Thimbleby Lodge, at Thimbleby in North Yorkshire, by 1845.[26]

Luke Thomas Crossley (1788–1857) is recorded in the *London Gazette* as 'in Leeds Yorkshire, trading with and carrying on business at School Close and Monkpitts Mills . . . under the firm Crossley, Robinson and Company, stuff and woollen-printers and dyers'. At abolition he had 670 slaves and received over £12,000 in compensation.[27]

Another Leeds slave owner was Eleanor Douglas. In her will of 1804, she informs us she was living in the fashionable and recently-built Park Square. The will recorded a settlement of 1792 under which a one-sixth interest in the Mount Pleasant estate in Hanover was to be used to raise £4,000 after her death for the benefit of her children: £1,000 to her daughter Helen Frances Catherine, wife of Rev. Daniel Sandford of Edinburgh, and similar shares to her daughters, Jane Wilhelmina Douglas and Eleanor Elizabeth Jackson.[28] At abolition her estate received £2,657 3s 7d. She died in 1810 living in Leeds.[29] Her son-in-law John Jackson had drowned on a voyage to Jamaica in 1787: the banker Edward Gale Boldero was one of his trustees. In the will he left his property in trust until his eldest son Thomas Witter Jackson was 21, to secure an annuity of £500 p.a. to his wife (given as Elizabeth Ellen) and to support his three children, and then to pay £3,000 each to the two youngest (John Montague Jackson and Mary Ann Jackson) at 21 and 18.[30]

The great Unitarian congregation at Mill Hill, Leeds included cloth merchants: the firm of 'Thursby, Hainsworth and Dunn' brought together three chapel trustees![31] The modern-day firm of Abimelech Hainsworth of Pudsey is the direct successor to this firm. Another major family were the Oates'. They were leading Unitarians and trustees of Mill Hill Chapel. The family became embedded in slavery through marriage with the Hibbert family.

Robert Hibbert (1717–84), second son of Robert (1686–1762), married Abigail Scholey. Their children married into leading families of the era:

- Thomas Hibbert (1744–1819) married Sophia Boldero, daughter of Edward Gales Boldero, slave owner and banker.
- Margaret Hibbert married Thomas Greg (?–1839), slave owner and industrialist of Manchester. His father, Samuel (1758–1834) was a trustee of Cross Street Chapel Manchester and owned Quarry Bank Mill. Thomas at abolition received around £5,000 compensation for 210 slaves.[32]
- Elizabeth Hibbert (1747–1828) married into the Leeds mercantile family of Markland. Robert Markland I (c. 1747–1828) was a check and fustian manufacturer and heir to an estate at Pemberton, near Wigan. His brother Edward was part of the partnership Markland, Cookson and Fawcett, the owners of the largest cotton mill in Leeds. Robert married Elizabeth in 1776. Their son Robert Markland II formed a slave-trading partnership with Simon Taylor, the richest man in Jamaica, and the Hibberts. Indeed, we note Robert Markland became overseer for the Hibberts until he left the island in 1808, being replaced by George Hibbert Oates. James Heywood Markland, Robert's younger brother, became an important pro-slavery lobbyist. Having trained as a solicitor in Manchester, he moved to London and joined the legal partnership Markland and Wright.[33] James

Heywood Markland, elected a Fellow of the Royal Society in 1816, left £30,000 at his death and was the most important figure on the Literary Committee of the London Society of West India Planters and Merchants in the 1820s as well as secretary and solicitor to the Standing Committee. The Literary Committee was established in 1823 as the agent of publicity for the pro-slavery cause through pamphlets, publishers, newspapers and journalists. At abolition he received compensation of £20,000 or thereabouts.[34]

- Mary Hibbert (1761–1844) married a Leeds cloth merchant, George William Oates, the son of George Oates.

George Oates (1717–79) was a successful cloth merchant and was named trustee of Leeds White Cloth Hall on 3 November 1774 along with his co-religionists John Bischoff and Arthur Lupton, both of Call Lane Chapel Leeds and Pemberton Milnes and James Milnes of Westgate Chapel, Wakefield.[35] He was a leading light in the Yorkshire Association.[36] George Oates had formed a partnership in the 1740s with Mill Hill man Thomas Woolwrich for dyeing and trading cloth. Sarah Woolwrich, Thomas's only child, married David Stansfeld of Halifax, who was a member of the well-known Unitarian family worshipping at Northgate End Chapel.

George had three sons and two daughters: Joseph (1743–1819) who resided at Weetwood Hall and married Elizabeth Raynor, the daughter of co-religionist and cloth merchant Joshua Rayner. Joshua Rayner (1703–57) was in partnership with Obadiah Dawson, said to be the largest stuff (cheap, coarse woollen cloth) merchant in England. Joshua Raynor took as his second Sarah Milnes of Chesterfield. She died aged 35 on 22 March 1753. Sarah was the daughter of William Milnes of Chesterfield: he was brother to Robert Milnes (1671–1734) and John Milnes (1677–1742) of Wakefield, and had married Elizabeth Lee. Their son William Milnes II married Ann Gaskell, sister to Benjamin Gaskell of Clifton Hall, the grandfather of Benjamin and Daniel Gaskell of Wakefield. Sarah Oates and Joshua Raynor had one son and two daughters:

- Milnes Rayner (1753–92) was a merchant and died unmarried, being buried at Mill Hill in August 1792.
- Elizabeth (1750–98) who married Joseph Oates, to whom the family estate passed to. Her daughter Sarah married Rev. William Wood's son, George William, whose sister Louisa Ann married the Rev. Samuel Crawford of Call Lane Chapel. Joseph Oates' children were George Oates, Joseph Henry Oates, Edward Oates, and Ann. The world of

Joseph Henry Oates is brought to life in *Men, Women and Property in England 1780–1870* by R. J. Morris.
- Sarah who married William Smithson of Heath Hall, near Wakefield. Smithson (1750–1830) was in business partnership with Milnes Rayner, and was Mayor of Leeds in 1781. George William (1757–97) of whom more anon Frederick Oates (1750–1803) marrying a daughter of William Read. Sophia Carolina Oates was wife of Thomas Robinson of Manchester, a West Indian Merchant and slave owner attending Cross Street Chapel. Louisa Ann (1758–1806) became the wife of the Rev. William Wood, minister at Mill Hill. His nephew was John Marshall, MP for Yorkshire from 1826 for the Whig cause.

George William Oates married Mary Hibbert. She was daughter of Robert Hibbert (1717–84) and Abigail Scholey (1723–95). Through the Hibbert dowry the Oates became slave owners. George William Oates children all profited from slavery:

- George Hibbert Oates (1791–1837) at abolition owned nineteen slaves. In 1824 he was subject to a stinging critique by the missionary Thomas Cooper who published details of his scandalous behaviour whilst in Jamaica in running a prostitution racket and fathering children by his slaves. Cooper revealed that Oates had been living in 'a state of illicit intercourse' on Georgia estate with a 16-year-old quadroon girl, who was pregnant with his child.[37] Oates was overseer to the Hibberts and clearly exploited his position for sexual gratification. He seems to have been, despite this, a semi-honest man. In his will, made 4 November 1837, he left his mother Mary an annuity of £100 per annum, and his sister Anna Maria £2,000; both women were at the time living in Bath. He left his brother Hibbert Oates £2,000. He left £100 cash each to his three 'reputed' children, Jane Oates, formerly a slave on Whitney; George Thomas Oates, formerly a slave on Hals Hall; and Mary Oates, a free girl of colour formerly a slave on Georgia estate. He left land to Elizabeth Williams formerly a slave on Great Valley estate and her 'mulatto child' (his reputed daughter) Anna Maria.[38]
- Hibbert Oates (1797–1843) was the owner of several estates in Jamaica. In 1823 he purchased Rowington Estate, with its twenty-six slaves,[39] and from 1825 owned the 'The View' estate. In 1832 he owned 52 slaves and by 1839 he had some 521 indentured workers. He worked as an attorney at law in Jamaica.[40] He died in Jamaica in 1843, and under the terms of his will he left £500 to his mother Mary Oates residing at

Bath and £1,000 to his sister Anna Maria Oates, also of Bath. He left George Barkley, an apprentice [*sic*] belonging to Rymesbury Pen, £50 cash and five acres of Hibbert Oates' estate called Rowington Park, and a similar legacy to Sarah Good on Rowington Park and her daughter Jenny Roberts. His residuary legatee was his housekeeper Frances Smith.[41]

- Robert Oates (1798–1876), was a captain with the West India Co. and died at Greater Antilles, Jamaica, captain of the ship *Wellington*.
- Anna Maria Oates (1799–1870), received monetary legates from her brothers Hibbert Oates of £1,000 and George Hibbert Oates some £2,000, and through her mother Mary Oates via her brother Thomas Hibbert, and her father. All of these sums were beyond reasonable doubt derived from slavery. She died in Bath in 1870 with an estate worth £20,000.

Chapter 6

North Yorkshire Slave Owners and Traders

Rural North Yorkshire was dominated by the country gentry. Lieutenant Colonel Thomas Browne of Newton House, at Falling Foss, Whitby, had 600 slaves on St Vincent by 1808. He was an American Loyalist, and was granted land that became Grand Sable estate on St Vincent, to which he moved over 600 enslaved people from the Bahamas in 1805–06. He had been granted a much larger tract of 6,000 acres, which included recently cleared Carib land in the possession of local planters, with whom there was a protracted conflict between 1806 and 1809. He was in Whitby in 1802, but died in St Vincent in 1825.[1] His son, the Rev. Thomas Alexander Murray Browne was vicar of Ellerburn 1817–24 when he moved to St Vincent. He was pro-slavery and against emancipation. He claimed £17,753 5s 7d at abolition, but failed to receive a single penny. His son, also Rev. Thomas Browne, sold the estate in 1846.[2]

Another army officer was William Grassett (1813–47) who served in the 7th Hussars. He was born on Barbados on 13 May 1813 to William Grassett. Educated at Eton and then Trinity College Cambridge, he was awarded a share in the compensation for Golden Grove in Barbados, in which his father William Grassett was owner-in-fee of 75 enslaved people and tenant for life of 132 more, of some £4,072 10s 11d.[3]

John Pickersgill, born near Ripon at Ellingstring, where he was baptised on 13 August 1785, was the son John Pickersgill senior. In 1810 he married Sophia, sister of Ellis Cunliffe Lister Kay (1774–1853), the first MP for Bradford in 1832. Pickersgill was a merchant shipping woollen goods to America and was a slave owner. He was a partner in George Wildes & Co, which was dissolved in 1842. At abolition he received compensation for three plantations on Trinidad: £1,251 11s 0d for fifty-one slaves, £893 7s 7d for thirteen slaves and £1,414 10s 4d for an undisclosed number of slaves.[4]

Scruton Hall in Bedale was home to Foster Lechmere Coore (1780–1837): he was awarded the largest share of the compensation for Pembroke estate in Trelawney with Thomas Fitzgerald as trustees and executors of Frederick Richard Coore. He was aide-de-camp to Sir George Prevost, Governor General of Lower Canada in 1802, succeeding Sir Robert Shore Milnes. He received £6,114 1s 0d at abolition. In 1818 he and his brother had 261 slaves.[5]

Bishop Burton was home to Richard Watt (1786–1855). He inherited George's Plain in Westmoreland, Jamaica as well as Speke Hall under the will of his grandfather. Some information about life on the plantation is available from the slave registers which were first produced in 1811 and then every three years from 1817. The returns for the George's Plain estate provide us with the first detailed account of those whose labour made the whole thing work. In 1817 the return lists a total of 331 enslaved workers, including 171 males and 160 females. One hundred and twenty-four had been born in Africa, and 207 had been born locally in Jamaica. By 1834, the high death rate caused by the harshness of the work and the inability to replace them with new slaves from Africa meant that the enslaved population had fallen to 255. There were 10 supervisors, 150 field workers (77 men and 73 women), 11 coopers, masons and carpenters, seven domestic servants, 19 children aged under six, and 58 who were classed as 'old', that is too unwell or infirm to work. At abolition he received £4,485 45s 9 for 256 slaves. His brother Francis received £2,210 16s 5d as his share of the compensation paid following the Emancipation Act of 1833, for slaves at a sugar plantation at Potosi in Jamaica.[6]

In 1791 the sugar plantation of Hyde, on Jamaica at St Thomas-in-the-Vale, was managed by Zachariah MacCaulay in 1791, who was from the East Riding.[7] The plantation was owned by Richard Welch, son and heir of Richard Macaulay Welch (c. 1733–82) and his wife Lucretia Mary Favel Dehany (1751–1813). Under the terms of his will: 'Philip Dehany and James Holder to manage conduct and carry on my plantation or sugar work called Hyde in the Island of Jamaica and the slaves, appurtenances and stock for the benefit and advantage of my estate'. To his children he gave:

the rents, issues and profits of my estate to pay and discharge all my lawful debts and also the following sums of money: to my younger son Robert Gregory Welch £5000 sterling and to each of my daughters £3000 sterling at the age of 21 or for my daughters at marriage if before the age of 21. If it is not expedient to pay the said portions then payments shall be postponed and interest at the rate of 5% shall be paid. If within 12 months after reaching the age of 21 my son Arthur shall think fit to make over to my son Robert Gregory his heirs forever one full and equal half part undivided of my said residuary estate then the said legacy of £5000 to Robert shall not be raised to paid to him.[8]

Adolphus Moffatt Bayard (d. 1827), a lieutenant in the 15th Hussars, lived in Bridlington. On his death, he passed to his brother Edward slave plantations in Jamaica, for which compensation of £2,522 12s 6d was paid for slaves at Blenheim Plantation and £2,524 1s 5d for slaves at Cranbrook.[9]

According to the Trans-Atlantic Slave Trade Database, several North Yorkshiremen took part in slave voyages:

- Thomas Parke (1730–1819) was from Swaledale, North Yorkshire. He was a linen draper who went into business as a linen merchant, initially with his brother John. He advanced from linen to investing in seventy-seven slaving voyages from 1781: fifty voyages as 'Parke & Heywood', and the remainder with William Davenport, Francis Ingram, Thomas Staniforth and others, before retiring in 1792. His nephew Christopher Wilson was a gunpowder merchant in Liverpool. It was one of Parke's captains, Joseph Frayer, who became their business representative in London – shipping slaves from Africa to bring back raw materials to make gunpowder in Kendal. After 1792 Parke ended his direct investment in the slave trade, and concentrated more on the production of cotton goods, a business in which one of his sons was involved. He became partner in Heywood's bank and was a director of the Liverpool fire insurance office established in 1777. A portrait of him by Joseph Wright of Derby survives.
- Thomas Wycliffe (1728–1809) from Richmond is recorded as undertaking 10 voyages between 1754 and 1768, transporting 4,423 slaves. Of these, 936 came from Central West Africa and were shipped to mainland North America and 2,987 to plantations in the West Indies.
- Thomas Foxcroft (1733–1809) of Thornton in Lonsdale, undertook 92 slaving voyages between 1768 and 1793, transporting 25,276 slaves of whom over 4,000 never reached their destination! He delivered 666 slaves – 526 from Benin and 140 from Sierra Leone – to tobacco plantations in America while 23,423 went to the sugar plantations in the West Indies. His sister Agnes married Robert Welch, whose brother John Welch was a major Liverpool slave trader. Foxcroft

invested with Edward Chaffers, William Siddall and Ambrose Lace in a ropery in Liverpool, supplying their ships with rigging.[10]

- Leonard Parkinson (1744–1817) was born in Kirklevington, Stockton on Tees, formerly the North Riding of Yorkshire. According to the Trans-Atlantic Slave Trade Database he was a slave trader, who with Colonel George Goodin Barrett of Doncaster, sold twenty-six ship-loads of enslaved Africans between 1789 and 1792 as slave factors at Montego Bay and other northern and north-western Jamaican ports. From the profits from the slave trade, Parkinson purchased the estate of Kinnersley Castle in Herefordshire, where he died in 11 July 1817, leaving his land in Herefordshire and Jamaica to his son Leonard Parkinson II and the castle was left in trust for the benefit of his daughter Mary Elizabeth Clarke.[11]

Chapter 7

Wakefield, Capital of Slavery

Wakefield was the capital of the eighteenth-century West Riding;
thus, it comes as no surprise that slave owners lived and
walked its streets well into the nineteenth century. Daniel
Defoe described the town in 1724:

> A large, handsome, rich clothing town, full of people, and full of
> trade...Wakefield is a clean, large, well-built town, very populous
> and very rich; here is a very large church, and well filled it is, for
> here are very few Dissenters; the steeple is a very fine spire, and
> by far the highest in all this part of the country, except that at
> Sheffield. They tell us, there are here more people also than in the
> city of York, and yet it is no Corporation town; and the highest
> magistrate, as I understand, was a constable.
>   Here also is a market every Friday for woollen cloaths, after the
> manner of that at Leeds, tho' not so great; yet as all the cloathing
> trade is encreasing in this country, so this market too flourishes
> with the rest; not but that sometimes, as foreign markets receive
> interruption either by wars, by a glut of the goods, or by any
> other incident, there are interruptions of the manufacture too,
> which, when it happen, the clothiers are sure to complain of loss
> of trade; but when the demand comes again they are not equally
> forward with their acknowledgments; and this, I observed,
> was the case everywhere else, as well as here.[1]

As a market town and chief administrative centre, the increasingly
wealthy town boasted such attractions as the 'New Wells' bath and
spa in imitation of fashionable Bath, while an increasingly important
racecourse brought thousands into the town. The theatre, racecourse and
the lending library established in 1768, as well as the assembly rooms
were funded by the value-chain economy of slavery. The race meeting

merged both social and economic functions. One of the town's richest merchants, Richard Milnes (1696–1755), the founder of his family's mercantile business, ran racehorses in the 1740s. Richard Milnes had been inducted into the Commission of the Peace on October 1736, and received his dedimus (a writ to commission private persons to do some act in place of a judge, such as to examine a witness, etc.) on 27 January 1744. He was a frequent correspondent with the 1st Marquis of Rockingham, and his successor the 2nd Marquis. He owned land in several counties and used his influence to mobilise the vote for the Whig cause.

Owning racehorses was part of the 'conspicuous consumption' culture of the elites: wearing the best clothes trimmed with gold lace, riding to business in a lavish coach, owning large mansions decorated by the best tradesmen money could buy, and including the ubiquitous portrait painted by the greatest living artists of the day: the Milnes family employed Michael Dahl, George Stubbs, George Romney and Joseph Wright of Derby for their portraits. This 'conspicuous consumption' of racehorse-owning was a tradition the family maintained into the nineteenth century: Richard Slater Milnes MP, Captain Robert Shore Milnes and Rodes Milnes all owned racehorses and lost staggering amounts of money on the turf. We look at the Milnes family in detail in a later chapter. Losing money was all part of the game: it showed other elites that these men had the money to lose! It was at the racecourse that the mercantile elite could be equals with the aristocracy and local gentry, making contacts for patronage and business. Racing went beyond mere masculine sociability: the racecourse was a venue to make good impressions, to foster alliances and to engage in social and political discourse which included abolitionism. In 1771 Rockingham and the Earl of Northumberland were at the Wakefield Races.[2] Sir James Lowther attended in the following year.[3] Before he came of age Lowther was reckoned the richest commoner in England. From his father he inherited estates in Cumberland and Barbados; from Lord Lonsdale, large estates in Westmorland; and in 1756 the Cumberland property of the Lowthers of Whitehaven, including Whitehaven itself – a fortune estimated at over £2,000,000. He was MP for Cumbria 1757–61, Westmoreland 1761–2, Cumberland 1762–9, Cockermouth 1769–74 and Cumberland again 1774–84. He used his huge financial resources to sponsor MPs. Lowther returned some distinguished members to Parliament. John Robinson, Sir Fletcher Norton, George Johnstone, Charles Jenkinson, Sir George Macartney and the younger Pitt were all first returned for a Lowther constituency. All either quarrelled with him or at the first opportunity sought to break the connection. But of the twelve MPs returned by Lowther at the general election of 1784 or at by-elections before 1790, only two (William Lowther and Michael le Fleming) are known to have spoken in the House – Lowther twice and le Fleming once. Of these twelve, three were Lowther's relations (William, John and James Lowther); four (Penn, le Fleming, Senhouse and Edward Norton) were personal friends; and the remaining five (Stephenson, Satterthwaite, Postlethwaite, Garforth and Knubley), were retainers, completely dependent on him. Not one of the twelve achieved any sort of distinction in the Commons, and most could never have been returned without a patron. Lonsdale died on 24 May 1802.[4] At the 1782 meeting Shore Milnes entered a horse. It ran alongside horses belonging to Mr Ayrton, Mr Edwin Lascelles MP for Northallerton, the Hon George Saville, MP for Yorkshire, and Sir John Ramsden. Richard Slater Milnes also entered a horse.[5] In 1786, Sir Thomas Gascoigne, MP for Malton, attended, along with Sir John Ramsden and Sir George Armitage. Stewards were Earl Fitzwilliam, Lord Mexborough and Lord Stourton.[6] The races were a place to be seen, a place to network, to renew and strengthen existing political and commercial alliances and foster new ones. Thus, it is hardly surprising that MPs from across the North of England, as well as the great and good, came together over the summer, when Parliament was in recess, to conduct business. At the races, Richard Slater Milnes was the equal of Earl Fitzwilliam and Rockingham: he was in the parade ring as an equal to these great men. Although an outsider to the political mainstream, but through family alliances with the Whigs on and off the racecourse, he became well known across Yorkshire. His alliance with the radical reformist Rev. Christopher Wyvill cemented his star in the local firmament.

After the races had finished, dressed in their finery the racegoers attended either Tate Wilkinson's Theatre, or danced until the early morning in the assembly rooms of the grandstand. Assemblies offered a variety of social functions: dancing, gaming, business discussion, eating and drinking, gossip, flirtation and courtship in an atmosphere of social exclusivity. The importance of the racecourse in eighteenth-century commerce and politics cannot be overstated. The Milnes were not unique in the town. Vast fortunes were made from the cloth trade and selling slave-produced goods. Of the great merchant families of the town, three families stand out for direct involvement in slavery: the Briscos, Ingrams and Heywoods.

The Brisco Family

John Brisco I, justice of the peace for Cumberland, married Catherine, the daughter of Sir Richard Musgrave, baronet. Their second son was Rev. John Brisco DD (1700–71) who married Catherine Hilton. He died on April 1771 aged 71. His eldest son was Sir John Brisco (1739–1805) 1st Baronet. He married Caroline Alice Fleming (1764–1822), daughter of Lieutenant General Gilbert Fane Fleming, a plantation owner on Jamaica and a major slave owner.[7] In the terms of her father's will Caroline was tenant-for-life of the slave plantations of Shadwell Park, Westhope, Grange and Salt Pond estates in St Kitts and tenant for life of Priddie's Salt Pond estate, also in St Kitts. Their first son was Sir Wastel Brisco I. She herself is the subject of Gainsborough's painting 'Lady Brisco'.[8] Their second son was Major General Horton Brisco (1741–1802). Of interest to our story are Rev. John Brisco's brothers Musgrave and Wastel II (?–1796).

Musgrave Brisco (1708–87) was John Brisco and Catherine Musgrave's fourth son. By 1766 he was living in Wakefield, and was an established member of the town's merchant community who requested free port status for sugar, rum and tobacco. He was a street commissioner in 1771 along with George Charnock, Robert Amory MD (Unitarian and author), William Serjeantson, John Sylvester Smith of Newland Hall, Loftus Anthony Tottenham, Benjamin Thompson, Daniel Maude, Joseph Banks and others.[9] The same year we find him paying £6 10s tax annually for a house on Westgate that stood alongside Pemberton House, valued at £4.[10] This was surely a fine and imposing mansion, far grander than Pemberton House which still stands today, which was valued at £3. He backed the Crown in the American War of Independence and in 1778 was a committee member for 'A voluntary Subscription for raising men for his Majesty's service', along with Sir Rowland Winn of Nostell, the Rev. Michael Bacon, vicar of Wakefield, Daniel Maude of Wakefield, John Atkinson of Huddersfield as well as great merchants from Leeds such as Thomas Wilson, John Blayds, John Wormald and John Beckett.[11] This placed Musgrave diametrically opposed to the Milnes and Westgate Chapel. Yet what brought him to Wakefield? We assume he was the English end of the family's West Indian plantation business.

Musgrave's brother Wastel Brisco II was a large-scale slave owner. He owned Cumberland Valley plantation on Jamaica as early as 1738. By 1754 he owned 297 acres in St Elizabeth, and 2,941 acres in Westmoreland. He was member of the Assembly of Hanover 1752–8. His total land holdings amounted to 7,676 acres. He married first, or was engaged to, a daughter of Peter Beckford (1673–1735), a Jamaican planter and slave owner. Beckford's sons William, Richard and Julines all became Members of Parliament. His daughter Elizabeth after the engagement (?) to Wastel ended, later married Thomas Howard, 2nd Earl of Effingham, and was the mother of Thomas Howard, the 3rd Earl, who was Governor of Jamaica in 1791 and a close friend of Jack Milnes the Democrat. Beckford was sole owner of nine sugar plantations and part-owner of seven. Beckford 'died in 1737 with land and personal property that probably exceeded £500,000'.[12] Wastel married again, to Deborah Campbell – of whom more anon. We also learn from slaving records that Wastel Brisco II was attorney to Barant Andries Woodstock who was listed in the Jamaican Quit Rent books for 1754 as the owner of 1,200 acres of land in Westmoreland and 3,635 acres of land in St Elizabeth, a total of 4,835 acres. John Hodges was listed in the Jamaican Quit Rent books for 1754 as the owner of 7,676 acres of land in St Elizabeth.[13] Woodstock's sister, Deborah, married firstly Peter Campbell of Fish River, and on his death Wastel Brisco. In her will of 1797, she left £5,000 in trust with the income to go to her daughter Elizabeth Woodstock Yorke, wife of John Yorke of Halton Place, Yorkshire, £2,000 for the benefit of her granddaughter Mary Ann Campbell, and £2,000 each to three other granddaughters.[14] Elizabeth would marry the slave owner John Yorke (1733–1813) as her second husband in 1769. John Yorke appears in a joint painting with his close friend Lieutenant Colonel Thomas Coore (1739–1821) who was a Liverpool merchant and uncle of Foster Lechmere Coore (1780–1837) of Scutton Hall. The Coores were major slave owners. Thomas Coore's brother Frederick Richard listed his slave property in his will as:

My freehold estate in Jamaica called Pembroke to my executors upon trust to manage the same and out of the profits to pay my wife an annual sum of £700 sterling for life as long as she remains my widow. Out of the same to pay to my wife or their guardians £100 a year each for the education and maintenance of my daughters. Then to pay a sum not exceeding £200 per annum for the maintenance and education of my son Frederick until the sum hereinafter to be raised shall be realised. Subject to the above-mentioned charges, the rents and profits to be accumulated until the sum of £20,000 is realised, for my daughters equally at age 21 or marriage. When this sum is realised and my son Frederick attains the age of 25, to convey the estate to him.

My wife and brother to be guardians of my children.

My father-in-law John Blagrove, my brother Lieut. Col. Coore and my friend Thomas Fitzgerald of Lincolns Inn to be trustees and executors.[15]

Foster Lechmere Coore we have already passed comment upon. Elizabeth Woodstock and John Yorke, we will meet again in a later chapter.

In returning to the Brisco family, recorded in the *Laws of Jamaica 1760–1792* we find reference to Barant Andrews Woodstock, Wastel Brisco, John Morse, George Raxtead, Francis Smith and John Armstrong obtaining by Act of Parliament uncultivated tracts of lands in the Parishes of St Elizabeth and Westmoreland in 1773. We note Wastel had been made secretary 'Of His Majesty's Island of Jamaica' on 12 September 1747. One can only assume that Musgrave was the English end of the business acting as the merchant in getting the slave-produced goods to market.

The accountant of the Cumberland Valley estate was John Morse and the overseer was Thomas Jeannes. In 1758 the estate was producing sugar, rum and pimento and also deriving income from 'renting enslaved people'. A year later the plantation was selling log wood dye; in 1762 the crops were sugar, rum, logwood and cattle; in 1770 Thomas Porter was overseer and John Brisco acted as attorney, the crops being sugar, rum and molasses; in 1781 sugar, rum and hire fees for the slaves generated the primary income, and cattle returned as a staple in 1796.[16]

The accounts of Holland Estate, St Elizabeth's, Jamaica, show Wastel owned the estate by 1762, its produce being sugar, rum, cattle and logwood in 1764; we find that copper was exported in 1766 and 1768, and molasses was exported in 1770. By 1775 sugar and rum were the sole exports, and in 1796 steers, cows, heifers and the 'hiring of slaves' was recorded as the income for the plantation in the year of Wastel II's death.[17]

Under the terms of his will Wastel II left £3,000 each to his daughters, Louisa Scarlett (the Scarletts were major plantation and slave owners), Elizabeth Campbell and Deborah Campbell, and £2,000 to his three grandsons, charged on his real estate in Great Britain and Jamaica. In a codicil he left £2,000 each to his two granddaughters. He specified his estates as Holland, Fish River and Petersville, and instructed that the produce from the estates be shipped to his consignees in London, 'Milligan, Robertson and Milligan', until his debt to them was repaid. The codicil also included provision of an annuity of £25 p.a. to Jacob Campbell, his 'servant of colour' then living with him, and a legacy to William Campbell, the son of a woman of colour named Mira or Mina of St Elizabeth, presumably his natural son with her. His heir was his legitimate son Peter.[18] Of note, Robert Milligan's statue in London has recently taken down because of his links to slavery.

On returning to Wakefield, Musgrave married Mary Fletcher Dyne in London on 7 March 1742.[19] The Dyne family had a slave plantation on Jamaica.[20] Musgrave I died in 1787. We can find precious little about Musgrave's life. His son Wastel Brisco III was to be a key player in the story of Wakefield and slavery. Musgrave appears to have spent considerable money buying land around Halifax, notably Barkisland. The family are buried at St Bartholomew's Parish Church, Ripponden. The tombstone reads:

> HERE lieth interred the Body of the Reverend Richard Horton Brisco, Clerk Eldest Son of Musgrave Brisco of Wakefield Esq. who died the 31st Day of October 1769 Aged 25 Years
>
> ALSO, the Body of the Said Musgrave Brisco who died the 3rd Day of May 1787 Aged 78 Years.
>
> ALSO, the Body of Mary Fletcher Brisco Widow of the above-named Musgrave Brisco. She died the 14th Day of July 1797, in the 84th Year of her Age.
>
> ALSO, the Body of Edward Dyne Brisco of Wakefield, Son of the aforementioned Musgrave Brisco. He died the 17th Day of Febr1815 Aged 65 Years
>
> ALSO, the Body of Jane Brisco of Wakefield Relict of the above-mentioned Richard Horton Brisco who died on the 5th Day of January 1839, Aged 92 Years.[21]

Under Musgrave's will, proved on 18 October 1787, he left £300 per annum to his widow, Broom Hall estate and house at Snowhill, Wakefield was passed to his son Wastel III, and to Edward passed the Cumberland estates and those at Barkisland. Musgrave II received £2,000 and his widow Jane Brisco received £500.

As the major benefactor of his father's will, Edward Dyne Brisco bought Westgate Mansion from Richard Slater Milnes in 1800.[22] This fine mansion was the fitting residence for a very wealthy landowner and merchant.

Widow 'Jane Brisco' aka Jane Brooke had married Rev. Richard Horton Brisco, Musgrave's eldest son. She was the daughter of Charles Brooke; her brother was John Charles Brooke (1748–94) and her sister Margaret Brooke. John Charles Brooke lived in Silver Street, Wakefield. He knew and visited Rev. Dr John Disney, a leading Unitarian minister.

Brooke was elected Fellow of the Society of Antiquities in 1775 and was a lieutenant in the West Riding Militia. He worked with the Rev. Joseph Hunter, a historian and genealogist of South Yorkshire. Brooke died in 1794 leaving an estate of £14,000, appointing his two sisters, Jane and Margaret, as executrix and legatees.[23] Jane died in 1839 whilst living in a fashionable new town house constructed in the 1790s on South Parade, Wakefield, no doubt with the proceeds of her inheritance.

Musgrave's widow, Mary Fletcher Brisco, sold two messuages on Westgate in 1787, no doubt to provide the cash settlements under her husband's will, and in September 1789 provided a mortgage for the new Dissenting chapel on Ebenezer Street, Leeds.[24] This was Ebenezer Baptist Chapel which was sold in 1797 to the Methodist New Connexion (we wonder if they were aware the chapel was built on the proceeds of slavery?) and was demolished in 1936. By 1797 a Mrs Brisco was renting a house taxed at 12s 6d a year from Mr John Charnock Esq on Kirkgate. The Charnocks' family home 'The Grove' was assessed at £11 a year tax.[25] As we note later the Charnocks were tobacco plantation and slave owners.

Musgrave I's son Wastel III was baptised on 29 April 1754 in Elland Parish Church.[26] Wastel III (1754–1834) had inherited from his uncle, Wastel Brisco II of Jamaica and Wimpole Street, 'all that my plantation estate containing one thousand and eight acres or thereabouts called the Salt Ponds plantation in the Island of St Christopher . . . by me lately purchased of the devisees named in the will of William Priddie of the said island . . . with the stock of slaves, cattle and other live and dead stock and stores of every sort'.[27]

By the time of his death Wastel Brisco III was described as of 'Wakefield and Devonshire Place'. He lived in the Milnes mansion on Westgate which he had purchased from his brother Edward. Wastel Brisco III is recorded as owner of Coffee Grove in Clarendon, Jamaica in 1804 and 1807 during the minority of his sons Wastel IV and Musgrave III. The estate had belonged to Jane Blinshall who had left it to her niece, 'Sarah wife of Wastel Brisco of Devonshire Place', and her children.[28] Jane had married Henry Booth Blinshall, who in 1778 appears to have mortgaged Amity Hall Plantation on Jamaica for £2,000 from the Goulburn family. Henry Goulburn Esq in 1753 owned 38 acres and thirty-two enslaved people in St Andrew, Jamaica, in 1753. He died in 1766, his probate recording ownership of ninety-eight slaves of whom fifty-seven were listed as male and forty-one as female. Eleven more were listed as boys, girls or children. The total value of estate at probate was £9,812.97 in Jamaican currency of which £5,820 was the value of enslaved people.[29] Henry's daughter Sarah marred Wastel III on 24 October 1785, her dowry being a whopping £7,000, no doubt entirely derived from slavery. Wastel III became very wealthy overnight and connected to a leading slave-owning family. In her will proved on 23 August 1799, Sarah left £1,000 to each of her children, and her personal estate and remaining monies to her husband.[30] Her nephew was Tory MP Henry Goulburn (1784–1856) who took ownership of Amity Hall in 1805. He was Chancellor of the Exchequer 1828–30 and Home Secretary 1834–5.[31]

In a document dated 1 December 1813 Musgrave III and Wastel IV – then both living in Wakefield – conveyed Coffee Grove Plantation to William Mitchell. The same document refers to the slaves belonging to Wastel Brisco, Musgrave Brisco, John Carmac (husband of Sarah Brisco, Wastel III's daughter) and John Booth Barton being conveyed to William Mitchell. In 1805 the plantation had just five slaves, but by 1809 it had seventy-three slaves, increasing to eighty-four in 1811, then dropping back to five slaves at point of sale. The Brisco family held five estates totalling over 2,600 acres.[32]

Wastel Brisco III died in 1834, and under the terms of his will, he left his son Sir Wastel Brisco IV (1792–1878) £12,000, his daughter Sarah Carmac £10,000 and his son Musgrave II (1792–1854) the remainder of the estate.[33] Musgrave III became MP for Hastings 1844–54.[34]

The man who bought some of the Briscos' estates was William Mitchell. He was both a plantation owner and an attorney who in his own estimate had 'perhaps 16 or 18' sugar plantations under his 'care' at various times. He informed a committee in 1807 that he had spent over £30,000 on the erection of a sugar works on one of his own estates which included Windsor Park in St Catherine, Bushy Park in St Dorothy, New Hall in St Thomas in the Vale and Georges Valley in Trelawny. Among others, Mitchell did business with and borrowed money from the powerful Jamaica planter Simon Taylor, who would move to Beverley and live at Etton Hall.[35] Mitchell was elected MP for Plympton Erle 1796–9. It was reported that he was 'a coarse looking man, but humane', who 'treats his negroes most kindly'.[36]

With Wastel III's death, the family's link to Wakefield ended.

Francis Ingram

Francis Ingram (1739–1815) was a Wakefield lad. After a brief career in the army, he began investing in slave voyages to make his fortune, financing his first voyage in 1758. By 1772 Francis was dealing in ivory and business included slave trading. The Trans-Atlantic Slave Trade Database records that he was responsible along with Thomas Staniforth (1734–1803), Thomas Earle (1757–1822), Thomas Parke and William

Joseph Denison for undertaking 97 slaving trips and enslaving 34,617 people. Francis used his fortune from these voyages to found the first bank in Wakefield.

The banking firm of Ingram, Kennett and Ingram played an important role in the commerce of Wakefield. Francis Ingram is recorded as agent for Staniforth's Bank, Liverpool in 1791–5, so clearly, he must have come to Wakefield some time after 1795, but he is listed as proprietor of Ingram & Sons of Wakefield and Halifax from 1791 to 1807, so we cannot be sure when he arrived in Wakefield or indeed ended his links with Liverpool. Certainly by 1792 he had built a large mansion on Westgate with banking premises fronting the street: it was one of the grandest of Wakefield's town houses. The building still stands and is today a nightclub, having lost most of its Georgian grandeur.

The bank experienced financial difficulties in 1808, when it was discovered that the Halifax co-partnership was in debt to the Wakefield co-partnership. In order to save the local, if not regional economy, John Leatham, James Jackson, Thomas Tew and Edward Trueman, bankers in Pontefract, bought out the failed institution.[37] Francis lived in a town house he built in the fashionable St Johns. As a tribute to his father, the east window of Wakefield Parish Church was filled with new glass by the terms of his son Abraham Richard Ingram's (1769–1865) will. The window was lost when the Pearson extension to what is now the Cathedral was built in 1901–02. A photograph of the window survives.[38] Following the failure of the bank, Francis left Wakefield and he died in Rome on 28 August 1815.

William Ingram

Eldest son of Francis Ingram, William (1768–1824) whilst living in Wakefield, in 1790 or 1791, entered into partnership with his brother Francis Ingram II (1775–1825) and James Rigby of Liverpool as slave traders, conducting 27 slaving voyages, transporting a minimum of 7,010 people:

1791
The *Ann* sailed from Liverpool captained by James Giles to Benin and thence to St Vincent and discharged 212 slaves.

1792
The *Mary* offloaded her cargo of 209 slaves in St Vincent.

The *Mary* offloaded slaves in Grenada.

1793
The *Ann* sailed from Liverpool to Porto Novo and thence to St Vincent and offloaded 198 slaves.

1794
The *Ann* discharged 210 slaves at St Vincent.

1795
The *Mary* offloaded 225 slaves at Kingston, Jamaica.

1796
The *Ann* docked in Barbados and discharged 213 slaves.
The *Mary* offloaded 228 slaves in Kingston.
The *Onslow* captained by William Cartmell docked on Barbados and offloaded 274 slaves.

1797
The *Ann* sailed to Cape Mount, thence to Demerara where she offloaded 200 slaves.
The *Mary* offloaded her cargo of men, women and children on Demerara.
The *Onslow* was captured by the French.

1798
The *Ann* sailed into Demerara and offloaded 175 slaves.
The *Ann* sailed to Porto Novo to Kingston, Jamaica where she offloaded 346 slaves.
The *George*, captained by Alexander Hackney, was captured by the French.
The *King George*, captained by James Rigby, sailed from Liverpool to Benin and thence to Martinique where she offloaded 388 slaves.

1799
The *Liverpool Hero* docked in Surinam and discharged a cargo of slaves.
The *King George*, captained by James Micklejohn, was lost with all hands at sea.

1800

The *Hughes*, captained by James Bailiff, docked in Demerara and offloaded 337 slaves.

The *Liverpool Hero*, captained by Alexander Laing, sailed from Liverpool to Porto Novo. She was wrecked on the voyage to the West Indies, all hands and the slaves trapped in the hold were drowned.

1801

The *Beaver*, captained by Christopher Brew, sailed to Surinam where he offloaded his cargo of slaves.

The *Dick*, captained by Walter Clements, offloaded her cargo of slaves at St Vincent.

The *Otter*, captained by Alexander Hackney, docked at Surinam where she offloaded her cargo of slaves.

1803

The *Dick*, captained by Alexander McLeod, sailed from Africa to Demerara where he offloaded his cargo of slaves.

The *Ford*, captained by Alexander Hackney, delivered 279 slaves to Trinidad.

The *Duke of Clarence* discharged 191 slaves at Trinidad.

1804

The *Dick*, captained by Alexander Laing, landed slaves in Demerara.

James Rigby was a major Liverpool slave trader who no doubt acted as Ingram's Liverpool agent. Ingram was a good Anglican and Tory. Between 1787 and 1802 the slave trade expanded exponentially: in 1787 36,000 slaves were transported, in 1802 some 56,621, the overwhelming majority via Liverpool merchants who it is reckoned had six-sevenths of the trade, the trade from Liverpool doubling in under a decade. The level of selling-on of slaves by slave factors in the West Indies, however, remained constant: 20,158 slaves sold in 1787 and 20,958 in 1802.[39] Huge profits were to be made; hence we see the Ingrams investing in slave trading once more after Francis senior gave up the trade by 1788. The Peace of Amiens in 1802 hugely disrupted the trade, with the total number of slaves being transported in 1803 dropping to 19,960. Traders, thankfully, went bankrupt. The Ingrams all worshipped at All Saints Parish Church every Sunday. He said his prayers and never felt his conscience pricked by his actions. He, his father and brother were denounced by the Rev. Thomas Johnstone from the pulpit of Westgate Chapel in 1801 – yet we suppose such denouncement was brushed off as 'the ravings of a blasphemer'.

Arthur Heywood

After Francis Ingram, the second great slave trader in Wakefield was Arthur Heywood (1715–95), whose sons would play a central part in the civic life of the town: we note that his son, John Pemberton Heywood, founded and financed the Lancasterian School on Bell Street, and was central in the funding and management of the Wakefield Dispensary. These august institutions, as well as the place of worship, of Arthur and his sons, Westgate Chapel, no doubt benefited from money generated directly by the slave trade.[40] We discuss Arthur and his extensive family network of slave ownership in our next chapter.

Other Slave Owners

Another great slave-owning family in Wakefield was the Watertons of Walton Hall, Wakefield. The family owned slave plantations over several generations. Charles Waterton (1782–1865) received compensation for 300 slaves on Walton Hall Plantation, British Guiana, and for a further 292 at La Jalousie Plantation. Indeed, we note he went to British Guiana to manage La Jalousie and Fellowship, the estates of his uncle Christopher Waterton. He claims to have never owned a slave, yet happily received over £30,000 in compensation for the loss of his slaves! Robert Waterton (1801–?) received compensation for 15 slaves on Guiana, 135 slaves at Philadelphia Plantation, 82 at Orangestein Plantation and 292 at La Jalousie. Between them, the two Watertons owned 1,116 slaves and received over £60,000, today many millions! Walton Hall, the home of these two slave owners, is a modern hotel which belies its origins as built on the backs of slaves. Robert's father Christopher Waterton owned La Jalousie, Le Bienfait, Windsor and Fellowship Plantations.[41] Like many slave owners he fathered children with his slaves as his will makes clear:

> To the Negress called Diana likewise during her lifetime 500 guilders and to both the mulatto children named Sally and Samuel in like manner yearly during their lifetimes each the sum of 500 guilders. Confirmation of the manumission of Diana and her children dated 27 May last.

65

To my trusty Bamba Ishaul as a reward for his services 300 guilders likewise during his lifetime, with confirmation of his manumission dated 25 May last.

The above sums to be paid from the revenues of La Jalousie.[42]

He left sums of money to his wife, £2,000 to the children of his brother Thomas, and £1,000 each to Thomas Daly and Christopher Waterton. Daly was the overseer of Mountain Valley estate in Hanover from at least 1796 to 1797. He was also owner of Woodville estate in Hanover, Jamaica. Deceased by 1815. He fathered a daughter Catherine, a 'free quadroon' baptised at Hanover 2 August 1798, and a son Patrick baptised the same day, also a 'free quadroon'.

At abolition, compensation claim records inform us that Thomas Picton Clapham (1801–41) of Sandal, Wakefield, owned eighteen slaves. Listed as 'gentleman', he married Hannah Knowles at St Peters Leeds. He was buried in the graveyard of St Helens Sandal Magna on 18 March 1841.[43] Wakefield Unitarian (he paid pew rent 1836–47 sitting in pew 24 with Mr Whitaker who ran the Wakefield Gas Light Company) and historian Thomas Norris Ince (1799–1873) was a solicitor in Wirksworth and in Wakefield from 1824. He and his sister attended Westgate Chapel. Thomas married Ann Lockwood in 1846: the Lockwoods being stalwart members of the congregation until the death of Phyllis Lockwood aged 106 in 2015.[44] Thomas's sister Mary married Charles Imhoff at Wirksworth on 22 October 1828. Their daughter Susan Catherine Imhoff was born on 17 September 1829. Imhoff, a Dutch national, was a slave owner on Demerara. He inherited or purchased 'Prosperity' Plantation from his father Killian Imhoff who had the property in 1798, and had died in 1806. In 1832 the plantation is listed as in lawful possession of Charles Imhoff having eighty-five slaves, forty female and forty-five male, its main product being coffee.[45] Presumably Charles had sold the plantation by 1835 as the compensation for seventy-nine slaves totalling some £4,192 17s 10d was awarded on 30 November 1835 to William Augustus Parker, who promptly invested £2,500 of this into the London and York Railway Co., which became the Great Northern Railway: this firm built the famous ninety-nine arches viaduct in Wakefield.[46] Mary and Charles' second son, Killian Rickards Imhoff, was born on Demerara on 26 November 1831, and another son Ernest was born 1832 in Guiana, and died on 17 July 1836 on Demerara. Imhoff himself died at Woerden Cottage, Demerara, on 21 January 1854.

Comment

What made Wakefield a regional capital of slavery? It was a regional centre for the cloth trade; it had a racecourse, assembly rooms, excellent schools – Heath Academy and the Grammar School – and was the largest town in Yorkshire: Wakefield was in the first half of the eighteenth century the economic powerhouse of the county, a position it rapidly lost to Leeds. Wakefield was ideally placed for merchants to import and export goods via Liverpool or Hull thanks to the burgeoning network of canals and turnpikes. The expanding transport network enabled the Milnes family to send woollen cloth to Russia via Hull, as well to Liverpool and Bristol; the Charnocks could easily send cloth to the Netherlands via Hull, so too the Steers into Germany. The town was also ideally placed to be a distribution hub for slave-produced goods like coffee and sugar, and had a ready market for log wood dye with the cloth merchants. The wine cellars of the Milnes family were no doubt stocked with rum as well as wine from Spain: the vaults were beneath the yard off Westgate, according to Richard Milnes's will of 1755. In the first half of the eighteenth century the Milnes family traded in wines and spirits, supplying the Wynns at Nostell on a number of occasions, and we know they petitioned the Marquis of Rockingham for duty-free importation of sugar and rum: slave-produced goods. The huge profits from trade with America from the end of the Seven Years War to the start of the American War of Independence were a boom time for the Yorkshire textile trade, allowing the 'merchant princes' to display their great wealth with the 'must-have' fashion accessory, a black servant. The 'merchant princes' got richer by investing in slave trading. Wakefield became a key location for the slave trade as our next chapter shows.

Chapter 8

Kith and Kin

Family ties were important in building commercial networks. Unitarians could, in theory at least, only marry other Unitarians. Therefore, it is not surprising that through well-placed marriages, a familial network built up across the North of England between nominal Unitarian families, the Hibbert and Heywood families being cases in point. The Hibberts dominated Manchester slaving interests while the Heywoods dominated Liverpool, Wakefield and later Manchester.

The head of the Heywood family was Arthur (1715–95), who, as we mentioned earlier, lived in Wakefield. He was the son of Benjamin Heywood (1687–1725) and Anne Graham. Arthur and his brother Benjamin (1722–95) were great-great-grandsons of Oliver Heywood (1629–1702) the 'puritan apostle of the north'. Arthur Heywood married twice: first to Sarah Ogden, and then Hannah Milnes. His children made advantageous marriages, as did his sister, nearly all into slaving families. Arthur funded his first slaving voyage in 1745, along with Thomas and John Backhouse of Liverpool, and funded a second voyage the same year with his brother and Samuel Shaw, James Crosbie and the Blundell brothers. During the 1760s, the two brothers, Arthur and Benjamin, had businesses in Liverpool and Lancaster, under the names Parke & Heywood, and Parke, Heywood & Conway respectively. The Parke family were major slave traders, conducting 132 slave voyages according to the Trans-Atlantic Slave Trade Database. The partnership between Parke and Heywood primarily was to trade linen, but the concern also dealt in 'African goods' which included ivory and slaves. Indeed, the Heywood family invested in 134 slave voyages and was responsible for the transportation of 43,388 people, of whom 37,124 survived the voyage.[1] Shortly before his death, Arthur and his sons Arthur and Richard obtained two plantations totalling over 80 acres of land in Jamaica via William Bramwell, but the sale fell through and the Heywoods were refunded £3,262 17s.[2]

Arthur never invested in plantations: he made his money from investing in slave voyages and importing back cargos. In relation to the produce from plantations, it was Arthur Heywood who on 11 May 1766 requested from the Marquis of Rockingham, in his capacity as Prime Minister, 'Of obtaining foreign cotton duty free, coffee for export at ¾ and the alteration of the tonnage of ships importing rum from our Islands and for export to Africa in the ships of 70 tons instead of ships of 100 tons'.[3] This concession gave Arthur Heywood a huge advantage over other merchants in Liverpool. The introduction to Rockingham was thanks to his nephew Pemberton Milnes and his late father-in-law Richard Milnes. Arthur used his family network of contacts to greatly bolster his own financial gain.

So important was Rockingham's patronage that Arthur Heywood named a slaving ship the *Marquis of Rockingham* after him. Launched in Liverpool in 1750, she was a two-masted brig, with a burthen of 119.3 tonnes and carried four cannon. Her first slaving voyage was in 1754 and the last in 1765, having made nine voyages in total. The second vessel of that name owned by Arthur Heywood was launched in 1767 and was registered as a slaving vessel in 1772. She had a burthen of 272.3 tonnes and carried four cannon. She made three voyages.

Arthur Heywood lived in Wakefield in the middle decades of the eighteenth century.[4] We know from the Westgate Chapel Archives that he was a Unitarian, as were his sons. From 1762 he rented pew 30 at Westgate Chapel: his name is neatly inscribed in the cover of the pew rent register. He stopped paying pew rent in 1768, and starts paying an annual subscription from 1 January 1778, paying £2 2s a quarter till 1 January 1787. His son Benjamin Heywood rented pew 10 from 1778 and then pew 22 from 1780, and we find him sat in pew 22 from 1799. Arthur's son John Pemberton rented pew 1 from midsummer 1804 till his death. The pew was altered to suit his very ample girth.[5] We will come back to Benjamin and his brother John Pemberton later.

During the period 1762–8 whilst he lived in Wakefield, Arthur Heywood undertook ten slaving voyages:

1762
The *Marquis of Rockingham*, captained by George Evans, sailed from Liverpool to the Gold Coast to Annapolis and delivered 188 slaves.
The *Rainbow*, captained by John Dawson, sailed from Liverpool to Kingston, Jamaica and offloaded 270 slaves.

1763

The *Hannah*, captained by Edward Prescott, sailed from Liverpool to Annapolis and delivered 315 slaves.

1764

The *Rainbow*, captained by William Gill, sailed from Liverpool to Benin and thence to Kingston, Jamaica and delivered 273 slaves.
The *Ingram*, captained by James Carruthers, sailed from Liverpool to Anomabu to Kingston, Jamaica and delivered 308 slaves.

1765

The *Marquis of Rockingham*, captained by George Evans, sailed from Liverpool to the Gold Coast and thence onto Jamaica and delivered 154 slaves.
The *Hannah*, captained by Edward Prescott, sailed to West Central Africa from Liverpool, and put into Charleston, delivering 297 slaves.
The *Rainbow*,captained by William Gill, sailed from Liverpool to Benin and was lost at sea with all hands.

1766

The *Ingram*, captained by Thomas Eagles, sailed from Anomabu to Kingston, Jamaica and delivered 283 slaves.

1767

The *Hannah*, captained by Edward Prescott, sailed from Liverpool via Anomabu to Grenada, discharging 268 slaves.

Arthur's first voyage set off in 1745 for Gambia. He directly financed 74 slaving voyages and transported 20,327 slaves, of whom 16,958 arrived in the West Indies or America. He was responsible for over 3,000 deaths.

Arthur was supplying slaves for both sugar plantations and tobacco plantations in Maryland. His kith and kin provided the captains: James Pemberton, Arthur's nephew, captained the *Nancy* from 1748, and then the *Britannia* from 1750 till she was lost with all hands in 1756. His ships were named after family members and benefactors; the *Ogden*, built in 1733, became a slave ship in 1741 and conducted nine slave voyages before being lost at sea in 1756; and the *Ingram* was built in Liverpool in 1761. Samuel Ogden and John Pemberton owned the *Hardman*, built in Liverpool in 1725, which carried ten guns. One of Arthur Heywood's captains was Edward Prescott, who appears to have been the nephew of Colonel Robert Prescott, who lived in Wakefield at this time. Arthur appears to have left Wakefield in 1768 and returned to the town in 1778.

The last voyage Arthur directly financed sailed from Liverpool in 1775. The vessel herself, the *Ingram*, was captained by James Paisley. She had a tonnage of 182.3 tonnes and was armed with six cannon. The ship sailed from Liverpool to Anomabu in Africa and thence on to Jamaica transporting 291 slaves.

Arthur, for whatever reason, stopped taking part in slave voyages. Was more money to made from other ventures? Had his minister of religion Rev. Thomas Johnstone's anti-slavery message made some impression on him? Most likely he moved into banking as it was less risky and more money could be made. In 1776, Arthur and his eldest son Richard entered into a banking partnership with Joseph Denison: Arthur owned 25 per cent, his son 25 per cent and Denison the remainder. He became the Heywoods' London agent.[6] Joseph and his son William Joseph Denison (1770–1849) were also backers of some of the slaving voyages Arthur undertook. In 1784, Arthur opened an office in Manchester, in response to requests from his customers there, but this closed in 1786. Arthur Heywood relinquished his interest in the bank to his son Richard after the latter's marriage to Mary Earle in 1784 and he died in 1795, 'one of the oldest and most respectable merchants in Liverpool'.[7]

Arthur invested his fortune locally: he owned £15,000 of stock in the Aire and Calder Navigation company for building the Selby Canal, which opened in 1779 and had cost £20,000 to build, and also owned £13,000 in turnpike securities, mostly in the Greetland and Weeland roads.[8]

The Caldwell Family

Arthur Heywood's sister Elizabeth married Charles Caldwell (1707–76). The Trans-Atlantic Slave Trade Database shows Charles Caldwell as investing in fifteen voyages between 1759 and 1767: nine with Benjamin and Arthur Heywood and others, five with William Ingram and others and one with Francis Ingram and others. Gill Slater (mentioned earlier) was a co-investor in fourteen of the fifteen voyages.

Elizabeth Heywood and Charles Caldwell were parents of Charles Caldwell II (1737–1814) merchant of Liverpool. He was co-owner of two estates in Antigua and one in St Vincent. His son was Rev. George Caldwell MA (1773–1848) who at abolition in 1832, owned three estates and received over £13,000 in compensation.[9]

We note that Elizabeth Heywood's youngest son, Benjamin (1739–1820) became an admiral in the Royal Navy; her daughter Catherine married Phineas Riall (1737–97), whose son was General Sir Phineas Riall (1775–1850). He married Elizabeth Scarlett in 1819 and through marriage became owner of a slave plantation and received £1,074 1s 4d compensation for fifty-three slaves.[10]

The Ogden Family

The family of Arthur Heywood's first wife, Sarah, were Liverpool slave traders. The first member of the family we have details for is Edmund Ogden, who married Phoebe (1666–93), daughter of John and Phoebe Buxton. Edmund Ogden I of Liverpool was the founder of dynasty of slave owners and traders via his children Edmund Ogden II and Samuel Ogden I.

A Liverpool merchant. Samuel (1689–?) married Sarah Pemberton in 1715 with a marriage settlement of 14 July 1715. Her father was John Pemberton of Liverpool. Her sister married Richard Milnes of Wakefield. Of their children, Sarah Ogden married Arthur Heywood and Phoebe Ogden married Arthurs brother, Benjamin. Of their children:

- Samuel Heywood was a lawyer – more of him anon.
- Benjamin Arthur Heywood (1755–1828) invested in thirty-nine slaving voyages between 1782 and 1787, transporting 14,629 people.
- Nathanial Heywood married Ann Percival, daughter of Thomas Percival MD of Manchester. Thomas Percival's uncle, James Percival, was a major Liverpool slave trader. The Trans-Atlantic Slave Trade Database records he conducted 46 slave voyages and transported 16,945 people into slavery. The son of Nathanial and Ann, Benjamin Heywood of Manchester, married Sophia Robinson, daughter of Thomas Robinson, merchant and slave owner of Manchester. The Percivals, Robinsons and Benjamin Heywood all attended Cross Street Chapel.
- Elizabeth Heywood married Joseph Birch (1755–1833). At abolition he owned eighty-six slaves and received £1,689 5s 3d compensation.[11] The Birch family were long-established slave traders; between 1764 and 1793, the family financed 45 slaving voyages and transported 12,496 people into captivity. Joseph Birch personally invested in nine slaving voyages between 1783 and 1793, transporting 3,016 slaves. Elizabeth's son, Thomas Bernard Birch (1791–1880) was High Sheriff of Lancashire in 1841, Director of the Liverpool and London Fire and

Life Insurance Co. and MP for Liverpool 1847–52. At abolition he had 147 slaves and received £2,722 8s 1d.[12] As an MP he voted 'to end those odious and intolerant laws which had so long disgraced our statute book', the Test and Corporation Acts, in February 1828, and voted to enfranchise Leeds and Birmingham in 1830 as well as voting to abolish slavery.[13]

- Sarah Heywood married Richard Bright (1754–1840) of Bristol. Bright was a merchant, partner in Gibbs and Bright with George Gibbs. George Gibbs (1779–1863) invested or co-invested with Robert Bright in the Bristol Dock & Canal Company, the Great Western Cotton Works and Clifton Suspension Bridge, as well as the Great Western Railway, of which both men were promoters and directors. Gibbs also invested in the Great Western Steamship Company. At abolition he gained £28,000 or thereabouts.[14] Richard Bright was a Unitarian and leading Bristol Dissenter. He attended Warrington Academy. Several of Richard's children were baptised at Lewins Mead Unitarian Chapel in Bristol and at least one of his children attended a school run by the Unitarian minister. Richard was buried in the family vault in the chapel in accordance with the instructions in his will. At abolition he owned 641 slaves.[15] His youngest son Robert Bright (1795–1869) was also a Unitarian and was a shareholder in the Great Western Cotton Works, Barton Hill, Bristol from 1837 and deputy chairman of the Great Western Railway from 1834 (with 259 shares). He left £80,000 in 1869. The money to invest in the railway came from slavery compensation: a whopping £28,000![16] This is roughly £3.3 million in 2020! The rich who could afford to buy slaves and invest in plantations got richer at the time of abolition. Their eldest son was Richard Bright (1784–1869), MP for Bristol 1820–30 as the representative of the West India Whig interest, and declared that his aim was to 'restore the constitution . . . to the standard' of 1688 by 'reducing the power of the crown to its legitimate bounds', voted to abolish the Test and Corporation Acts, and supported the 'practical proposition' for enfranchising Birmingham, Leeds and Manchester.[17]

Edmund Ogden II (1748–1812) was baptised a Unitarian and attended Warrington Academy. He married the daughter of Richard Gildart Esq, MP for Liverpool. The Trans-Atlantic Slave Trade Database reveals Samuel and Edmund Ogden funded 43 slaving voyages between 1723 and 1759, transporting 12,136 people, of whom over 2,000 died on the voyages! The money from these voyages made the family very wealthy indeed. Edmund's father-in-law Richard Gildart (1667–1770) was in the same business. The Database shows that Richard and his son James conducted 66 slaving voyages between 1715 and 1775, transporting 17,438 people, with over 3,000 dying during the crossing. Of the slaves, 2,659 were sent to American tobacco plantations, 13,202 to West Indian sugar plantations, 310 to Brazil and 237 to unknown destinations. Gildart was a partner with his father-in-law Sir Thomas Johnson (1664–1728) in shipping tobacco and rock salt from the Americas. He was Whig MP for Liverpool 1701–23. It was he who was responsible for the floating dock at Liverpool, and the building of two new parish churches, St Peter's and also St George's. In 1716, he became infamous over the way he treated prisoners. When some of the Jacobite prisoners taken at Preston pleaded guilty and begged for transportation rather than execution, Johnson submitted proposals to the Treasury for transporting them at 40s. per head, the prisoners to serve Johnson or his assigns for seven years as bonded labour. The prisoners pleaded that they would not 'consent to be slaves', and Johnson had them 'turned into a dungeon . . . and fed only with bread and water'. In the end, all 639 prisoners were transported by Johnson. In increasing financial difficulties, in 1723 he resigned his seat to take up the post of Collector of Customs in Virginia, leaving his son-in-law, Richard Gildart to cope with his debts.[18]

Gildart was Lord Mayor of Liverpool 1714, 1731 and 1736 and MP 1734–54. By the time he stepped down as an MP 'he had become one of the leading Liverpool slave traders, sending ships to the Gold Coast to barter tobacco for slaves for the West Indies'.[19] Two wealthy MPs in the wider family no doubt helped the Ogden, Heywood and Milnes family.

The Milnes Family

Richard Milnes (1696–1755) was one of the great 'merchant princes' of Wakefield. He married Bridgett Pemberton on 20 February 1718. Under the terms of the marriage settlement of 18 February 1717 the dowry was £2,500.[20]

Her father, John Pemberton, was a merchant and slaver. The Trans-Atlantic Slave Trade Database records he funded a slaving voyage in 1733 with Samuel Ogden, and financed voyages in 1714 and 1718 from Africa to Virginia – the destination tells us he was shipping slaves to tobacco plantations. The Database records other members of the Pemberton family, invested in 31 voyages, transporting 6,662 people of whom 5,782 were disembarked. Many of these voyages were conducted with Thomas Birch, father of Joseph Birch, and Mayor of Liverpool in 1777, who we shall meet again later in the story. Under the terms of the will of John Pemberton of 6 December 1737, proved in 1744, he left his wealth to his three daughters, Elizabeth, Sarah and Bridgett. The girls each received £500. The remainder of Pemberton's estate was to be held in trust and the resulting interest paid to the children of Elizabeth, Sarah and Bridgett. His widow received £100 of plate, £100 in hard cash and £500 from the estate. The executors were Elizabeth Pemberton his widow, Samuel Ogden – who married his daughter Sarah on 14 July 1715 – and Richard Milnes of Wakefield.[21]

Richard, like his father Robert (1671–1734), was a wealthy cloth merchant as well as a dealer in spirits, wine and tobacco. He had built a grand town house on Westgate next door to his fathers' own mansion: both of these imposing houses have long since been demolished. In the extensive yard behind his house Richard had wine vats and storage cellars for rum, as well as warehouses for fleeces, and cloth. The rum and tobacco would have been slave produced. Despite owning no slaves and not funding slaving voyages, as a merchant Richard Milnes was part of the wider slave-based economy of the eighteenth century. Very few aspects of the economy were very far away from slavery. The £2,500 fillip from his father-in-law – roughly £500,000 in 2020 – generated almost certainly from slavery, no doubt helped cement the family's position as leading merchants, with 'friends in high places' in Liverpool. Under the terms of his will of 13 May 1745, proved on 14 March 1755, £1,500 went to his widow Bridgett, £300 to the executors of Samuel Ogden's estate, the dwelling house, land, warehouses, shops, plate, pictures, furniture etc went to Robert the eldest son along with £3,000, Pemberton Milnes received £2,400, and to his four daughters Penelope, Hannah, Elizabeth and Sarah £4,800, each to receive £1,200. The will settled £10,000 in cash on his children – roughly £2.5 million today![22] In the 1740s Richard had supplied uniforms for a 55-strong company of foot, i.e. infantry, in the 1745 Jacobite Rebellion. Some £39 was spent on cloth, each man's 'suit of clothes' costing 14s 3d, the fifty-five hats cost 2s 6d, 'sheets and cords' for hats cost 8s and canvas for the hats 9s. We also note, that Richard owned two ships, *Old Noll* armed with twenty carriage-mounted cannon and fourteen swivel guns, and *Thurloe* with sixteen carriage-mounted cannon and fourteen swivel guns. Milnes transported Jacobite POWs[23] as well as operating as a privateer, licensed by the state. Milnes was very successful in this role: on 31 July 1744 the *Old Noll* captured a French slave ship and a French privateer 'armed with 12 carriage guns – six pounders'. On 14 August 1744 three French ships were captured, one laden with indigo, the *Anne* laden with fish and oil, and the *Hannah*, laden with ginger, sugar and cotton from the West Indies. The *Old Noll* was captured and ransomed in October 1744 for £1,500, which was easily paid for by the prize money awarded by the Admiralty of £29,000 on 23 October 1744. In March 1745 the *Old Noll* took 430 hogsheads of sugar, five tons of indigo and hides. Her sister-ship, the *Thurloe*, took a French slave ship returning to France from Martinique laden with sugar and coffee in April 1745.[24] In 1765–6 when the Marquis of Rockingham was premier, the leading merchants of Wakefield sent a petition requested for themselves 'free port at Dominica and Jamaica and for facilitating and enlarging the trade to Russia...'. The petition was headed by John Sylvester Smith of Newlands Hall, seconded by General Loftus Anthony Tottenham, and signed by Richard Kennet, William Turner, Henry Zouch (magistrate), Richard Buxton, Dr Cookson, Colonel Robert Prescott, Samuel Zouch, Timothy Heald, John Lumb, Musgrave Brisco, Joseph Shephard, William Nevinson, Francis Maude, William Maude, George Cotton (who had married Richard Milnes's sister Elizabeth), John Milnes, Pemberton Milnes, John Milnes Jnr, James Milnes, Robert Milnes, Richard Buxton, Mary Naylor, Thomas Holdsworth and Peregrine Wentworth, amongst other names.[25] Of the signatories, well over half attended Westgate Chapel. Wakefield merchants, seconded by Leeds, sent a similar request in 1766 dated 16 August signed by the Mayor of Leeds Joseph Dixon, as did Sheffield, signed by 200 persons of note, requesting free port rights for sugar and rum.[26] As we noted earlier, these were slave-produced goods and in high demand. The less tax they incurred in importing the goods, the more profit could be made.

Richard and Bridget's children married into slave-trading families: Robert (1718–71) married first Joyce Slater (of whom of more anon) and then Esther Shore (of whom more anon), Pemberton (1729–95) married Jane Slater (about the Slaters more anon), and their daughter Elizabeth (1726–1807) never married. Penelope Milnes (1720–99) married John Tarleton in 1751.[27] The Milnes family, it seems, struggled to raise the dowry, and Pemberton sold land in Wakefield in 1755[28] and paid the final £600 of the £1,500 owing on 22 October 1757.[29] When Bridgett Milnes died, £879 9s 4d out of Bridgett's legacy of £2,275 was passed to Penelope.[30] John Tarleton was the only son of Edward Tarleton, who married Isabel, daughter of Jonathan Livesey. Edward is recorded as transporting slaves from the West Indies to Virginia and owning the ship *Clayton Golby*.[31] This is not unexpected as Edward's brother, Thomas, was in exactly the same trade. It is very likely that John continued the 'family trade'. Thomas Tarleton (1690–1731) was a slave trader, and petitioned the Crown in 1728–9 against the duty on slaves imported to Virginia; his ship *True Blue*, built in Bermuda in 1729, transported slaves from the West Indies to New York. His son, John (1719–73), was Mayor of Liverpool in 1764.

In 1752, as members of the Company of Merchants Trading to Africa, two ships, the *Swan* and the *Tarleton*, transported 740 slaves from Africa to Jamaica, making £8,607 14s 2d on their sale . John Tarleton had interests in the Leeward Isles and South Carolina, and owned at estate on Dominica. His sons Clayton Tarleton, John Tarleton Jnr and Thomas Tarleton formed the trading firm of Tarleton & Backhouse with Daniel Backhouse: in 1788 the firm had a contract to provide 3,000 slaves and had eight vessels at sea. By 1790 the Tarletons had ten ships, which had cost the firm £85,725 to fit out, insure and buy the 'cargo'. John Tarleton died in 1773 with a fortune of £80,000.[32] John Tarleton's son Major General Banastre Tarleton, of American War of Independence fame, was MP for Liverpool 1790–1812.[33] According to the Trans-Atlantic Slave Trade Database, the Tarleton family as a whole undertook 184 slaving voyages, transporting 52,674 people of which 45,561 were disembarked – some 7,000 or so human beings perishing on their forced removal from homes and loved ones to work on plantations. We note that John Tarleton (1719–73) was a slave owner, and was the owner of an estate at Carriacou on Grenada inferred to have been Mount Pleasant, and a further estate not yet traced named Belfield on Dominica. His sons John (1755–1841) and Thomas (1753–1820) retained ownership of these estates. Thomas Tarleton & Co. were also shown as the owners of La Resource in Demerara in 1798.[34] His son Clayton was a major slave trader. He and his brother Thomas undertook 66 slaving voyages and moved 18,649 people, of whom 16,210 arrived in the Americas according to the Trans-Atlantic Slave Trade Database.

Sarah Milnes (1731–?) married William Goodwin in 1755.[35] He, along with other members of his family, were slave traders, often financing voyages with Arthur and Benjamin Heywood, their kinsmen, according to the slave voyages database, they conducted 19 voyages, transporting 4,965 slaves, with nearly 1,000 dying on route.

Richard Milnes's youngest brother, John I (1710–71) married Mary Shore. This marriage alliance, united two powerful Yorkshire Unitarian families, the Milnes and the Shores, of whom more anon. Mary's nephew was Samuel Shore (1738–1828). She was the daughter of Samuel Shore I (1676–1751), who was in business with the Cotton family as Iron founders, their iron being shipped from Liverpool: George Cotton would marry Elizabeth Milnes, sister of the aforementioned Richard Milnes. The children of the marriage included:

- Hannah Milnes (1742–1802) a courtesan.
- Robert Shore Milnes (1747–87) went on to be Governor of Martinique, where he was known for his liberality and fair treatment of the slave

and free black population, and Deputy Governor General of Lower Canada. A baronetcy was conferred on him on 21 March 1801. Milnes left for England on 5 August 1805 but remained administrator until 12 August 1805 and Lieutenant Governor until 29 November 1808. Thomas Dunn assumed his duties as administrator until Governor Sir James Henry Craig arrived in October 1807. He became Colonial Agent for Martinique thereafter. He was named trustee of Westgate Chapel in 1812, and his daughters would become trustees in 1831 – perhaps the first female trustees in a Unitarian chapel in the country!

- Jack Milnes (1751–1810) was educated at Warrington Academy in business and theology, and took up the reins of the family business in 1771 on the death of his father. He had an estimated personal income of £7,000 a year. Jack was, as we shall see was a key player in Whig national politics. Joseph Hunter, the South Yorkshire historian, recalled about him 'but during the few years I had his acquaintance, I found him an ever ready and assiduous friend, a cheerful and pleasant companion, an amiable, and I may say interesting man'.[36] The Rev. Martin Naylor, added: 'A man not withstanding his eccentricities, highly respected by a very numerous acquaintances for his many amiable qualities'.[37] Like his father he had been a JP, and Deputy-Lieutenant of the West Riding.[38] By the 1780s, Jack Milnes believed that the family business purchased over 50 per cent of all white cloth produced in the county and he could rely on the political support of the leading manufacturers of the county.[39] Jack, as we shall see, takes a leading role in the story of abolition in the third part of our narrative.

- Esther Milnes (1754–82) married James Torre of Snydale Hall at Normanton on 22 August 1774. She died in aged 28 on 14 June 1782. He married again to Caroline Coates. James and Caroline's daughter, Anna Margaret Caroline married firstly in 1815 Charles Herman Cornelius van Baerle of Demerara and secondly in 1836 Humphrey Jeston RN. We note that van Baerle owned the New Bee Hive estate in British Guiana.[40]

The Blundell Family

Arthur Heywood's first marriage to Sarah Ogden produced an only child, Sarah Heywood. She married James Mason of Shrewsbury. Her daughter married firstly General Bryan Blundell, son of Jonathan Blundell of Liverpool. He was Lieutenant-Colonel of the 45th Regiment of Foot, with the rank of Major-General. He died in 1799 and is buried in Exeter

Cathedral. He had taken part in General Sir Charles Grey's action in the West Indies in 1794 against the French to capture Martinique. Sarah's daughter went onto marry Comte de Mesnard, a French Royalist émigré, in 1806.

The Blundells were a major slaving dynasty. There is much evidence to document deep and lucrative involvement in the slave trade by the Blundells and their partners Thomas Leyland, William Earle, Samuel Warren and Edward Chaffers. The Trans-Atlantic Slave Trade Database records that Jonathan Blundell (1723–1800) undertook 75 slaving voyages and transported 22,009 people. He was the son of Captain Bryan Blundell, founder of Liverpool Blue Coat School, who made 67 slaving voyages, transporting 16,381 people. The family as a whole made 113 slaving voyages, transported 31,341 people of which 25,313 were disembarked: over 5,000 perished in their hands!

Bryan Blundell's brother, Jonathan Blundell II (1758–1800) was a Liverpool and Jamaica slave factor, partner with Samuel Rainford and Robert Rainford senior at first in Kingston and then returning to Liverpool. He died in 1800 aged 42. The family invested their fortune in coal mining in the Liverpool area. Indeed, we note it was construction of the Leeds-Liverpool Canal that opened up large-scale coal production in the Wigan area in the 1770s. We find Bradford men John Hustler and Thomas Hardcastle, wool staplers and merchants, as well as the slave traders Jonathan Blundell, William Earle and John Hollinshead from Liverpool, as members of the Leeds-Liverpool Canal Committee and providing some of the earliest substantial investments to develop waterways, railways and collieries.

The Slater Family

Adam Slater MD (1696–1758) of Chesterfield was brother to Thomas Slater (1699–1739) of Wakefield. Adam married Elizabeth Johnson. Under the terms of his will proved in 1758 he bequeathed £200 a year to his wife Eliza, £2,500 to each of his children Jane, Joyce, Elizabeth, Thomas, Gill, Richard and Silas, £20 to his 'father Johnson', and all rest and residue to his eldest son Adam.[41] Adam's children married into slaving families or became slave traders:

- Jane Slater (1731–1812) married Pemberton Milnes (1729–95). He was born on 27 September 1729, son of Richard Milnes (1696–1755) and Bridget Pemberton. He married Jane Slater in January 1754, his brother Robert's wife's sister. Known in his own lifetime as Pem

Milnes, he was brought up in the family's cloth business. Pemberton Milnes had his name inserted into the Commission for the Peace on 25 May 1762, with John Milnes and Robert Milnes inserted as JPs the same day, although they never seem to have acted. He took his dedimus on 7 June 1765, the same day as John Milnes, but neither went on to swear oaths. Pemberton swore his oath at Rotherham in July 1770. His decision to act was probably influenced by the Marquis of Rockingham, in light of the coining affair of 1769–70, to see more JPs in the manufacturing area of the West Riding. He was appointed the same day as the Rev. Henry Zouch, Richard Wilson and Joshua Horton – all four men had taken their oaths over five years since being inserted into the Commission of the Peace which was unprecedented. Pemberton was the second most active JP in the West Riding after Henry Zouch. Pemberton was also a Deputy Lieutenant of Yorkshire: he was also a major player in politics. He was a frequent correspondent with the Marquis of Rockingham and his successor Earl Fitzwilliam. He owned land in several counties and used his influence to mobilise the vote for the Whig cause. He supported the American Colonists in 1776, in direct contrast to his erstwhile cousin Banastre Tarleton. Pemberton Milnes was one of the first committee men of the Wakefield Library established in 1786, and subscribed to the York Emanuel Charity Fund formed in 1782. He became guardian for his nephew Richard Slater Rich upon his father's death. He was recognised as the leader of Yorkshire Dissent, and managed to combine the duties of magistrate, merchant, banker and landowner as well reportedly being the largest consumer of port in the county. He built Bawtry Hall as his main residence in 1779. He continued his interest in the cloth trade, and was a committee member for the building of a new White Cloth Hall in Leeds in 1774, as well as being chairman of the Joint-Stock Ossett Mill Company in the 1780s. Pemberton & John Milnes gave £10 10s to the Leeds cloth hall, as did James Milnes & Co. Fellow Unitarian Robert Lumb gave £1 1s, as did John Naylor, also a Westgate chapel man.[42] Pemberton and his brother John were trustees and subscribers to the Piece Hall in Halifax, along with James Milnes & Co, whose agent was Titus Rideal, a Westgate Chapel man. Another Chapel man was Timothy Heald. Others included the Oates family from Mill Hill in Leeds.[43] Halifax Piece Hall opened in 1779. The roof trusses for Westgate Chapel were brought back from the Baltic – the Milnes family had the sole contract to clothe the Russian army, and the timber was a back cargo. The family financially supported the establishment of the first avowedly Unitarian Chapel in London, in the mid-1770s, the leading lights of the congregation being the Dukes of Richmond and Norfolk, Sir George Savile, the Duke of Grafton and Attorney General Lee. His only child, Mary Bridgette Milnes (1754–1835), married firstly P.A. Hay Drummond, son of the archbishop of York, and then Viscount Galway in 1803. His widow, Jane, died on 21 September 1812 aged 81.[44]

- Joyce Slater (1733–64) married Robert Milnes (1718–71), eldest son of Richard Milnes (1696–1755), and elder brother of Pemberton. Joyce and Robert were parents of Richard Slater Milnes (1759–1804). Known as Dick, he was educated at Bolton School, and later at Glasgow University, where James Milnes Jnr was educated. A classmate at Bolton was the son of Josiah Wedgewood. Bank Street Chapel in Bolton was under the ministry of Philip Holland at the time. With the death of his father in 1771, Pemberton was his nominal guardian. Unlike English universities, Glasgow and Edinburgh had no tests on religious grounds on those wishing to study. Glasgow graduates included Benjamin Heywood, a banker from Manchester, John Kenrick, and Rev. Lant Carpenter. Edinburgh was where the great Unitarian Josiah Wedgewood sent his son for his education. We discuss Dick Milnes again later as an abolitionist. Joyce Slater died in childbirth on 7 January 1764 aged 31. She along with her son, infant daughter Joyce, husband Robert, and sister Jane are buried beneath Westgate Chapel, Wakefield. Robert Milnes married secondly Esther Shore, daughter of Samuel Shore, whose elder sister Mary had married John Milnes in 1737.

- Thomas Slater (1736–1817) was apprenticed to Arthur Heywood, 'their kinsman', in 1756. In 1775 Thomas is recorded as co-owner of two estates on St Vincent known as Queensbury estate or plantation and the Vermont estate. He married Mary, daughter of William Todd of Wakefield, and under his will proved in 1818 the two estates were placed in trust, the trustees being his daughter Mary, sons Silas and Leonard and nephew Mark Whyte of Barrow Hill, for the benefit as to three-eighths to his son Silas, two-eighths each to his sons Anthony and Leonard, and one-eighth between his daughters Joyce and Mary. He gave permission for the sale of the estates but sought to limit the sale of the shares in them outside the family. He left two further sons, Robert and Adam, annuities of £300 per annum each.[45] Thomas's son, Leonard Slater (1780–1858) at abolition received £4,125 11s 5d for 144 slaves.[46]

- Gill Slater (1737–1802) was a slave trader and was also apprenticed to Arthur Heywood. He co-owned plantations with his brother Thomas. On 19 September 1759 he also invested in the privateer *Prince*

Tom, a 200-ton brig with a crew of forty, along with Benjamin Heywood, Arthur Heywood, William Ingram (brother of Francis Ingram the slave trader) Edward Cropper, and Charles Cooke of Liverpool: Cropper (1704–76) undertook thirty-four slaving voyages, and Cook (1724–98) forty. The *Prince Tom* was armed with sixteen carriage-mounted cannon.[47] Gill Slater married Isabel, daughter of George Farringdon Esq of Shaw Hall – their daughter Elizabeth married John Peel, brother of Sir Robert Peel. The Trans-Atlantic Slave Trade Database records that Gill Slater conducted 48 slaving voyages between 1759 and 1793, transporting 13,623 slaves of whom 11,894 arrived in the West Indies. As well as solely financing voyages, he partnered with Joseph Birch, Thomas Staniforth and Joseph Brookes Jnr, as well as Francis Ingram, Arthur and Benjamin Heywood. He was declared bankrupt in 1793.[48] Under the will of Peter Haffey, plantation owner, his estate was to be sold: three-ninths of the proceeds were to be given to Gill Slater and made provisions to free seven named enslaved people, to pay £50 and give two named enslaved people to 'Little Sally', a free black woman formally belonging to him, and to pay legacies of between £50 and £200 each to several individuals in Liverpool and London. Haffey instructed in 1798 the freeing of his 'negro boy Luck, son of Louis and Sally' and left him an annuity of £8 p.a.[49] It seems that Haffey and Slater were close friends and possibly business partners as correspondence between the two men,[50] points to Haffey being based on St Vincent, and Slater as the Liverpool end of the business.[51] Henry Haffey died in 1836 and had been owner of Mount Alexander and Wallalibou estates in St Vincent, which he had sold before the slave compensation process of the 1830s.[52] Haffey had taken on 36 acres from William Henry Masterton in 1793 at Mount Alexander, St Vincent.[53]

- Elizabeth Slater (1740–71) married Anthony Whyte of Liverpool on 4 April 1763. The Trans-Atlantic Slave Trade Database reveals he invested in a slaving voyage in 1768–9 along with Robert Erskin, John Natham, Robert Green, John and Thomas Tippin. Their ship *John* had been constructed in New England in 1763 and carried 80 tons of cargo and was armed with four cannon. They delivered 200 slaves to Barbados.

The Shore and the Digges Families

The Shores were one of the richest families in Sheffield. Samuel Shore I (1676–1751), was an iron founder in business with George Cotton.

He married Jane Sykes (1681–1750) in November 1700. As alluded to earlier, their children married into notable local families:

- Samuel Shore II (1707–85) married Margaret Digges, daughter of Robert Digges of Manchester, whose sister Esther married the slave owner Thomas Hibbert. The children of Samuel Shore II included the radical politician Samuel Shore III (1738–1826) and Hannah, who married the radical Manchester politician Thomas Walker, who had very pronounced Unitarian beliefs despite being nominally Anglican. In August 1766 Samuel Shore II led a group of Sheffield merchants to petition for free port status for goods imported from Dominica and Jamaica – sugar, coffee, cotton rum, molasses and log wood.[54] The Shore family as merchants were involved in the import of these goods and their sale in Sheffield. Samuel senior was trading iron to Liverpool and we assume that since his son married a Digges girl, that he must have been known to the Digges family and may even had exported his iron on their ships and imported the rum, sugar and other goods produced on family plantations. We note that Robert Digges was a slave trader working out of Liverpool. He was uncle to Thomas Digges, a slave trader who delivered cotton into Liverpool in 1716.[55] Margaret's sister, Esther Digges (1714–72) married Samuel Bayley (1717–78). The marriage into the Digges family brought a dowry derived almost certainly from the slave trade into the Shore family, as well as further connections with the trade.
- Esther married Robert Milnes, a widower. Robert's son, Richard Slater Milnes, known as Dick from an early age, is a key player in this story, as is his sister 'Bessy' who married Samuel Thornton MP.

The Heywood Family of Wakefield

Returning to Arthur Heywood and Hannah Milnes, their children married into leading merchant and slaving families.

Richard Heywood (1751–1800) married Mary Earle, a member of an extremely wealthy slaving family in Liverpool. William Earle (1721–88) was a plantation owner, father of the aforementioned Thomas (1754–1822), and also of William (1759–1838), the father of Mary. He was partner with his brother Thomas in T & W Earle & Co. According to the Trans-Atlantic Slave Trade Database, the Earles invested in 200 slaving voyages, transporting 57,903 people, of whom over 8,000 died during the voyage from Africa to the West Indies. Thomas Earle was Mayor of Liverpool 1787–8 and died in 1822, leaving £70,000.[56]

This Heywood-Earle marriage joined two great Liverpool slaving families together. Thomas Earle's son, Hardman Earle (1792–1877) was Mayor of Liverpool in 1836. It was to him and Richard Heywood (son of John Pemberton Heywood of Wakefield) that Charles Turner of City Chambers London and of Liverpool had assigned all his real and personal estate, along with John Hayward Turner as trustees 'to sell same . . . for equal benefit of all creditors.' At abolition Hardman received over £20,000 compensation for 1,378 slaves.[57] Hardman Earle founded Earlestown in Lancashire. He invested his slavery compensation in railway shares, becoming Chairman of the London and North Western Railway. A rich man had become considerable richer on the back of slavery. He was also a cotton broker, importing slave-produced American cotton. Nicholas Salisbury & Co. had been established in 1808, and the partnership was expanded to include John Hayward Turner and Hardman Earle, in 1812 the firm becoming Salisbury, Turner and Earle. Nicholas Salisbury and Turner were significant slave owners.[58] Liverpool cotton brokers were vitally important links in a chain that supported at first British colonial-produced cotton and then American slave-produced cotton which led to the development of the Lancashire cotton industry, an industry that virtually 'enslaved' its employees to extract maximum profits.

Benjamin Heywood (1752–1822), second son of Arthur, lived in Wakefield at Stanley Hall, and lies buried beneath Westgate Chapel. He purchased Stanley Hall estate in 1802 for the considerable sum of £23,500- likely this was funded by both his own financial interest in the wool trade as well as inheritance from his father which was derived largely from the slave trade. He became a major figure in the Lake Lock Railway Company and held the trust deed of the company in January 1803. Capital for the railway was raised through the issue of 128 shares and it was the world's first public railway. His political allegiances shifted from the Whigs to Tory loyalism in the 1790s: like many other Unitarians he was pragmatic in his politics, following the majority rather than ploughing his own furrow like Jack Milnes. Heywood was an officer in the Wakefield Armed Association cavalry, headed by James Milnes as captain commandant. He was admitted to the grand jury at York in 1799 along with James Milnes, and was listed as Commercial Commissioner for the Wapentake of Agbrigg. He was involved in the county elections of 1807 and 1818 for the Fitzwilliam interest.[59] He was brought into the Milnes' textile business by his father in the 1770s and in 1787 invested heavily in Healey Mill Company at Ossett, being one of the five trustees who owned and managed the concern, the board being chaired by Pemberton Milnes. The other trustees were Jeremiah Naylor, Ebenezer Aldred and Thomas Lumb – all Unitarians at Westgate Chapel – and Joshua Haigh of Ossett.[60] Without doubt, Benjamin's investment came via slavery. Benjamin married Elizabeth Hobson, daughter and heir of James Hobson of York, widow of William Serjeantson, on 29 March 1784. Via his father's business links and through his children, Benjamin was embedded in slavery. His wife Elizabeth had married William Serjeantson on the death of his first wife Jane Leeds in 1768. The marriage of William and Jane Leeds had produced a single child, to whom Elizabeth was stepmother to William Rookes Leeds Serjeantson. William Serjeantson's sister, Susanna married Lieutenant Colonel Robert Prescott, whose son Lieutenant Colonel Serjeantson Prescott died in 1816. Robert Prescott was a professional soldier and slave owner. William Serjeantson died 16 April 1782. William Rookes Leeds Serjeantson married Elizabeth, daughter of Henry Dawkins MP (1728–1814). Henry Dawkins was spectacularly wealthy: he owned 20,000 acres in Jamaica and lived there from c. 1751 to 1759, when he left to reside permanently in England. In 1759 he married Lady Juliana Colyear (1736–1821), daughter of Charles Colyear, Earl of Portmore, and Juliana Hele. He sat as an MP from 1760 to 1784.[61] William and Elizabeth's son, George John Serjeantson, married Emma, daughter of Robert Chaloner MP, banker and slave owner. Their eldest daughter Juliana married Henry Bowen Cook on 27 June 1822, grandparents of Charles John Bowen Cooke, Chief Mechanical Engineer of the London and North Western Railway. Of Benjamin's children:

- Arthur Heywood, a captain in the 3rd Dragoon Guards, married Mary Duroure, niece to Edmund Winn Baronet.
- Mary married Daniel Gaskell.
- Hannah married Edward Hawkes Brookesbank.
- Elizabeth Heywood was baptised 11 December 1784. She married Hugh Jones, a successful banker from Liverpool. He died in 1842 leaving £200,000 and was a partner in Heywood's Bank. Their daughter Mary Ellen Jones married Robertson Gladstone (1805–75) on 28 January 1836 – the Jones family were Unitarians and the Gladstones evangelical Anglicans. Robertson was brother of the future Prime Minister William Ewart Gladstone, and Mayor of Liverpool 1842–4. Robertson was a West Indian merchant. He left £120,000 at his death. At abolition he owned 468 slaves and received £21,011 2s 7d. He invested this in railway shares: £3,000 into the Shrewsbury, Oswestry and Chester Junction, £2,500 to the West Yorkshire Railway, a massive £92,580 into the Trent Valley Line,

£5,000 into the Derby and Crewe Junction Railway, £40,300 into the Shrewsbury and Birmingham, and £16,300 into the Birmingham and Oxford Junction Railway, amongst other investments.[62] In August 1845 he was appointed Deputy Chairman of the Grand Junction Railway and was also on the committee of the Birmingham and Oxford Junction Railway. The Gladstones were in business partnership with the Serjeantsons – Benjamin Heywood's wife's first husband's family – as Gladstone & Serjeantson Cotton Factors trading from America: this was slave-produced cotton. Robertson was one of the trustees of the Great Western Cotton Company, a company that imported slave-produced cotton.[63] Both families were embedded in slavery. It was William Ewart Gladstone who was the childhood friend of James Milnes Gaskell, son of Benjamin Gaskell. Gladstone was a guest in 1829 and 1832 at Thornes House. When Gladstone returned there in 1871, he experienced 'a vivid recollection of the place as it was associated with much kindness received and with my first stepping out from a very retired childhood and youth into the world'. Indeed, Mr and Mrs Gaskell and Daniel Gaskell appear several times in Gladstone's numerous diaries. Gladstone was drawn to Gaskell's wife, who mothered and inspired him, by a common interest in religion – they were both Anglicans.[64] Indeed, we have to note that Robertson's father John Gladstone (1764–1851) was a politician and merchant, trading cotton and sugar, and then invested in buying plantations in British Guiana (Demerara as was) in 1803 including the Belmont Estate amongst several others. The largest estate was the Vreedenhoop estate in Demerara which he bought in 1826 for £80,000. It had 430 enslaved people working on it. Throughout the 1820s Gladstone expanded his sugar estate holdings in the Caribbean, despite the rise of abolitionism, and was a vocal defender of slavery. With the ending of slavery, he sold most of his West Indian properties and moved into Bengal sugar. At abolition he received over £112,500 – roughly £13 million in 2020! He invested in railway shares: £4,000 into the Birmingham and Oxford Junction Railway, £37,500 into the Caledonian, and £20,000 into the London and Manchester.[65]

John Pemberton Heywood (1765–1835), younger brother of Benjamin, married Margaret Drinkwater in 1797 and received a hefty £10,000 dowry from Peter Drinkwater, a cotton merchant in Manchester. On his death in 1801, John Pemberton received a further £10,000. He was actively involved in the Yorkshire Association and Whig politics in the county.

We have no clue as to his inheritance from his father Arthur, except to assume it was fairly substantial. John Pemberton was a lawyer active in London and retired from the bench in 1811. He used his vast wealth to build Wentworth House on Wentworth Street Wakefield, and to found the Lancasterian School. He subscribed to the Music Saloon on Wood Street in 1822 as well as to the Wakefield Dispensary: three Wakefield institutions benefitted from slave money. His son Richard was a banker and partner in Milnes and Heywood with Richard Rodes Mines.[66] Richard Heywood was named co-trustee with his cousin Hardman Earle and John Hayward Turner in the bankruptcy of Charles Turner, a West Indian merchant and slave owner. Heywood was to receive a percentage of the £4,747 5s 3d paid out as compensation for the 331 slaves Turner owned on Antigua. By the time the claim was completed on 23 January 1836 Richard Heywood was dead.[67] Heywood had died aged 32 on 16 December 1833 and lies next to his father in the catacombs beneath Westgate Chapel. His father John Pemberton died aged 79 in 1835, morbidly obese, the size of his 'funeral vault' being a noted talking point of visitors to the catacombs along with the 'leg space' of his pew. His son, John Pemberton Heywood married his niece, the daughter of Elizabeth Heywood and Hugh Jones in 1836.

Comment

At his home in Wakefield Arthur Heywood sat in the middle of a web of familial ties with major slave traders. The extended Milnes-Heywood family's slave-trading activities based on the Trans-Atlantic Slave Trade Database are as follows:

Birchs: 45 voyages, 12,496 slaves
Blundells: 113 voyages, 31,341
Brights: 23 voyages, 7,853 slaves
Caldwells: 14 voyages, 4,066 slaves
Earles: 200 voyages, 57,903 slaves
Gildarts: 66 voyages, 17,438 slaves
Gladstones: 1 voyage, 439 slaves
Goodwins: 19 voyages, 4,965 slaves
Heywoods: 134 voyages, 43,388 slaves
Ogdens: 43 voyages, 12,136 slaves
Pembertons: 31 voyages, 6,662 slaves
Slaters: 45 voyages, 13,623 slaves
Tarletons: 184 voyages, 52,674 slaves
Whytes: 1 voyage, 200 slaves

At a conservative estimate the grim tally is 265,184 men, women and children dragged from their homes by the extended family of Arthur and Benjamin Heywood. Over a quarter of a million people!

Heywood was not unique, far from it, even in Wakefield. Francis Ingram and his sons transported 41,412 people and Ellis Hodgson 55,010 – the latter not being a Wakefield resident when he did so. Three men who lived Wakefield and its district transported between them 139,810 men, women and children, of whom over 15,000 died on the voyages. Wakefield has a dark past and played a not-insignificant part in the slave trade. The truth is, of the roughly 1.4 million men women and children transported by the slave trade, 25 per cent transported between 1700 and 1807 were sent into slavery by Arthur Heywood, his extended family and slave traders in Wakefield.

This crime has been ignored until now and needs to be brought into the light, explored and discussed. The town of Wakefield's late eighteenth century prosperity rested on the profits of the transatlantic slave trade. Yorkshire has a hidden past that requires greater exposure than this book allows for. This book is, I hope, a springboard to understand the dimensions of the crime committed against African people by people from Yorkshire, without which contrition and gestures are meaningless. Slavery is utterly absent from museums across the county: it has been airbrushed from the past. This too is a crime: wilful ignorance? We can no longer hide the fact that Yorkshire played a pivotal part in the slave trade. Yorkshire men and women committed a great crime in the name of money. Liverpool has begun the process of restitution for its links to slavery, yet Yorkshire and indeed towns and cities like Halifax, Wakefield and Leeds have made no attempt to acknowledge the slave trade.

Chapter 9

Island Governance

Yorkshire was also birthplace and home to those involved in the governance of West Indian islands and who had ultimate powers of arbitration over the slaves on the islands they ran:

- Marmaduke Robinson (1757–1836). Baptised in Malton, the third son of Marmaduke Robinson, on 17 February 1757, he was a solicitor and agent in the West Indies before settling in London. He was awarded the compensation as mortgagee for two estates in Antigua belonging to Sir William Lewis George Thomas, 4th Baronet, with some 535 enslaved persons, and it seems acted as trustee for the Arthur Freeman estate on Antigua as part of an arrangement within the Freeman/Thomas family under indentures dated 1801 and 1811.[1]
- Sir Fitzroy Jeffreys Grafton Maclean (1770–1847), 8th Baronet, son of Donald Maclean of Brolas and Margaret Wall of Clonea Castle, was the owner of Sixmens estate in Barbados which had belonged to his first wife Elizabeth Bishop née Kyd. As a serving army officer, he had been present at the capture of Tobago in 1793 and a year later took part in the capture of Martinique as a company commander in the 60th Regiment of Foot. He was granted command of the island, his successor being Robert Shore Milnes. In 1803 he commanded the Batavian soldiers received into British service on the surrender of the Dutch West Indian colonies. In 1805 he was present at the capture of St Thomas and St John. He was named governor here from 1808 to 1815 when the islands were returned to Denmark under the Treaty of Paris. By 1809, the only remaining French foothold in the Americas was the island of Guadeloupe. The French used the island to resupply privateers who preyed on British trade routes. Britain invaded Guadeloupe on 28 January 1810 in which operation he participated. He returned to Britain in 1815 and lived at Nether Hall in

Doncaster, an early Georgian mansion that still stands. At abolition he received £3,676 1s 8d for 185 slaves.[2]

- George Metcalfe (1758–1821) of Rigg House, Askrigg, near Hawes, North Yorkshire. He was Governor of Dominica from 1805 to May 1808. His tombstone in Hawes Parish church reads:'In memory of George Metcalfe, Esq., of Rigg House many years President of the Counsel [sic] of Dominica and Colonel of the St George's Militia in that island. He died on 13th February 1821 aged 63. Also, of Elizabeth Metcalfe his wife, daughter of William and Margaret Davis of Gargrave in this county, who died 4th January 1846 aged 60 years.'[3] As well as governor, he was a sugar planter and slave trader. Between 1796 and 1807 he conducted 10 slaving voyages and transported 3,166 slaves.[4] In 1833 his widow Elizabeth in 1833 received compensation for 359 slaves. His will proved on 21 February 1822 states:

This is my last will. I am in plorable good health but think it necessary to have a will by me. I give and bequeath all my property of whatsoever kind Real and Personal to my beloved wife Elizabeth for and during her natural life and at her decease I bequeath Birk Rigg Estates, Rigg House Estate, Mossdale Moor Estate, Gayle Estate with all my property in Hampton Court Estate, Negroes and all my estate Negroes and houses in the Island of Dominica to Robert Atkinson now in Richmond To Thomas Davis now in Gargrave and to Isaac Metcalfe now in London each one third as Tenants in Common with this proviso that Robert Atkinson and Thomas Davis assume and bear the name of Metcalfe and qualify at the Herald's Office before they enter into possession and subject to pay the following legacies viz Margaret Coats £50, Nancy Atkinson £100 and if she marries well £100 more. One shilling per day to George Atkinson during his life and £10 to Isaac Atkinson now in Dominica. I appoint W T Roberts Esquire, London, Mr John Davis of Liverpool, Anthony Davis in Philadelphia son of Thomas, and Mr John Routh of London to be to be my executors and I bequeath £1,000 sterling to each of them from the Hampton Court Estate as a reward for acting zealously. I further will that my dear wife shall not marry again and that should she marry the whole of my property shall as heretofore devised. I bequeath the shop at the East End of Hawes Market and my half the pew in Hawes Chappel to my wife Elizabeth for ever and to her executors her heors and admons and further it is my will that the Mortgages and other Incumbrances shall be paid prior to the legacies and that the legacies to my executors shall be the last paid. Given under my hand and seal at Rigg House this twenty first day of September 1820 . . . George Metcalfe, signed and acknowledged in the presence of Chris Moor, Alexander Metcalfe, Mary Hunter. I further will by way of a codicil that the male heir of each of the legatees to the estates after the death of their father and if it be descended to a person not named Metcalfe that then the said person shall qualify and take the name of Metcalfe before he shall enter into possession and I recommend to each of the three principal legatees to curtail by will the said properties to the heir male of each and I give power to my executors to sell my Dominica property except the Negroes that may be removed to Demerara.[5]

- Thomas Wilson (1724–1808), Chief Justice of Dominica 1775–9 and father of Admiral George Wilson. He died at Camberwell in 1808 aged 84. His wife Lucinda née Holt had been buried at St Giles and St Mary at Pontefract on 11 October 1792. His daughter Isabelle married firstly Henry Grove, Collector of Customs on Dominica, and then John Belson: the announcement of this second marriage in 1792 also showed her father as Thomas Wilson of Pontefract Yorkshire.[6]

- From Wakefield came Sir Robert Shore Milnes (1754–1837), eldest son of John Milnes and Mary Shore. After a military career in the Royal Horse Guards, Milnes left the army in 1788 with the rank of captain. Seven years later he was Governor of Martinique. On 4 November 1797 he was appointed Lieutenant Governor of Lower Canada, and on 15 June 1799, at 53 years of age, he was sworn in; on 30 July 1799 he replaced family friend Governor Colonel Robert Prescott – who married Wakefield lass Elizabeth Serjeantson and his sister Hannah was witness to the marriage – as administrator of the province. A baronetcy was conferred on him on 21 March 1801. Milnes left for England on 5 August 1805 but remained administrator until 12 August 1805. Thomas Dunn assumed his duties as administrator until Governor Sir James Henry Craig arrived in October 1807.[7] Milnes acted as agent for Martinique from 1809, working under Governor General Broderick and his successor Governor Wale for a number of years and was noted for his enlightened governance. He took up the cause of both the Creole elite as well as freed slaves, as well as French nationals. The slave revolt in 1811 was Milnes's greatest moment of triumph. With no access to international markets to trade sugar and other goods, the island's economy collapsed, and Milnes recognised that the island's economic distress was directly linked to Martinique's racial imbalance and racist culture: he warned that continued economic stress may lead to larger slave revolts, and to take increasingly violent ends, and invoked the spectre of the St Dominique rebellion. Driven by famine, the possibility of a West Indies-wide rebellion was a real possibility unless the British government allowed the French plantation owners to sell their coffee and sugar in home markets in France. The British government of course ignored Milnes, refused to grant Creoles status as subjects of the Crown and refused to allow Martinican ships into home ports. Milnes managed to keep the lid on rebellion, but matters were made worse with a devastating hurricane in 1813, which witnessed Milnes petitioning London for aid, and the government finally allowed Martinican ships to trade their sugar into British ports.[8] In 1774 he was named a trustee of Westgate Chapel in Wakefield and was president 1812–37; his two daughters became the first female trustees in the chapel's history. He married Charlotte Frances Bentinck, daughter of Captain John Bentinck and Renira van Tuyll van Serooskerken, on 12 November 1785. Milnes died at Tunbridge Wells on 2 December 1837 and was survived by two daughters and three sons: two sons were army officers, John Bentinck Milnes was killed in the War of 1812, and William Henry Milnes was killed at the Battle of Waterloo. Mrs Milnes died in 1850.[9]

Like every county in the country, Yorkshire had its slave traders who made vast fortunes. Not only slave ships owners came from Yorkshire, but so did captains. Thomas Pratt was captain of the *Hibernia*, which under his command made four slaving voyages from 1804 to 1808. According to the Trans-Atlantic Slave Trade Database, the *Hibernia* with Thomas as captain embarked 984 Africans and disembarked 885 – 99 people lost their lives en route, so one in ten did not survive these voyages. Pratt lies in Askrigg Parish Church graveyard.[10]

These are just some of the slave owners and traders – each of these people had a vested interest in keeping slavery: they provided, it must have seemed at the time, an insurmountable obstacle not only to abolishing the slave trade, but also slavery. Yorkshiremen captained slave ships, owned slave ships, owned slaves and plantations and governed islands.

Chapter 10

Yorkshire and the Slave Trade

As we leave Part 1 of this book that has dwelt on slave traders and owners, how do we assess these people across Yorkshire? From parsons to MPs, high sheriffs and the middling sort, slavery was part and parcel of their moral judgement on the world. By the 1830s, the cotton industry could not operate without slaves. The sugar industry, and its allied trades, was just as reliant. Slave-produced goods were embedded into the economy. 'King Cotton', the material that made Lancashire and Manchester rich, relied on American plantations. Without slavery in America, the boom time of 'Cottonopolis' would not have happened. Even when the abolition of slavery in the British Empire came in 1833, slavery was the cornerstone of the economy. Big business, as well as everyday people, had a vested interest in it. Slavery was not the preserve of just the elite – the bulk of the slave owners in Yorkshire seem to have been from the burgeoning middle class, who, no doubt wanting to make handsome profits, invested their money in merchant houses and plantations as they were safe businesses which guaranteed a return year on year. For many, the rents and income from slave plantations were their sole income – the abolitionists were fighting against vested interest both great and small, as well as the mercantile interest. Yet this opposition was overcome, as we shall see in Part 3 of this work.

Many saw no moral conflict between slavery and their Christian faith. Indeed, the Bible is full of scripture supporting slavery:

> Leviticus 25:44-46 'As for your male and female slaves whom you may have: you may buy male and female slaves from among the nations that are around you. You may also buy from among the strangers who sojourn with you and their clans that are with you, who have been born in your land, and they may be your property. You may bequeath them to your sons after you to inherit

as a possession forever. You may make slaves of them, but over your brothers the people of Israel you shall not rule, one over another ruthlessly.'

Here was the divine right to own slaves. Yet the Bible also presented texts against slavery: Exodus 21:16 'Whoever steals a man and sells him, and anyone found in possession of him, shall be put to death.'

Both slavers and abolitionists believed they were doing the work of God. It was a theological debate as much as a moral crusade. For thousands of men and women, slavery was acceptable, it was the way the world was and their religion supported their moral judgement on slavery. To our eyes and to the people of the early nineteenth century slavery was wrong; today air travel is accepted as normal, yet it is destroying the planet with its carbon emissions. It is too easy to condemn the past and ignore the failings in our own time: 'Let he who is without sin cast the first stone,' as the Bible comments. Yet we must make some form of conclusion and moral judgement. The weight of public opinion from the 1770s showed that moral attitudes to slavery had changed: perception had altered. The paradigm had changed dramatically. Change is always hard thing to accept, so much so the pro-slavery lobby blocked bids to abolish the slave trade and slavery from 1788 to 1833. Yet change occurred. It is those men and women who blocked the moral crusade to treat all people as equal that we must pass judgement upon. The ideals of the French Revolution of *liberté, égalité, fraternité* changed the world for the better. Opposition to notions of equality under the law, protectionism of religious rights, exclusion from government of the vast majority of the people, discrimination on the grounds of race, gender and religion were at the heart of late eighteenth-century politics and the shift of public morals against slavery. The self interest groups who wanted to openly discriminate we can judge as bigots and racists, which we discuss in the third and final part of this book.

As historians we have to avoid painting people as monsters who are beyond understanding – the past is a foreign country, after all, that no one can visit! Rather than describing these people as monstrous, we also need to avoid as far as is possible any tacit apologizing for the acts a person carried out in the past, and make it clear that we find their actions morally repugnant. As true today as in the past, morality is complicated: it changed and moved and was not necessarily reflected perfectly in the law.

Armed with these ideas, how do we judge men like George Hibbert Oates? He ran a prostitution racket which is morally wrong, and he also fathered children with the women he slept with; yet he also made financial provision for them in his will. He took some degree of responsibility. Many fathers today do not do that, and many in history did not either. As we shall see in our next chapters concerning Africans in Yorkshire, he and Waterton were not unique in fathering children with their slaves. Today it is wrong to have sexual relations with a child aged 12: but that was the legal age of consent from the 1790s. George Hibbert Oates slept with girls aged 14 – legally and morally he did nothing wrong in the eighteenth -century world. In modern eyes, yes, he was a paedophile, a monster, and we acknowledge that his moral judgement in his lifetime was singled out by his peers as wrong. His moral actions and judgement were shaped by his own experiences of the culture he found himself in which was harsh and very brutal, which was different to the moral codes of England. Was the moral code of his environment wrong? Yes. Slavery dehumanised people, it treated people as things that were disposable. Yet how can we make objective judgements from all of this that are meaningful? Our own modern values of course affect our understanding and view of the past. The Holocaust was legal, yet morally wrong. Slavery was legal, sexual intercourse with a 12-year-old was legal. How do we judge the slave owners who fathered children with their slaves? Many fathers left provision for them in their wills, others gave them full legal rights, yet others could leave their children as slaves as we shall see. How do we judge these men? Compared to some plantation owners, Oates was a good master: Thomas Picton, the hero of Waterloo, was also known as the 'Butcher of Trinidad' and committed torture, mutilation and murder and burnt a slave alive.[1] Condemned in his own lifetime, his status as a hero somehow assuages the blood he spilled. Was Picton a monster? Yes. He was put on trial by his peers and found guilty. Was Oates a monster? Were all slave owners monsters? This is perhaps an impossible question to answer.

But how far have we really come in 300 years? Fathers today abandoned their children, sex tourism and sex slavery still exist, and wage slaves in sweatshops around the globe make the bulk of the clothing we wear. We are culpable of the same crimes as our ancestors. This is not the space to discuss eighteenth and nineteenth-century sexual morality, but we do acknowledge that the actions of past to us are morally questionable. It is indeed an alien world. We need to allow the past to judge itself, and rely on the judgements of the time to aid us in our judgements. In 1750 slavery was acceptable. By 1830 it was not, and those who chose to maintain slavery were on the wrong side of history. Slavery existed because the economy of the country relied upon the exploitation of free or bonded labour. It is still the very basis of the capitalist economic system of the world. Our goods are made in China, Taiwan and Cambodia by workers who earn a year less than we do in day, because we want cheap goods, to get value for money. These cheap goods are then shipped to Europe for us to buy and make merchants rich. How is this any different to the slave plantations of the eighteenth century? Before we judge the past on our morals, surely, we must look to ourselves?

PART 2:
AFRICANS IN YORKSHIRE

Chapter 11

Slaves in Yorkshire?

As our earlier chapters have shown, Yorkshire was a key player in the slave trade, yet it is saddening to note that slaves lived in Yorkshire. It is heart-breaking to relate that people could be fashion accessories.

Regretfully we acknowledge that black servants were 'the must-have fashion accessory' in the eighteenth century. Yet for these people in many cases it was a virtual death sentence. Dragged from Africa and exposed to European diseases, most frequently, as we shall see, they lived for no more than 18 months. Like other counties Yorkshire had rich families who 'had to have' a black servant: the culture of 'conspicuous consumption' in action where capitalism relegated people to the status of objects. It is the largely forgotten story of these men and women which now follows. It may be disturbing to some to realise that our communities in Yorkshire were very diverse: black and Indian men and women walked the streets of Yorkshire, accompanied by French, Germans, Portuguese, Dutch and many other nationalities besides. The story of Yorkshire is not just about white 'Anglo-Saxon' men and women.

The *Gentleman's Magazine* estimated 20,000 people of colour working in London as servants in 1764.[1] Yorkshire has been a safe haven for immigrants for centuries. In Wakefield there were economic migrants – the Gotthardt family had settled in the 1770s from Bavaria; the O'Dwyer family had fled France as Royalist émigrés seeking sanctuary and safety; the Fernandes family had fled seeking sanctuary when Portugal was invaded by French troops in 1807; Spencer van Strawbenzee had fled the Netherlands a decade or so earlier and came to Wakefield. At the start of the eighteenth century Hans Busk was worshipping at Call Lane Chapel, Leeds, and had migrated from Gotthenburg in Germany. Here he lived amongst a large immigrant community that worshipped at Call Lane:

Bernard Bischoff, a Swiss national.
John Berkenhout, a Dutch national.

Johannes Koster, a German national.
The Noguier and Gautier families from France.
The Clerkenbrinkes, a Dutch family.[2]

These foreigners were discriminated against by the Leeds merchant community at large: they had to pay taxes at double rate.[3] They sought a new life: how different are they to thousands of British citizens living in Spain, France and other parts of the globe seeking a new life? It depends on the view point and latent racism of the observer. An expat in Spain is as much an immigrant as a refugee from Iran. My own ancestors, the Van Bootlandts, were technically illegal immigrants from Frisia who sought refuge from religious persecution. Without my immigrant ancestors, I would not have been here to write this book.

In relation to the slave trade and slavery, we find slaves living in Yorkshire. Until the Somerset case of May 1772 (see Chapter 12) these servants were legally slaves. Often, based on period portraits, these servants were dressed in elaborate and expensive clothing, and wore a silver collar about their neck, as a mark of their slavery. Such collars could be quite elaborate indeed. In the county town of York, we find a Yorick. Mr Waite had his black servant baptised at St Olave York, and at St Crux we find Dolly and Tamar baptised in the eighteenth century, again servants in the city. John Buxton, who described himself as a 'Blackman, native of Bengal', was arrested for vagrancy in Thornton in the North Riding in 1802. He had come to Britain from Ireland with his master, Captain John Warrington, who had suddenly died, leaving him 'to the mercy of all well-disposed Christians to enable him to procure his passage to his native country as this climate does not agree with him, [he] would wish to return as soon as convenient'.[4]

East Yorkshire

The earliest reference we have come across for a black servant comes from 1600 when we find a reference to 'a negro woman belonging to Mr Burnet'. She is listed in the tax records as a member of the household of Bartholomew Burnett of Hull from 1598 to 1600.[5] We have been unable to find a place or date of death for her.

In the early 1740s, a black servant was brought to the region from the East Indies by William Draper. After his appointment in 1743, the new Archbishop of York, Thomas Herring, wrote to all the clergymen within his diocese requesting information. In response to a question about whether his parishioners were baptised, Thomas Mease, curate at

Beswick wrote: 'I know of none who come to church in this place that are not baptised, except one call'd Beswick, a Black, who is about twenty years of age; he was in the East Indies, sold to Mr William Draper, Esq of this Town. He is a Youth of no learning, and but of very slender capacity.'[6] The same record goes to state that Beswick was baptised in Kilnwick on 30 November 1746 and given the Christian name John. We can find no further reference to this man.

In 1739 Lady Burlington, at Londesbrough Hall, provided to her black servant James Cambridge a coat and veste. He was drawn by William Kent in 1735 and painted by Van Loo as part of a family portrait which now hangs at Chatsworth House, Derbyshire. Indeed, in July 1725 Joseph Caesar, black servant to Lord Burlington, was baptised in London, and was appointed by Lady Burlington as her footman, earning £105 a year, from which he was to pay turnpike toll charges.

Peter Horsfield, a footman to Sir George Strickland, married Elizabeth, daughter of the Rev. George Lawson, vicar of Weaverthorpe at Boynton on 25 March 1780. Their son, one-day-old Henry Horsfield, was baptised at St. Cuthbert's Peaseholm Green in York on 21 December 1780. The baptismal record identified his father as 'a negro'.[7] Further confirmation that Horsfield was of African descent comes from a letter sent to Boynton Hall from a Mr. Stedman, addressed to 'Peter the Negro, Servant to Sir George Strickland'.[8]

Richard Pompey, a 'grown-up person', was baptised at Boynton on 26 September 1746.[9] There is no mention of his race in the parish records, but Pompey was a name typically given to many black servants. Was he a servant of the Strickland family? Presumably.

Records show that 'John Robinson, about 18 years of age, an African servant to Mr. R. Graham . . . residing in Kell Gate' was baptised in Beverley Minster in 1796.[10]

In the early eighteenth century, black servant John Scampston was employed by Sir William St. Quintin, 3rd Baronet of Harpham. The record of his baptism in Rillington on 21 August 1720 reveals that he was a 'Black boy'.[11] He was buried on 27 August 1725 recorded as 'John Scampston Black servant to Sir William St Quintin'.[12] St Quintin sat for Hull as a Whig MP in eleven successive Parliaments. He was appointed to the Treasury Board at George I's accession, and lost his post in 1717, when he followed Walpole into opposition. Supporting Walpole, he obtained a lucrative Irish sinecure on Walpole's return to office. He died on 30 June 1723.[13]

West Yorkshire

In West Yorkshire we have a number of people of colour baptised, and are clearly identified as such on the baptism records. These people were likely born as slaves and brought to Yorkshire as servants.

A 'merchant prince', Thomas Charnock, of the Grove, Wakefield, a member of an extremely wealthy family of cloth merchants, owned a black servant in Wakefield. Richard Brown, a 16-year-old, was baptised in Wakefield on 12 August 1763. He had been brought from North or South Carolina to work as a servant:

> Wakefield October 30 1762
>
> May it please your Grace To read first the inclosed Letter directed to me, and then Your Lordship will see the reason of my writing to You at this time, and also of the Request to Your Grace.
>
> This Mr Thomas Charnock, a Native of this Town, having lived many Years in North- or South-Carolina, came back to his Mother two or three years ago, bringing a Black Boy along with him. He told me, some time after he had been here, that as soon as the Boy could read and understand, he intended that he should be baptised. I let him know, both then and since, that Notice must be first given to the Archbishop. The Boy seems to be sixteen years of Age. Mr Charnock is in no kind of Business, has an opportunity of speaking to me every day: but has not exchanged a word with me for above six Months. Now, the last Thursday in the Afternoon, when the Bells were ringing for Prayers, the Parish Clerk came to tell me, that Mr Brocklebank, Mr Scott's curate for Horbury, who was going to read Prayers, would baptise Mr Charnock's Black, if I would give leave. I replied, by no means till notice was given to the Archbishop and another Person coming to me with the Boy, and I not complying, but referring to the Rubrick, received this inclosed Letter from Mr Charnock in the Evening. I desire therefore the Favour of Your Grace, that your Lordship would be pleased to appoint my Curate Mr Armitage or Mr Scott the Lecturer or any other Clergyman, to examin this Boy, and you will greatly oblige, my Lord, Your Lordship's most Obedient Servant.
>
> Benjamin Wilson[14]

The boy was baptised during the tenure of Archbishop Drummond, whose second son married the daughter of Pemberton Milnes, Mary

Bridget Milnes. Benjamin Wilson was vicar of Wakefield 1751–64. From the records of Wakefield Parish Church, we find: '1763. Augt. Richard Brown, a Black from Carolina, 12th.'[15] Was this actually Thomas Brown? Or are we dealing with his brother? He was baptised at All Saints and not St Peter's Horbury. From the letter, Charnock was a merchant in Carolina. We know Thomas owned an extensive tobacco plantation and several hundred slaves. Members of the wider Charnock family also owned sugar plantations on Jamaica at the same time, the plantation in Barbados being called 'Charnocks'.[16]

Thomas Charnock (1709–?) was brother of George Charnock (1720–83), both sons of William Charnock. George Charnock was an Anglican, a Tory, governor of Wakefield Charities and in 1755 Constable of Wakefield. He had built Grove House by 1750. William (1718–61) built Burneytops House on part of the Grove Estate, which by 1786 was developed as 'West Burney Tops Close' the first planned Georgian development in Wakefield with plans drawn up by Charles Watson of Doncaster. This development became 'South Parade', home to the Charnock, Johnson and Tootal families by 1790. Both William and George were cloth merchants exporting to the Netherlands and Portugal. George's sons Thomas (1758–1831) and John (1752–1811) became partners in Robert Smithson's Low Laithes colliery.[17] William Charnock senior (1679–1746) was a cloth merchant, and had Timothy Reveley apprenticed to him on 25 July 1716.[18] William Charnock and Mary Ryley were married on 30 March 1725 at Westgate End Chapel, the precursor to the current Westgate Chapel. A Timothy Reveley was named trustee of the chapel on 25 December 1735 and of the new chapel in 1753 and had been allocated burial vault 27 under the chapel on 16 March 1752. Timothy's sister married Thomas Lee, parents of John Lee (1733–93), Attorney General in 1783. The Charnocks for a time were squarely with the congregation that would become Unitarian in the middle decades of the eighteenth century, and above all else, worshipped alongside the Milnes, Reveley and Naylor families who dominated the cloth trade in the area.

Living at Wentworth Woodhouse was Charles Watson Wentworth, 2nd Marquis of Rockingham. He was a great player in national and international politics. He was a personal friend of Pemberton Milnes of Wakefield. A 'black boy' named Henry Friday is recorded in 1770 as a servant at Wentworth Woodhouse.[19] Presumably he had been christened or re-named after the character in *Robinson Crusoe*. He was buried on 18 August 1773.[20] However, he was not the sole black servant at Wentworth Woodhouse.

Mary Bright, the wife of the Marquis of Rockingham, had two black people as servants. Governor Wentworth, reporting the capture of Long Island in 1776, wrote that he 'sends two negro slaves "Romulus" and "Remus" two accomplished musicians', as a gift to Lady Rockingham.[21] The fate of these persons is not known

In Birstall Parish Church, Tom Granada, 'a negro', was baptised 8 January 1769. He was buried there on 14 December 1769.[22] No parents are listed, and we presume he was baptised as an adult and was a servant in a nearby large country house, and that he originated from Grenada. Such a place of birth implies he was a slave.

Born in 1747, John Lewis was a 'Negro' living in Bawtry, near Doncaster. Bawtry Hall had been built by Pemberton Milnes in the 1770s and became the principal residence of his daughter, Mary Bridgett and her first husband Peter Auriol Hey Drummond. Lewis was buried in Bawtry 18 December 1802 aged 55, an 'Anglican'.[23] The suspicion is, he was a black servant to either Pemberton or Mary Bridgett, very much likely the latter as her husband was son of the Archbishop of York. This is guesswork: we cannot prove that that he was a slave or indeed a servant, and could as easily have been a free man. However, given his name, John Lewis, and that slaves tended to take the names of their masters, we find that in the 1750s John Lewis of Westmoreland, Esquire who died in 1769 was a major slave owner with 429 slaves at the time of his death.[24] Buried at Bawtry Parish Church on 9 February 1789 was Mary Ann Rose, 'a Negro Woman'. Was she related to John Lewis above?[25]

At Nostell Priory, Wakefield, we find reference to Jean-Philippe 'a young French speaking black servant' and Sir Roland Winn endeavouring to exchange a loaf of bread for a 'black boy' to circumvent the law about selling black people in England in 1775.[26] Arguably therefore a black women had become pregnant on the estate and the unwanted child was to be cruelly disposed of. Who was she? What became of the child?

The baptismal records of All Hallows Church, Harthill records the baptism of Thomas Pompey on 7 November 1725, described as 'a youth about 14 years of age and a native of Guinea in Africa. . . . The Right Honourable Marquess of Carmarthen and James Frymer Esq., the Godfathers and the Right Honourable Lady Carmarthen and Lady Pitt, Godmothers.'[27] The Marquis of Carmarthen was Peregrine Osborne (1656–1729), 2nd Duke of Leeds, MP for York in 1689.[28] The family home of the marquis was Kiveton House. Pompey was clearly a servant in this grand house, and his baptism was clearly one of social exuberance, no doubt to celebrate 'a pagan' becoming a Christian. We know nothing more about Thomas: we find a burial record of a Thomas Pompey in

Stepney, dated 12 September 1727 and a second dated 1757. These could be Thomas of Harthill, or indeed two further black servants named Thomas Pompey living in London with no connection at all to Yorkshire!

We find a second baptism in 1764 in Wakefield of a person of colour. In February 1764 the vicar sought permission for the baptism of a young Black man of over twenty who 'belongs to Colonel Prescot':

Wakefield February 18 1764
    May it please Your Grace,
    There is a young Man, a Black, above twenty years of Age, who has given notice to my Curate Mr Armitage that he desires to be baptized.
    He belongs to Colonel Prescot, who now resides in this Town. I wish Your Lordship and all your Family good Health and I am, my Lord,
        Your Lordship's most Obedient and most Humble Servant
        Benjamin Wilson[29]

The word 'belongs to' leaves us in no doubt that he was a slave and the personal property of the colonel. When we consult the baptismal records of All Saints we find:

1764. April. John Wakefield, a child left at a house in Kirkgate, abt. 2years of ages. 12th
Octr. John Vernon, a black from Antiga, abt. 22yrs old. 4th.[30]

This is undeniably the same man as mentioned to Archbishop Drummond by the vicar of Wakefield. He was undeniably a slave: the surname Vernon may refer to Vernon's plantation, Antigua, owned by John Vernon.[31]

Who was Colonel Prescott? A career soldier and administrator, Robert Prescott married Susanna Serjeantson in Wakefield. Her brother William's widow would marry Benjamin Heywood of Westgate Chapel in 1782. Thus, Prescott became, inter alia, a member of the Milnes cum Heywood family. Indeed, we note that Robert's marriage was witnessed by Hannah Milnes – older sister of Robert Shore and John Milnes, sons of John Milnes, again all of Westgate Chapel – and also by Margaret Cookson, daughter of Dr Cookson, the leading physician in the West Riding till his death in 1779 aged 79. Margaret Cookson was known as Maria, and was dancing and socialising a great deal with Jack Milnes.[32] Prescott began his career in the British army on 22 June 1745, when he was appointed an ensign in the 15th Regiment of Foot, promoted lieutenant three years later and captain on 22 January 1755. Four years later on 5 May 1759 Prescott received the prestigious appointment of aide-de-camp to Major General Amherst. On 22 March 1761 he bought himself the position of major in the 95th Regiment of Foot. His regiment was sent to Martinique in 1762, arriving shortly after the capture of the island, and proceeded to Cuba in May. Prescott exchanged into the 27th Regiment of Foot in July, and on 10 November 1762 he purchased the rank of lieutenant-colonel in the 72nd Regiment of Foot. With no regiment from 1763 he lived in Wakefield. With the outbreak of the American Revolution, Prescott was gazetted lieutenant-colonel of the 28th Regiment of Foot on 8 September 1775. Made brevet colonel in August 1777, he fought at Brandywine on 11 September and was in action at the Battle of Monmouth in June 1778. He was commander of the 1st Brigade in the attack on St Lucia, and from August 1779 into 1780 he commanded British troops in the Leeward Isles. Colonel of the 94th Regiment of Foot on 13 October 1780, he was on half pay from 1783, then made colonel of the 28th Foot on 6 July 1789. In October 1793 promotion to general came and he was ordered to command Barbados, being involved in the capture of Martinique and named governor. Appointed lieutenant governor of Lower Canada on 21 January 1796, he was succeeded on Martinique by Robert Shore Milnes. Prescott remained till April 1799 when he was recalled to Britain and Milnes took over as governor. Prescott died in Battle in Sussex aged 89 in December 1815.[33] Prescott was clearly a very close family friend of the Milnes. He had served in Martinique under the orders of Robert Monckton, MP for Pontefract 1751–4, 1774 and 1778–82. He owned 4,000 acres on St Vincent that he sold in 1775 to a syndicate comprised of William and Robert Gemmell, Henry and Duncan Davidson and James Baillie the elder for £31,750.[34] His nephew, Robert Monckton Arundell would marry as his second wife Mary Bridgette Milnes, only daughter of Pemberton Milnes. He would also be MP for Pontefract, and York 1783–90.

Robert Wadeson was baptised at Sedbergh, then in the West Riding, on 20 November 1753, listed as 'black'.[35] He was undeniably a slave cum servant owned by Robert Wadeson (1717–67) who was born in Dent, near to Sedbergh, and was a plantation owner. About Wadeson the slave, we know nothing more: we have been unable to trace a date of death or place of burial. In his will of 1767 Robert Wadeson left £20 to Elizabeth Kirke of Bridge Town in Barbados 'as a small token of her care for me and I bequeath to my servant Amelia Snowden [illegible] for the [illegible] and care she has given proofs of in the service my family the sum of fifty pounds'. The will goes onto mention land in Barbados. His sister Agnes married Robert Vanbrugh.[36] Without doubt, Robert Wadeson was a plantation owner, and seemingly was in business with James Leigh Perrot.[37] Perrot married Jane Leigh Cholmeley, aunt and patron of Jane Austen and heir to her father Robert Cholmeley of Barbados.[38] We find reference to the baptism of a child, Samuel Weyman Wadeson, on Barbados by 'Eva' to Robert Wadeson in 1740.[39] A clandestine marriage then takes place at St Andrews Holborn on 10 May 1742 between Wadeson and Eva Weyman, two years after the birth of the child.[40] A full eight years pass before a more legal marriage takes place on 11 June 1750 between Eva and Robert, not in London this time but at Whaplode Drove, Lincoln![41] On 6 February 1753 we find the baptism of Mary, daughter of Robert and Eva Wadeson, and 21 September 1754 Samuel Weyman Wadeson is baptised.[42] Is this the same Samuel? Baptised in Barbados as a bastard and then baptised as a young man once his legal status was determined? Samuel Weyman Wadeson was articled to Thomas Fell, lawyer, on 22 June 1775.[43]

Robert Vanbrugh was baptised on 31 July 1728 at St Dunstan in the East, London, son of George Vanbrugh, presumably a relative of David Vanbrugh, a merchant in Kingston, Jamaica. The will of David Vanbrugh was proved in Jamaica in 1746, and he possessed twelve male slaves and eleven females valued at £951 5s 6d and had plate valued at £31 9s 1d. The total estate was valued at £951. In 1754 the estate is listed as 900 acres.[44]

At Fishlake near Doncaster we find 'Cesar Watson, negro boy servant of Mr Watson' baptised on 27 January 1788.[45] The Watson family bought and sold land with Robert Milnes of Wakefield.[46] We have been unable to find out anything more about Cesar.

At St Giles Parish Church, Pontefract, Thomas Wharton was baptised on 19 December 1763, recorded as 'a Negroe aged 23 years'. Seemingly he was a black servant in a large mansion close to the town.[47] The Wharton family were local land owners in nearby Carleton.

At Darfield, the vicar reported the adult baptism of an East Indian servant of Lieutenant John Marriott who was 17 years old.[48] Church records reveal this person to have been Thomas York, who was baptised on 9 December 1762, described as 'an east Indian'.[49]

North Yorkshire

In rural communities, rich elite families were the predominant slave owners: both the ownership of plantations and the prestige of a black servant led several landowners to obtain slaves to serve in their mansions. In Scarborough, a wealthy spa town, Africans – presumably servants – were baptised. The earliest is Thomas Matthew Pompey, in

1765, followed by George Hill in 1767, John Amity, 'being an Adult and a Blackamore', in 1782, and lastly John Pittess, 'Negro servant to Captain Winter', was baptised on 19 January 1798, all of which took place at St Mary's Church.[50]

On the bleak moors we find in 1758 a newspaper report about a runaway slave:

> From Dent in Yorkshire, on Monday the 28th of Aug last. THOMAS ANSON, a Negro Man, about five Feet six Inches High, aged 20 Years or upwards, and broad set. Whoever will bring the said Man back to Dent, or give any Information that he may be had again, shall receive a handsome Reward from Mr. Edmund Sill of Dent, or Mr. David Kenyon, Merchant in Liverpool.[51]

The Sill family were major plantation owners. On abolition, the family benefited from the compensation of £3,783 1s. 8d. paid for the 174 enslaved workers on Providence plantation. Thomas Anson found safety in the army with other runaways, serving as a trumpeter. He was discharged from the 4th Dragoons in 1768 – his papers recorded he was born in Africa and was aged 30. He served alongside James Williams and Joseph Williams, who were discharged for 'being the property of' their masters. Another trumpeter in the 4th Dragoons but decades later was James Goodwin, who was born in Bridgetown, Barbados c. 1788–9. He enlisted in the 18th Dragoons in Arundel, Sussex in June 1809 and served with the regiment until 1821 when he transferred into the 4th Dragoons with whom he served until 1840. In India he married Ann Julien in 1825 and rose to the rank of Trumpet Major. On discharge he was 52 years old and 5ft 10in tall, with black woolly hair, black eyes and a black complexion. He was a carpenter by occupation. He was described as 'a good and efficient soldier, seldom in hospital, trustworthy and sober' and died in 1865.[52] Yet we ask, did the Sills have more black slaves working on their estates in Yorkshire? Was Thomas a servant, or working the local quarry? Perhaps. Buried in 1777 at St Thomas Allerton Mauleverer was Larr Brittain 'A negro'.[53] Nearby Allerton Castle, the home of Richard Arundell MP for Knaresborough and thence of William Monkton Arundel (1749–74) and Robert Monkton Arundel, 4th Viscount Galway. It is likely Brittain was a servant in the Monkton Arundel family.

At Hinderwell we find James Berwick baptised on 30 June 1773 described as 'aged 19 yrs. a negro born Senegal'.[54] Clearly, he was born in Africa, enslaved and either taken to a plantation or brought directly to England to work as a servant in a large country house.

Living in Dent in 1762 was Harry, a mulatto. We know about his existence from the will of William Forbes, merchant of Jamaica, made on 10 December 1762 and proved on 26 June 1773. In his will Forbes left £500 to his reputed 'mulatto' son Harry, then at Dent in Yorkshire, and appointed Samuel Kilmer of Lancaster and John Sill of Kingston as the boy's guardians, the Sills being the 'owners' of Thomas Anson (above). Was Harry a house servant or an estate worker? In a codicil dated 17 December 1762 Forbes awarded his brother and sister £200 each as long as they paid their mother interest at 5 per cent p.a. on his legacies. The headline news for us is that by the terms of the codicil he manumitted a 'negroe boy' named Tom then with him in England.[55]

At Hutton Rudby the vicar recorded the adult baptism of 'George Othello, an adult whose age is uncertain, [on] 27 July 1763. This George Othello is a black.'[56] We note that many black slaves were given classical or literary names by their masters, so the surname Othello suggests he may have been a slave. Scipio Africanus was a common name for a black servant-cum-slave in England, or 'Sambo'.

Baptised at Saint Oswald King and Martyr, Oswaldkirk, was Pembroke 'a negro boy from Guinea' on 8 June 1718.[57] Born in Africa, enslaved and brought to England, he was very likely a servant at Oswaldkirk Hall, built c. 1690 for William Moor, whose daughter, Mary, married Edward Thompson, MP for York 1722–42.[58]

Major Francis Peirson (1757–81) was a major in the 95th Regiment of Foot, which was raised in Yorkshire. The major was killed at the Battle of Jersey in 1781 fighting against the French. His servant was, so history suggests, called 'Pompey', the property of a named captain in the regiment then on leave. After the battle, Pompey returned to England, worked in London and then appears in York. A diarist recalls:

> The black servant of the late Major Pierson applied at the Mansion House, York, for relief, having travelled with a pass from Portsmouth to visit the parents of his excellent master . . . Contributions to assist the distressed man were received at the York banks to enable him to provide clothing and the means of returning to Jersey.[59]

One assumes Pompey returned to Jersey. A figure based on Pompey appears in John Singleton Copley's famous painting 'The Death of Major Pierson, 6 January 1781' (1783), bravely avenging his master's death at the hands of the French. The actual model for 'Pompey' was the black servant of the London auctioneer James Christie.

In rural Marske, near Richmond John Yorke was baptised in 1776. The baptismal record states:

> Thursday Augs the 8th. A negro servant belonging to Mr Hutton and who had been in the family above 4 years and [illegible] then to be about 17 or 18 years of age and says his catechism in a tolerable way was baptised in the Church of Marse by the name of John Yorke. The sponsors were Mr Huton, Mr Paull of Beedal and the housekeeper Ane Liny. The next day the said youth was confirmed in Richmond Church . . . [60]

The 'Mr Huton' mentioned was without doubt John Hutton (1730–86), grandson of John Hutton (1659–1731) MP for Richmond 1697–1702, owner of Marske Hall. John Yorke the servant married a Yorkshire girl, Hannah Barker, at Kirkby Ravensworth church in 1799.[61] His descendants live in Bradford.

It is likely that John Yorke was named after John Yorke the plantation owner, of nearby Bewerley Hall, Richmond, now demolished. Yorke had married Elizabeth Woodstock Campbell in 1769. Elizabeth's mother, Deborah Campbell, had married Peter Campbell, who owned Cumberland Valley Plantation on Jamaica. Peter at the time of his death in 1740 owned 341 slaves, of whom 180 were listed as male and 161 as female, 73 being boys, girls or children. Total value of estate at probate: £19,429 13s.[62] On Peters's death, Deborah married Wastel Brisco II who we mentioned earlier. The link between John Yorke the slave owner and John Yorke the servant is not proven.

Chapter 12

Free Black People in Yorkshire

As well as slaves and indentured labour, Yorkshire was home to black people who carried out their day-to-day lives like anyone else. The earliest documentary reference we have found comes from 1687, when John Moore was given the freedom of the city of York, listed in the freemen's rolls as ' – blacke'. Moore appears to have been a fairly wealthy member of the community. He was in a position to-pay the requisite amount of money to the corporation for this status: records show that he paid two amounts – 20 nobles (equivalent to 13s 6d) to the Common Chamber of the city of York and £4 to the city council – to the mayor to enjoy all the privileges of the freedom of the city. Belonging to this elite body, he could bear arms, he had the right to fish in the city's rivers and, since freemen were beneficial owners of the meadows, he could graze his animals on them.[1]

We find 'Sarah daughter of John Thomas, a negro sojourner in Brafferton, baptised 27th day of September' 1795.[2] Clearly, he was a free man, able to work where he pleased. Buried at Tickhill Parish Church on 11 September 1837, aged 52 was James Tine, described as an 'emancipated negro slave'.[3]

As well as people of African origin, Yorkshire was the home to mixed-race people. Their background is rather distasteful to modern ideas: many slave masters used their slaves for sexual gratification – George Hibbert Oates ran a prostitution ring. In other cases, 'marriages' seem to have taken place as well as extramarital affairs with slaves. In some cases, the slave masters seem to have genuinely cared for their mistress and children, and did try to do the right thing by their children.

One such man was George Goodin Barrett of Doncaster. He was a slave factor trading as 'Barrett and Parkinson, slave factors' in business with Yorkshireman Leonard Parkinson.[4] Barrett owned Spring estate on Jamaica with its 371 slaves and also Thatchfield Pen, again on Jamaica with its 175 slaves. Barrett's plantations were producing sugar, rum, molasses, cattle, barrelled herring, salt fish and coffee for export to America and England. Barrett had a relationship with a mulatto woman, Elisa Peters, and the six children resulting from this relationship were sent to live with John Graham Clarke in Newcastle, because, under the terms of his will made 1794 and proved in 1808, 'They should not fix their abode in Jamaica but do settle and reside in such countries where those distinctions respecting colour are not maintained'. In a codicil to the will made in 1795 he freed Elisa Peters, a 'mulatto woman' lately conveyed to him by his father Edward, and left her an annuity of £50 per annum. He left £2,000 each to his six children.[5] Barrett clearly cared for his children and mistress. Sadly, we have been unable to trace the whereabouts of these children in England. But Barrett was not alone in bringing his children back to England. Black people were part of English society, working as sailors, tradespeople, businessmen and musicians. They married and had families. Perhaps the most famous was Henry Redhead Yorke, who for a time lived in Sheffield. He was a radical politician.

Ann Bruce

She was a woman of colour, and was one of many extramarital partners in Jamaica of George Kirlew, who was an attorney and slave owner, who returned to England in the mid-1830s. George was born on 31 December 1779 at Hemingbrough, son of William Kirlew and Hannah Richardson. He was a major slave owner. At abolition he received £89 11s 8d for 4 slaves, £474 13s 7d for 25 slaves, £202 15s 4d for 10 slaves, a whopping £2,756 3s 7d for 155 slaves at Camp Savanna, Westmoreland, Jamaica, a further £303 15s 9 for 13 slaves, £296 14s 9d for 18 slaves, a further £1,297 1d for 70 slaves and lastly £19 10s 10d for a single slave at plantation 90 on Jamaica. He was attorney for Fort William, Geneva, Hertford, Logwood, Prospect, Roaring River, Williamsfield, and Windsor Forest plantations, trustee of Walbro plantation and guardian of Wilton upon Wye plantation, all being on Jamaica.[6] George was in the Westmoreland militia. He had slaves, cattle and property in Prospect Estate (Savanna), Camp Savanna (Frome Estate) and Phoenix Park (near Savannalamar) He was an important man in local society, acting as both a judge and a church warden.

In 1805 George had married in Jamaica Elizabeth Colgrave (1796–?) a slave girl and fathered a son William in 1805 who died young, and a son James in 1808. At some stage he began sexual relations with Ann Bruce (1796–1874), another slave, and fathered a daughter Jane, who was born in 1810 and a son William in 1812. We assume Elizabeth was dead at some time before 1835 as George Kirlew and Ann Bruce married in Jamaica on 9 July 1835. Ann Bruce was born in 1796 at Savannalamar, Westmoreland, Jamaica, as a slave. At some stage she was freed and was baptised on 27 January 1810. In 1817 she is recorded as a slave owner: Gamma alias Joseph Kirlew age 22 – possibly a bastard child of George Kirlew – James Alderson age 4, Rachel Graham aged 28 'Negro', Maria Boddington aged 16 'Créole', and Judy Frost and Susanna Wilson aged 18 months. James and Susanna were the children of Rachel by an unknown father. By 1841 Ann Kirlew was living on the Mount in York, with her husband George. George died on 18 September 1854. According to the 1871 Census she was living at 148 'The Mount' with two servants, Hannah Wilson aged 60 the cook and Hannah Ripley a housemaid aged 32. Ann died aged 78 on 14 May 1874.[7]

George Kirlew's nephew, Henry Kirlew (1805–29), lived with George in the 1820s on Jamaica. Under the terms of his will, he left to George Kirlew and Ann Bruce both of Phoenix Park all his estate as tenants-in-common for life, specifying that he owned South Duffield Hall in Yorkshire and his leasehold messuage at 4 Union Place, both then rented out. After the death of George Kirlew and Ann Bruce the property was to pass to his (the testator's) uncle Edward Kirlew coal merchant of Essex Wharf. Furthermore, he left £1,000 in trust with George Kirlew and Ann Bruce for the education of any child to be born within eight months of the date of the will being proved to Mary Smith 'a slave belonging to the Prospect Estate' in Westmoreland.[8]

William Flemming

Recorded as an 'Indian Black' he buried his daughter Harriet, aged 3, at Wentworth Parish Church 9 July 1784.[9] Was William a servant or a free man? We have been unable to trace his place of death or burial.

John Lewis Friday

He enlisted in the 33rd Regiment of Foot in May 1813. At the time, the headquarters and depot were based in Hull, whilst the 1st Battalion was serving on ceremonial duties in Windsor. He fought at Waterloo, listed as 'private Jns L Friday' and received a Waterloo Medal.[10] He married Mary Woodall in Sculcoates on Tuesday, 29 December 1817.[11] Friday named the place of his birth as 'Mossambasse', which could be a transliteration of Mozambique in Eastern Africa. He was without doubt a drummer or musician in the regiment. By 1819 he was living in

Kirby Moorside. The church records report on 21 July 1819 the baptism of John Friday, son of John Friday, a 'musician in the 33rd Regiment'.[12] On 15 February 1821, and less than seven months after leaving the 33rd Foot, he re-enlisted in London in the 2nd Battalion of the 1st Foot Guards, but sadly he died in the regimental hospital in Rochester Row on 18 June 1821.[13] His widow Mary Woodall gave birth to a daughter Elizabeth, baptised on 30 January 1822 at Kirby Moorside.[14] Mary may have been living in Scarborough at the time of the 1861 Census with her brother Robert Woodall. She was then aged 66, making her born in 1795, a year younger than her husband. We have failed to trace her parents or the fate of her two children.

In this military context, we note that the 1st West Riding Militia had a black musician. Henry Clarkson recalls: 'The regiment had a fine band, at the head of which marched two negro boys, one playing the triangle, and the other the cymbals.'[15] Regimental records note that in November 1807 Adjutant Butterfield of the 1st West Yorkshire Militia wrote to his colonel that 'Major Dearden has this moment directed me to express his wish to have a Black, taken from the Prison here, as a Tamboreen in the Band to complete our number'.[16]

Ann Harris

Ann Harris was described as 'a Coloured Woman formerly of Demerara now at Startforth near Barnard Castle in Yorkshire'. She had a relationship with a married man, Henry Underwood, who fathered a child with her. In his will of 1818 Henry Iles Underwood directed she be paid £50 per annum and £1,000 to her daughter Eliza on becoming 21. Ann Harris, a 'free coloured', is listed as having paid tax for the ownership of three enslaved people in 1808, left Demerara 'with 4 servants and a child' and appears next as 'an adult aged about twenty-one' was, baptised in Startforth in 1814. Her daughter Eliza was fathered by Underwood. Ann married Edward Lawson in 1817 and had eight children baptised in Startforth.[17] In the 1841 Census she is living at Lower Startforth with Edward aged 60, Sarah aged 35, John aged 15, Mary aged 15 working as a tailor, Lered aged 13, Charles aged 10, Francis aged 7, Septimus aged 5 and Elora aged 3.[18] Ten years later, Francis is recorded on the census working as a joiner, Septimus and tailor and Eliza was a scholar; all three were still living at home, along with Edward and Ann's grandchildren Margaret aged 9 and Edward aged 4.[19] Ann was aged 70 at the time of the 1861 Census. Daughter Eliza was still at home working as a dressmaker, and grandson Edward was a shoemaker, living

David Hartley MP. The largely forgotten founder of Yorkshire abolitionism in 1776, over a decade before Wilberforce's involvement. He was a Whig, and associated with both Charles Watson Wentworth, 2nd Marquis of Rockingham, and the Milnes family of Wakefield who financed his election campaign against William Wilberforce in 1780.

The Rev. William Turner, minister of Westgate Chapel 1761–94. A firebrand Whig, he masterminded the organisation and political direction of the Yorkshire Association. An ardent admirer of the work of Jean Paul Marat and also the abolitionism of David Hartley, he preached the first avowedly abolitionist sermon in Yorkshire in December 1776. His gravestone is in the grounds of the Orangery, Blacklane, Wakefield.

The Rev. Thomas Johnstone, assistant minister of Westgate Chapel 1792–4, and minister till 1834. A passionate supporter of the ideals of the French Revolution and abolition throughout his life. He masterminded the campaign of his closest friend Daniel Gaskell to be elected first MP for Wakefield. He is buried in the catacombs beneath Westgate Chapel alongside his second wife, his son-in-law and the wider Milnes family.

The gravestone of Thomas Lang, chairman of the Wakefield Committee for the Abolition of the Slave Trade in 1788. He was a lifelong Unitarian, attending Westgate Chapel, where he is buried.

Daniel Gaskell, first MP for the enfranchised town of Wakefield. He voted in favour of the abolition of slavery as well as a reduction in the compensation of the slave owners, which he felt was unjust as the slaves themselves received nothing. He was a lifelong Unitarian, attending Westgate Chapel, Wakefield where he is buried.

The Rev. Dr Joseph Priestley, Minister of Mill Hill Unitarian Chapel in Leeds, passionate advocate of the abolition of the slave trade.

Major John Cartwright, abolitionist and political reformer, founded the Society for Constitutional Information in 1780. He lived in Liversidge in Yorkshire where his brother owned a mill.

MAJOR CARTWRIGHT, 1789.

John Milnes aka 'Jack Milnes the Democrat'. Firebrand Jacobin, abolitionist and political activist. He did much to transform the political fortunes of the Whigs in the West Riding, leading to the election of Walter Ramsden Fawkes on an abolitionist ticket as MP for Yorkshire in 1806 and Lord Milton the following year. His elder brother, Robert Shore Milnes, was Governor of Martinique, Deputy Governor General of Lower Canada and Agent for Martinique, where his enlightened leadership of the new dominion earned him universal respect. He was a lifelong Unitarian, attending Westgate Chapel, Wakefield where he is buried.

Richard Slater Milnes, Whig MP for York 1784–1802. He voted for abolition at each reading of the bill in the House of Commons. He was friends with Wilberforce. He was a lifelong Unitarian, attending Westgate Chapel, Wakefield where he is buried. His wife Rachel Milnes was visited by Wilberforce in 1788 to talk about abolitionism and politics. Their son Robert Pemberton Milnes was MP for Pontefract and her grandson Richard Monkton Milnes was elevated to the peerage as Lord Houghton. She was a lifelong Unitarian and was intended to be buried at Westgate Chapel, where her empty funeral vault remains. She died in while London visiting her daughter and was buried there.

The interior of Westgate Chapel, Wakefield as it was when Rev. William Turner thundered his denunciation of slavery in December 1776. The author has preached from this pulpit perhaps thirty times in the last 20 years.

Walter Ramsden Fawkes, MP for Yorkshire 1806–07, left-wing Whig and ardent abolitionist. He was the voice for reform and for making peace with Napoleon's France across the county. Fawkes was a friend and political ally of the Rev. Thomas Johnstone. His election in 1806 was in essence a referendum on the ideals of abolitionism.

Robert Prescott, Deputy Governor General of Lower Canada, predecessor to Sir Robert Shore Milnes. His black servant, John Vernon, was baptised in Wakefield in 1763.

Rev. Dr Coulthurst, vicar of Halifax, founder of Halifax Dispensary, and slave owner. A supporter of the abolition of the slave trade, he advocated for 'captive breeding programmes' of slaves to offset the abolition of the slave trade. As a slave owner, he had no moral or religious qualms about slavery, and fully supported the institution as it made him a very rich man.

Cobblers Hall, Heath, Wakefield. Here was established Heath Academy in the mid-eighteenth century. It was here that the slave trader from Sheffield, Thomas Staniforth, was educated. Staniforth funded 79 slaving voyages and transported 24,621 slaves. It was also at Cobblers Hall that abolitionist John Cartwright was educated. Today it is an innocuous house. Perhaps it needs a plaque to remind passers-by of houses links to both slavery and abolition?

Westgate Chapel, Wakefield. Completed in 1752, the primary benefactor to the building of the chapel was Richard Milnes, a man made rich on the cloth trade and privateering. He was also a beneficiary of the slave trade. His wife, Bridgett Pemberton, was daughter of a slave trader. Both he and his wife are buried beneath the chapel in the Milnes family catacombs. Indeed, we note, the Milnes family traded cloth and other goods to slave plantations in America and the West Indies, the profits from their cloth trading built Westgate Chapel. The chapel's links to slavery, and those of the City of Wakefield, have largely gone unacknowledged.

The Wakefield headquarters of the Aire and Calder Navigation Company. Arthur Heywood, a Wakefield Unitarian, invested £15,000 entirely derived from his slave trading activities into the concern, and was a member of the board that ran the canal. Heywood directly financed 74 slaving voyages and transported 20,327 slaves of whom 16,958 arrived in the West Indies or America. He was responsible for over 3,000 deaths.

The Wakefield home of the hugely wealthy slave trader Francis Ingram. He was responsible along with Thomas Staniforth (1734–1803), Thomas Earle (1757–1822), Thomas Parke and William Joseph Denison for undertaking 122 slaving trips and enslaving 41,412 people. He spent his fortune founding Wakefield's first commercial bank.

The banking premises of Milnes & Heywood on Burton Street, Wakefield. The senior partner was the grandson of Arthur Heywood, Richard Heywood, it drew on the reserves of Heywood's Bank, whose capital was entirely from the slave trade and slave plantations. The second partner was Richard Rodes Milnes, second son of Richard Slate Milnes MP.

Wentworth House, Wakefield. Built by John Pemberton Heywood, third son of Arthur Heywood, who inherited vast wealth from his father, which had been earned from slavery.

The Rev. Richard Munkhouse was vicar of the newly-built and fashionable St John's Church in Wakefield. He was a slave owner, and his children married into slave-owning families. Perhaps unsurprisingly, he preached no sermons against slavery or the slave trade, and instead concentrated his efforts in endeavouring to close down Wakefield Lending Library and Westgate Chapel as they were hotbeds of political dissent.

Burney Tops House, Wakefield, home of members of the slave-owning Charnock family.

South Parade, Wakefield. A development of Georgian housing using the vast profits made from tobacco plantations in Maryland by the Charnock family.

Interior of Wakefield Parish Church, now the Cathedral, c.1870. The great window behind the altar is a memorial to Francis Ingram, pious Anglican and slave trader.

Normanton Parish Church, where the slave owning Rev. William Mason was vicar in the mid-nineteenth century. Whilst at Normanton, it is recorded, he owned eleven slaves at Port Royal on the Eden Estate St George, and a further twenty-four slaves at St George, all in Jamaica. Upon abolition of slavery received just shy of £4,000 compensation.

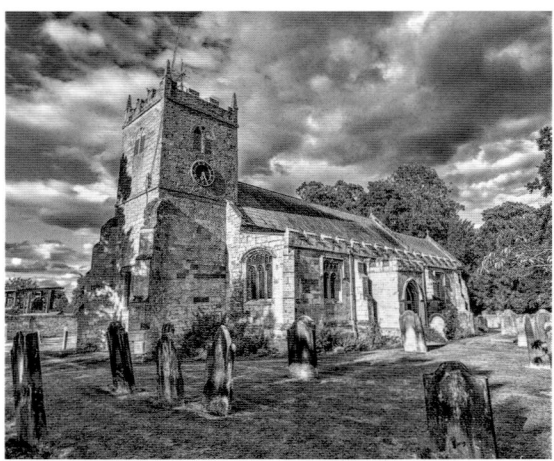

Kirby Misperton Parish Church where Rev. Charles John Sympson was rector. His father Robert Sympson received one of the largest single compensation awards at abolition for 704 slaves. He lived at Kirkby Misperton near Pickering. The good reverend's father received compensation for 94 slaves on St Ann at Phoenix Park, 64 at Angels Pen, 179 at New Hall, 244 at Georges Valley, 244 at Money Musk and 174 at Riverside. In total he owned 1,703 people and received almost £70,000 compensation. He was one of the largest slave owners in the county. He willed 'whatever sum can be afforded' from his estate of Monymusk in Jamaica to his three daughters, Harriet Fowler (to receive one-third more than the two others), Emma Charlotte O'Neill and Isabella Theophania Weguelin, but left the amount to the discretion of his son-in-law William John Law, 'who most kindly and nobly took up the heavy mortgage' on the estate. He also left £2,000 each to his sons Charles John Sympson and George Frederick Sympson.

Shibden Hall near Halifax. Made famous by the TV series *Gentleman Jack*, the Lister family, who would own Shibden Hall estate, received £3,500 a year rents from the Adelphi Plantation. Louisa Grant, the daughter of Major Charles Grant, a slave owner, married Dr John Lister. He had inherited the estate from his sister Ann in 1840, whose uncle James had inherited the estate in 1826. The income from the slave plantation was the sole income of the doctor, along with his small army pension for the maintenance of the estate. At abolition Louisa Grant received £12,65o 13s 8d for her 485 slaves!

George Kirlew was born on 31 December 1779 at Hemingbrough, son of William Kirlew and Hannah Richardson. He was a major slave owner. He had sexual relationships with a number of his slaves: Elizabeth Colgrave with whom he fathered two sons, an unknown slave girl whose son Joseph, born a slave, became property of George's third mistress and future wife Ann Bruce when she was given her freedom! At abolition, he received over £5,000 compensation for his slaves. George Kirlew and Ann Bruce used this money to move to York, living on the Mount.

The funerary monument to Ebenezer Robertson, a major slave owner who appears in the slave register for Kingston, Jamaica in 1817.

The grave of Margaret Boghurst. She was the daughter of Ebenezer Robertson and Margaret Dunbar, who was described as a 'free quadroon'. i.e. a woman of colour. Margaret Dunbar had been the mistress of James Tierney, brother of radical MP George Tierney, and had given birth to a daughter Sabrina Eleanor Tierney.

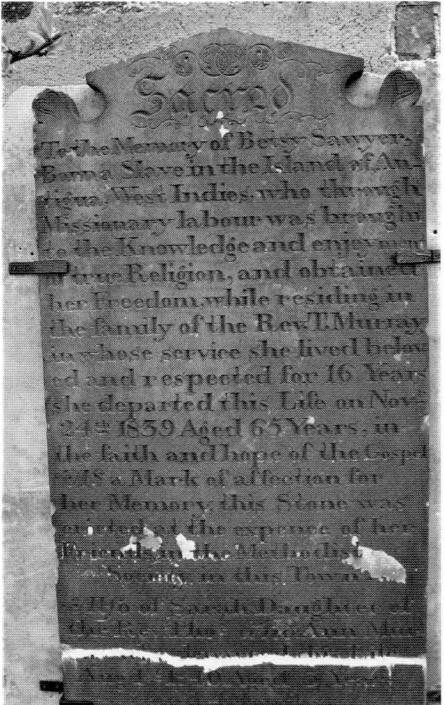

Memorial to Betsy Sawyer, a freed slave who lived in Leeds.

Northgate End Unitarian Chapel, Halifax. It was from the previous building that stood on the same site as the now lost 1870s chapel, that the Halifax Committee for the Abolition of the Slave Trade was founded and managed from 1788.

Mill Hill Unitarian Chapel, Leeds. The current building replaced the much earlier chapel of the 1690's where Rev. Dr Joseph Priestley preached and where the Rev. Charles Wicksteed did much good work to organise abolitionism in Leeds. Here too worshipped the slave-owning Oates family.

Nostell Priory, home of Sir Rowland Winn who endeavoured to exchange 'a black boy' for a loaf of bread. The grand stately home was also home to Jean-Philippe 'a young French speaking black servant'.

Henry Redhead Yorke. Born a slave and freed, he became a lawyer, militia officer and thence a leading Jacobin and supporter of radical politics in the 1790s. He moved to Sheffield in 1793 where he attended Upper Chapel and was engaged to the sister of Joseph Gales, Unitarian newspaper editor and ardent abolitionist. In 1794 Henry chaired a mass meeting at Castle Hill which called for the immediate abolition of slavery. He was arrested for treason and imprisoned in Dorchester. His son was the first black MP.

St Giles Parish Church, Pontefract. Here was married Ruth Swaby, the daughter of a freed slave and slave master John Swaby to Thomas Oxley a local chemist in 1816. Born in Jamaica in 1792 she was buried in Pontefract in 1853. It was here at St Giles in 1792 that Lucinda Wilson, wife of Thomas Wilson, Chief Justice for Dominica, was laid to rest.

Holy Trinity Parish Church, Wentworth. Here William Flemming, recorded in church records as an 'Indian Black', buried his daughter, Harriet aged 3 on 9 July 1784. Was William a servant or a freeman? We have been unable to trace a place of death or burial of William or any reference for his wife.

with his grandparents at 98 Startforth Village. Ann died in April 1862 aged 72. Ann and Eliza received compensation for three slaves in 1833.

The Parkinson Family

Ralph Parkinson, was a slave owner and fathered children by his slaves, as he admits in his will of 1805:

> Ralph Parkinson of the parish of St. James in the County of Cornwall and Island of Jamaica. Will dated 12 June 1805. If I die in this parish, I desire to be buried in the churchyard near to my nephew and nieces, and that an elegant tomb of marble be sent for and put over my grave with my age and place of nativity. I was born at Pickton in the North Riding of Yorkshire on the 14 Aug. 1762, and came to this Island on the 12 April 1778. Not one of the name of Scarlett to be asked to my funeral, and if I should die in the parish of Westmoreland, I desire to be buried at White Hall my Pen, near to my brother Robert, and that my tomb be placed there with an iron railing. To my four quadroon children which I have had by a mulatto woman, Betty Grant, that I purchased from Tryall Estate in Hanover and set free - the names are Richard, Jane, John and Robert Parkinson - £2000 sterling each. They are to be educated in England and never return to Jamaica. My negroes Rose, Lilly and Minerva and wench Sally to serve them, and upon the said children going off the island I give these negroes to Betty Grant, together with Moggy and her two daus. Nancy and Mary, and Nancy and her children may be sold to Mr. William Tonkin for £100 each. I give her also £50 a year, and at her death the negroes to my goddau. Ann Watson, to whom I also give my beaufet with all my china therein, to be handed to her father and mother, and if she die to her sister Ruth.[20]

We have been unable to trace the whereabouts of these children in England.

The Robertson Family

According to his memorial in Beverley Minister, Ebenezer Robertson of Beverley was born at Tain in Scotland on 25 February 1761. He was a slave owner. His epitaph reads 'Exemplary in all relations of Life. Exalted the Moral virtues into Christian graces by guiding his conduct of the principles and by resting his hopes on the promises of the Gospel'. In 1790 he conferred his legal status on his children by Margaret Dunbar, a quadroon woman:

> Mary Blake of the Parish of Kingston a free mulatto woman and James Blake and John Blake free mulatto men, the reputed children of Nicholas Blake decd; late of the parish of St Elizabeth, Margaret Dunbar a free quadroon, daughter of the said Mary Blake and Sabena Eleanor Tierney, Margaret Robertson, Francis William Robertson and Mary Anne Robertson the infant children of the said Margaret Dunbar to all rights and privileges under certain restrictions.[21]

He went on to father seven more children: Gilbert (born 29 April 1792), Ebenezer (born 15 November 1793), William (born 11 February 1795), Jane (born 10 March 1797), Robert (born 11 September 1798), another Robert (born 25 October 1799) and William George (born 12 July 1801). All the children were baptised in Kingston and in each record, Margaret is recorded 'as a free quadroon woman'. By the time she began her relationship with Ebenezer Robertson, Margaret had already given birth to a child: Sabrina Eleanor Tierney (1784–1844). The father of the child was James Tierney. He was a barrister who died in Kingston, Jamaica, in 1784, brother of George Tierney MP and brother-in-law of Abram Robarts MP. The will of James Tierney names Margaret Dunbar as his housekeeper: he leaves her £1,000 and 'all my household furniture and utensils, pictures, plate, china, linen and carriages and any one of my horses which she may choose for herself'. The will also mentions Sabina's half-sister Eleanor Frances Tierney. Sabrina died in 1844 and left her estate to the Rev. Ebenezer Robertson, her nephew.[22] James Tierney's brother, George[23] was a radical politician, known to the Milnes family, Richard Sheridan,[24] John Cartwright and Lord John Russell. James and George's sister, Sabine, married London MP and banker Abraham Robarts, who on his death left his son £350,000 and was described as 'an eminent banker, loan contractor, West Indian factor and director of the East India Company, Royal Exchange Insurance and a partner in Lechmere's bank in Worcester'. Robarts had over 300 slaves at abolition.[25]

Ebenezer Robertson is known to have been a slave owner, and assigned the mortgage of the Craig Mill estate in St George to Thomas Jameson in 1801, yet we note an Ebenezer Robertson appeared in the Slave Register for Kingston in 1817.[26] Of his children fathered with Margaret Dunbar we know:

- Francis William joined the East India Company as a writer. The will of Francis William Robertson, 'Principal Collector and Magistrate at Bellary of Bellary, East Indies', was proved on 14 January 1840.
- Margaret married Edward Boghurst (1791–1870) of the Royal Artillery on 5 June 1815 at St John and St Martin, Beverley. By the time of the 1841 Census, Edward Boghurst was living in Surrey and was aged 50. Eldest son Francis Edward was aged 20, twin daughters Emily and Laura were aged 15. They were living at Catherine Place, Walcot, Somerset. Margaret Boghurst, born in 1788 in Jamaica, appears on the 1851 census at 31 Walkergate of Beverley as an 'annuitant' aged 63. At the time the Census was taken, in the house was John Giles, aged 53 a wheelwright, a visitor; Martha Giles, aged 55 housekeeper, Becky Giles aged 26 servant, Catherine Johnson aged 36 servant, John Giles Jnr aged 17 an apprentice carriage trimmer, Alice Giles aged 14 and Edward Giles aged 4.[27] She died in 1856 aged 68, and lies in the same grave as her father who died in 1825 and her estranged husband who died in 1870.[28]
- Ebenezer Robertson Jnr attended Charterhouse School and was a Carthusian 1809–11. He gained a BA from Trinity College, Cambridge in 1828 and in 1830 married Harriet, daughter of J. Lockwood. Rev. Ebenezer Robertson was of 1 North Bar Street, Beverley, 9 January 1840 when he sold his furniture by auction. He was rector of Motistone with Shorwell on the Isle of Wight from 1840 until 1854 when he 'resigned being desponding in his mind that he should fall into poverty'. In 1847 in St Peter's Church, Shorwell he erected a memorial to his nephew Francis Edward Robertson Boghurst, only son of his sister Margaret, who died on 24 January 1847 aged 29. Ebenezer Jnr committed suicide by jumping off the Shakespeare Cliff in Dover, 16 August 1854.
- Robert Robertson was still alive in 1824 when he was left a legacy of £5,000 by his father.[29]
- Gilbert Robertson received compensation in 1833 for ten slaves and may have married Maria Martinbough in 1829, both of them being recorded as persons of colour.[30]

Alas, we have not found a date or place of death of Margaret Dunbar. We have found no mention of her in Beverley.

Betsy Sawyer

Betsy Sawyer died in Yeadon. She had been emancipated by the Murray family and had moved there from Antigua, presumably as a servant. There is a memorial to her at Yeadon Methodist Church, which reads:

> To the memory of Betsy Sawyer, born in slavery in the island of Antigua, who through missionary labour was brought to the knowledge and enjoyment of true religion obtained her freedom whilst residing in the family of the Rev. T Murray in whose service she lived loved and respected for 16 years. She departed this life on 24 November 1839 aged 65 years in the faith and hope of the gospel. As a mark of affection for her this memorial stone was erected at the expense of her friends in the Methodist Society of this town.[31]

Ruth Swaby

She was the daughter of John Swaby (1758–1825) and Francis King, described as a 'free mulatto' born in 1792 in Jamaica. John Swaby was a slave plantation owner on Jamaica. Francis King had at least ten children with him. It's not clear where Francis came by the finance but between 1817 and 1820, she purchased around ninety enslaved people from the estate of Charles Loughman and between 1820 and 1823 she purchased around 100 enslaved people from the Crown under escheat of the estate of Joseph Williams. Between 1829 and 1832 she conveyed ninety-one enslaved people from Waltham estate in Manchester in trust to John Griffith, James Swaby her natural son, and others. At abolition she received just under £4,700 compensation for her slaves. It appears she died in 1838 aged 71.

Ruth married Thomas Oxley, a physician, at St Giles Pontefract on 15 June 1816. Frances Ann Oxley was baptised 3 November 1817 at St Giles Pontefract.[32] She married Samuel Pyemont Smith on 22 September 1841 in Doncaster. According to the 1851 Census, Frances Ann was living in Leicester at 54 Silver Street, Whitwick. Samuel aged 36 was curate of Whitwick, Frances was aged 34, born in Pontefract with a large brood of children: Ruth Amelia Remont aged 8 born in Camspall, Emma Pyemont aged 6 born in Selby, Francis aged 5, Frederick aged 3, and Arthur Cyril aged 9 months. The household included Arthur Walker and James Johnston as pupils, Annie Edmonds aged 27 the governess, Mary Palick aged 21 servant, Hannah Richard, aged 24 servant and Harriet Oliver aged 15 servant.[33] Frances died in 1892 aged 75.[34] Elizabeth Eleanor Oxley was baptised at St Giles on 12 December 1825. According to the 1851 Census she was living with her brother John Swaby Oxley at

Willburton, but sadly we have not been able to trace her whereabouts after this date. John Swaby was baptised at St Giles on 9 September 1818, and his brother Thomas Louis was baptised on 5 December 1819. John Swaby was admitted to Queens' College Cambridge 10 June 1836, and married Mary Sarah Pearson (1819–82) on 9 October 1855 at Hagley in Worcestershire. The 1881 Census lists him living in York, and he died aged 77 on 15 July 1895.

According to the 1841 Census Thomas and Ruth were living at Belle Vue Terrace in Campsall, Yorkshire, with daughters Frances aged 20 and Eliza aged 15. Thomas Oxley was aged 70, and Ruth 50 according to the census.[35] By 1851 Ruth was a widow and according to the census was 'a Gentlewoman' living with her brother-in-law John H. Smith at 8 Finsbury Place South in London. In the same household was Sarah Ann her half-sister – her father also fathered five children with 'mulatto' Ann Eliza French and Ann Eliza went on to have two more children with Anthony Britton after Swaby's death – as well as half-brother Charles (French) Swaby (Gentleman) and her sister Marie A. (Antoinette) Dunn, a widow age 29.[36] Ruth died in 1853 in Pontefract where she was buried in September of that year.[37]

Henry Redhead Yorke

Perhaps one of the most important black politicians of the late eighteenth century was born a slave. Henry Redhead Yorke (1772–1813) was given his freedom, and became a lawyer, militia officer and radical abolitionist – a man whose life deserves to be made into a film. Yorke was a black English Jacobin radical, who for a time attended Upper Chapel Sheffield, and sat in the pews with the radical Jacobin newspaper editor Joseph Gales (1761–1841), and Samuel Shore, the reluctant radical. Yorke's politics, like that of Gales, was radical French Republicanism, for which beliefs he was imprisoned. It was Gales in 1789 who acclaimed the victory of 'our French brethren over despots and despotism', and marked this by roasting an ox and carrying it in a procession through the town which was fired on by local authorities. It was Gales who burnt effigies of Edmund Burke and the Duke of York at the stake and celebrated the French victory at Valmy against 'the forces of oppression'. We discuss both men's involvement in Sheffield later. We know a great deal about Henry's life as he wrote it all down whilst in prison: an active radical in Derbyshire, he had attended the French National Convention in 1792, whilst in Paris at White Hotel and the 'British Club': it seems highly likely he met Jack Milnes here. It seems he was in Sheffield by 1793 and became engaged to Joseph Gales's sister; the relationship must have blossomed quickly as he was in Sheffield for under 12 months, during which time he had cemented his place in Sheffield radicalism and the religious community at Upper Chapel.

Yorke was directly involved in the Sheffield Constitutional Society, as he had been in Derby, writing in 1794 'Thoughts on Civil Government: Addressed to the Disfranchised Citizens of Sheffield'. He called for an immediate abolition of the slave trade and slavery at a mass meeting in April 1794. The Sheffield magistrate the Rev. James Wilkinson branded the meeting illegal and seditious and ordered the ringleaders to be arrested. Yorke fled Sheffield. He was thought to be hiding in the home of the Manchester radical George Walker.

The Rev. Wilkinson wrote to Henry Dundas MP on June informing him that Yorke, the runaway demagogue was likely in Manchester with Mrs Henstock 'his natural mother'.[38] In a letter from John Brookfield, solicitor, of Sheffield, he records that Rev. James Wilkinson JP had sent him to Manchester to apprehend Yorke, but he had failed to do so. The letter also tells us that letters with a description of Yorke – 'a black' – had been sent to the chief magistrates of Liverpool, Newcastle, Sunderland, Shields, Hull and Carlisle with a view to prevent him leaving the country. The intercepted letters seemed to show that Yorke had come from France to 'sow seeds of discord'.[39] He was caught and put on trial with Joseph Gales and Richard Davison for 'a conspiracy and unlawful meeting for seditious purposes at Castle Hill, Sheffield, Yorks, 7 April 1794'. He was charged with conspiracy and sedition on 10 July 1795 and sentenced to two years imprisonment in Dorchester gaol. At the trial he was described as 'Mr. Henry Redhead Yorke, a Mulatto, by birth, and equally tropical, and verging to extremes, in disposition'. His son became the first Black MP and sat for York from 1841.

Yorke's mother, Sarah Anne Bullock (1745–1804), had married Edward Henstock (1747–?) in 1787, a linen draper. His son or nephew, another Edward (1761–?), was working in Wakefield at the end of the 1770s as he had been taken on as an apprentice by Thomas Smith in 1776.[40] The household in Manchester included a daughter and a son who was a physician who had lived in London, who had fled to Switzerland. Mrs Henstock was described in 1794 as a mulatto and 'as a freed slave from Barbuda'. Sarah was a slave, owned by the Codrington family, the daughter of a black slave and a white man. She was manumitted in 1771 with her eldest son Joseph. Sarah had four children, Jane (1760–85), Joseph (1763–93?), Henry (1772–1813) and Sarah Ann (1774–1811). The father of the children was Samuel Redhead (1704–85). He fathered children with other slaves, likely Elizabeth Davy mentioned in his will who had born him many children. Sarah in 1779 was 'a domineering wife', but how legal the marriage was we do not know. As a slave planter, Samuel was a wealthy man.[41] The family were in England by 1784 and on his death, Sarah inherited all the contents of his London house and £1,050 in cash. Other slaves were in the household, a 'Negro Hester' and 'Mulatto William' who passed to Sarah Ann Redhead along with £1,500. Joseph and Henry each received £1,500 and ownership of two Antiguan slaves, Stephen and John.[42] The eldest child, Jane, was married by this time and died in January 1785, shortly before her father. Edward Henstock was at 23 Faulkner Street, Manchester, with a warehouse on Market Lane according to a directory of 1795.

About Joseph, the letters written in 1794 tell us he was a physician, living in Bartlett's Buildings, Holborn London, and he travelled or fled to Switzerland.[43] He presumably died fighting for the French Republic as Henry collected his ashes in 1802 from France.

Comment

Slaves lived and worked in Yorkshire. No museum, library or book to date acknowledges this fact. Slaves with silver collars, kept on a leash, walked the streets of Yorkshire and adorned the houses of the well-to-do. Some attitudes to these servants may have changed with the Somerset case of 1772 in which Somerset, a fugitive enslaved African, brought a case against his owner who was attempting to force him to return to the West Indies. Lord Justice Mansfield ruled that it would be illegal to remove Somerset from the country against his wishes. This case partially extended the rights of enslaved Africans in Britain and formed the beginning of a much wider campaign against slavery. Yet black servants did not gain full legal status until 1838.

What we have noted is that these black servants often died young: being dragged from Africa and taken to Yorkshire, assuming they survived the voyage, they were exposed to new illnesses to which they had no natural immunity. It was a virtual death sentence: culpable homicide for fashion's sake. Yet Africans lived free lives in Yorkshire and one of them was to play a key part in the story of abolition in Yorkshire: Henry Redhead Yorke. Ignoring the contribution of Africans and Indians to the story of Yorkshire is racist. The human past is common to all regardless of gender, creed and ethnicity.

We cannot leave this section without mention of the first black Unitarian minister and abolitionist. For our Unitarian story we must mention Robert Wedderburn (1762–1835). He was born in Kingston, Jamaica, the illegitimate son of James Wedderburn Colville and an African slave, Rosanna. Rosanna was sold when five months pregnant and her son was deemed 'free' at birth. He joined the Royal Navy, and arrived in Britain in 1778, working as a tailor. He was licensed as a Unitarian preacher in 1813, opening his own chapel in Soho that year. He became involved in radical politics and abolitionism. In 1824 he published an attack on the institution of slavery 'The Horrors of Slavery', which was widely circulated by the abolitionist cause and provoked a furious reaction from James Wedderburn Colville's eldest son and heir, Andrew Colville.[44]

PART 3: ABOLITION

Chapter 13

The Road to Abolition

One man is inextricably linked to abolitionism: William Wilberforce. Yet he was not the first abolitionist nor the founder of the movement. We must look back to the middle decades of the eighteenth century for the first glimmers of abolitionism. Dr Adam Smith (1723–90), a Scottish philosopher and erstwhile Unitarian deist, in his *Theory of Moral Sentiments'*, published in 1759, declared:

> There is not a negro from the coast of Africa, who does not, in this respect, possess a degree of magnanimity which the soul of his sordid master is too often scarce capable of conceiving. Fortune never exerted more cruelly her empire over mankind, than when she subjected those nations of heroes to the refuse of the gaols of Europe, to wretches who possess the virtue neither of the countries they came from, nor of those they go to, and whose levity, brutality, and baseness so justly expose them to the contempt of the vanquished.[1]

Smith is arguably one of the founders of the abolitionist movement in this country, whose legacy has been overlooked in the homogenisation of history which accords credit to Wilberforce in popular imagination. In 1760, the Scottish jurist George Wallace argued that slavery was 'against nature' in his book *System of the Principles of the Law of Scotland*.[2] Another pioneer of abolition was the Bishop of Gloucester, Rev. Dr William Warburton (1698–1779), who preached on 21 February 1766:

> . . . the vast multitudes yearly stolen from the opposite continent, and sacrificed by the colonists to their great idol, the GOD OF GAIN . . . Gracious God! to talk (as in herds of cattle) of property in rational creatures! creatures endowed with all our faculties,

possessing all our qualities but that of colour; our brethren both by nature and grace, shocks all the feelings of humanity. . . nothing is more certain in itself, and apparent to all, than that the infamous traffic for slaves directly infringes both divine and human law. Nature created man free, and grace invites him to assert his freedom.[3]

Building on the groundswell created by Smith, Wallace and others, in 1769 Granville Sharp (1735–1813) published *A Representation of the Injustice and Dangerous Tendency of Tolerating Slavery . . .*, the first tract in England attacking slavery. Within it, he argued that 'as freedom is unquestionably the birth right of all mankind, Africans as well as Europeans, to keep the former in a state of slavery, is a constant violation of that right, and therefore of justice' and 'true justice makes no respect of persons and can never deny to any one the blessing which all mankind have an undoubted right'.[4] Sharp argued for political and civil liberty, his thinking and ideas harked back to the Wilkesite phase of English radicalism of a few years previously, and argued that political liberty went hand in hand with civil liberty, and tellingly said not a word on religious liberty.[5]

Abolition of slavery and the moral implications of slavery was, simply put, not a 'big issue' till May 1772 when slavery was thrust dramatically into the public sphere. In that month a significant court judgement by Lord Mansfield in the case of James Somerset, who was an enslaved African, versus Charles Stewart, a customs officer. In this case, the slave who had been purchased in Boston and then transported with Stewart to England had managed to escape. Lord Mansfield gave his ruling that slaves could not be transported from England against their will. The case therefore gave great impetus to those campaigners such as Granville Sharp who saw the ruling as an example for why slavery would be unsupported by English law.

Nevertheless, the ruling did not advocate the abolition of slavery completely. Those backing Somerset argued that colonial laws which permitted slavery were not in conjunction with the common law of Parliament, thus making the practice unlawful. The case in question was still argued very much along legal lines rather than humanitarian or social concerns, but it would mark an important step in a trajectory of events which ultimately culminated in abolition. Granville Sharp published *An Essay on Slavery: proving from Scripture its inconsistency with humanity and religion* in the following year.[6]

In Yorkshire, it was David Hartley, MP for Hull and a friend of the Milnes family of Wakefield and a supporter of the Marquis of Rockingham, who brought slavery into the political sphere, long before Wilberforce. He was the son of the famous philosopher of the same name, David Hartley (1705–57) whose religious idealism directly inspired Rev. Dr Priestley. Little wonder that Hartley Jnr was drawn to fellow Unitarians. A friend of Benjamin Franklin, he wrote in November 1775 that slavery was 'contrary to the laws of God and man'.[7] A matter of months later, Hartley brought the matter of slavery to the House of Commons, saying that 'the Slave Trade was contrary to the laws of God and the rights of men'. He dramatically laid shackles on the table of the House during the debate to emphasise the point.[8]

1776 was a fateful year for the advancement of abolitionism: Dr Adam Smith boldly asserted that slavery was not as profitable as free labour and that forced servitude took away the motivation to succeed. Smith argued that slaves were the most inefficient and costly form of labour that could be used. Sugar could be produced more cheaply by free paid workers in India.[9] Wilberforce, who met Adam Smith in 1787, quoted Smith often in placing the economic argument for abolition at the forefront of the debate. Indeed, the Quaker abolitionist James Cropper quoted Smith's ideas about slavery's economic inefficiency. Closer to home in Yorkshire the radical Whig Rev. William Turner spoke from his pulpit at Westgate Chapel.[10] Turner subjected his congregation to a vehement denunciation of the corruption of the ruling class. Impassioned by the idealism of Marat and the anti-slavery rhetoric of David Hartley MP, Tuner argued that on a nationally-appointed fast day, ostentatious self-mortification was nothing more than

> pride, vanity, self-confidence and even the basest sensualities and most odious debaucheries in secret, as well as of morousness, haughtiness, censoriousness, hardness of heart, oppression, fraud, falsehood, and cruelty towards others. Who finding themselves possessed of power, assume the right to invade, and make property of their fellow creatures, and use them for their own advantage, pleasure or caprice, though it were to their bitter suffering and cruel oppression, both in body, mind and outward estate . . . whoever shall persist in the commission of unrighteousness, oppression and cruelty to their brethren, and, at the same time, attempt by fastings, however solemn, to bribe the righteous ruler of the world to connive at the wickedness,

will only bring down on themselves his heavier vengeance for the aggravated insult.[11]

About the rights of man Turner thundered:

> I trust my brethren, that none of us is chargeable with any flagrant acts of injustice and oppression, violence or cruelty against any if our inferiors; that we have no bands of wickedness to loose; no heavy burdens imposed by us on our brethren, to undo; that we have none oppressed or enslaved to set free, not any unreasonable or burdensome yoke to break; yet, let us strictly examine ourselves upon this head; and if we find, that in any respect we have approached the borders of oppression against any of our brethren, let the solemnities of this day engage us, without delay, to rectify and redress it, as far as we can, and in all our future conduct, to adhere closely to that golden rule.[12]

Turner preached that the power to govern was to be given by common consent, for the common good and not for the particular interests of a narrow group, noting men had been 'blinded by ambition and avarice, hardened against the feelings of humanity, and having perverted or lost all principle fear of God and righteousness to man'.[13] Here was an attack against the government, the ruling classes and slavery, radical words that 20 years later would have been at home in Republican France or spoken by Thomas Paine. Rev. Turner was amongst the first men in the country to articulate these feelings, supported by his colleague at Newington Green, Rev. Dr Richard Price and Rev. Lindsay. Benjamin Franklin purchased a printed copy of the sermon, starting a long friendship between the two men. Rev. Lindsay was the London agent for distributing copies to men like John Lee, Richard Price, Dr Priestley, Abraham Rees,[14] Andrew Kippis,[15] Jonathan Shipley, the Bishop of St Asaph[16] and William Rose[17] – the great and good of radical Whiggism of the day. Turner inspired Price and Newcome Cappe[18] at York to issue even more forthright political polemics. Indeed, it was Turner who in 1780 devised the principles and strategy of the Yorkshire Association which we will return to in more detail later.[19] Turner's sermon echoed the words of Jean-Paul Marat in his 1774 treatise 'Chains of Slavery': Marat's ideas would have a huge influence on later generations of English radicals. The purpose of Marat's writing was to encourage his readers to attempt by any means to destroy the chains of destitution imposed upon them by their rulers who governed not for the good of the people, he argued, but for the good of their social order, class and religion. We must 'espouse the cause of any individual oppressed', Marat declared. His ideals of the oppressed shaking off the chains of slavery and tyranny would inspire a generation of English radicals. It was Rev. Dr Richard Price who solidified Marat's idealism into a blunter, more obtuse instrument of debate, comparing slavery and liberty unfavourably with the British state.[20] Price (1723–91) was a Welsh moral philosopher, Nonconformist preacher and mathematician. He was also a political pamphleteer, active in radical, republican and liberal causes such as the American Revolution. He was well-connected and fostered communication between a large number of people, including several of the Founding Fathers of the United States, notably Benjamin Franklin who was known to Rev. William Turner who we met earlier. Price spent most of his adult life as minister of Newington Green Unitarian Church, on the outskirts of London. He also wrote on issues of demography and finance, and was a Fellow of the Royal Society. In November 1789, Richard Price's sermon commemorating the Glorious Revolution of 1688 concluded by hailing events in France as the dawn of a new era:

> Behold all ye friends of freedom . . . behold the light you have struck out, after setting America free, reflected to France and there kindled into a blaze that lays despotism in ashes and warms and illuminates Europe. I see the ardour for liberty catching and spreading; . . . . the dominion of kings changed for the dominion of laws, and the dominion of priests giving way to the dominion of reason and conscience.

Mary Wollstonecraft was a member of Price's congregation, and the ideas she absorbed from the sermons at Newington Green pushed her towards a political awakening. She later published *A Vindication of the Rights of Man* (1790), a response to Burke's denunciation of the French Revolution and attack on Price, and *A Vindication of the Rights of Woman* (1792), extending Price's arguments about equality to women.

At the same time as Turner and Price were preaching against slavery and the government of the day, the radical firebrand Major John Cartwright (1740–1824) declared to the abolitionist Granville Sharp that:

> The child of a slave is as free-born according to the law of nature, as he who could trace a free ancestry up to the creation. Slavery in all its forms, in all its degrees, is an outrageous

131

violation of the rights of mankind; an odious degradation of human nature. It is utterly impossible that any human being can be without a title to liberty, except he himself have forfeited it by crimes which make him dangerous to society.[21]

Cartwright, a native of Nottinghamshire, was educated at Heath Academy, Wakefield, and knew Yorkshire very well indeed: along with his brother, he ran a mill in Liversidge and attended Westgate Chapel in Wakefield for time between 1810 and c. 1818. He was a radical from early age and gathered around him like-minded gentlemen. The war with America was hated by English radicals, and the government's perceived incompetence led to two major radical campaigning groups emerging. 'No taxation without representation' became a rallying cry. To pay for the war taxes increased: those paying the taxes objected as they had no voice in Parliament or no right to vote! Cartwright and fellow radicals sought a more equal Parliamentary system in the country. They supported the abolition of 'rotten boroughs' and aimed for the enfranchisement of millions of voters by extending suffrage and creating new constituencies in the rapidly-growing towns across the country. Cartwright believed in the establishment of annual Parliaments and universal suffrage and wrote several pamphlets on the matter. As well as political reform Cartwright and those gathered around him argued for religious toleration, disestablishment of the Church of England, and the abolition of slavery. In 1780 he founded the Society for Constitutional Information, sought to appeal mostly to the middle classes rather than the country gentlemen who supported Wyvill. Following the anti-Catholic Gordon Riots the society, as with other radical groups, slipped into decline, but the Duke of Richmond granting his patronage to the society in 1783 changed its fortunes. The firebrand Unitarians John Horne Tooke, John Thelwall, Granville Sharp, Josiah Wedgwood, the famous potter, Thomas Walker (a Unitarian radical who married Samuel Shore's daughter), Rev. Dr Richard Price, Thomas Brand Hollis, Rev. Dr John Jebb, Capel Lofft, Joseph Gales and William Smith were all members. The leading West Riding Dissenting family, the Milnes of Wakefield, were core members: Dick Milnes was elected to the Society on 18 April 1783, sponsored by Cartwright and Jeremiah Batley; James Milnes Jnr was elected a member on 30 January 1784 and Jack on 13 February the same year, being sponsored by William Smith MP and Thomas Brand Hollis. The society was an organisation of social reformers, many of whom were drawn from the rational Dissenting community, dedicated to publishing political tracts aimed at educating fellow citizens on their lost ancient liberties. Here was a radical abolitionist group that included most of the Unitarian clergy of the country and political reformists.

One of most prominent figures amongst the Unitarian clergy that gathered around John Cartwright and the Society for Constitutional Information was Rev. Dr John Jebb (1736–86): he championed religious toleration, political reform and abolition of slavery. He wrote to Granville Sharp in 1776 thanking him for sending him a copy of his essay on slavery and remarked that he had 'for many years maintained that no considerations of trade, or any other consideration whatever can be offered in excuse for so horrible a practice . . . this practice is as offensive to the supreme being, as it is contrary to reason and Humanity. Indeed, a stronger and more wanton violation of Man's Rights cannot be justified'.[22]

Four years later in 1779 Rev. Dr Jebb remarked, with almost crystal-clear foresight of how the slave trade and slavery would be abolished.

> Let us suppose that a member of the commons' house of Parliament is instructed to declare his dissent, in case a bill should be introduced, which has for its object the abolition of the slave trade; a practice, so abhorrent from the dictates of humanity, and the principles of our religion, that I make no scruple of affirming, with a very excellent citizen, and respectable writer, that it ought not to be tolerated in a Christian country.
>
> Let us further suppose, that the majority of the representatives of the people have also been instructed by their constituents, to promote the introduction of a bill, for its immediate abolition.
>
> Let us, lastly, suppose that the principles, on which such a bill is founded, accord with the feelings, and the judgment of the member, who has received instructions to oppose it.
>
> In these circumstances, it is demanded, what is that line of conduct, which it would become such member to pursue, who, attentive to the dictates of conscience and honour, is also willing to approve himself a friend to the rights of human kind?[23]

Here was the blueprint to bring about abolition and exactly the same route that Rev. Christopher Wyvill was taking contemporaneously with the Yorkshire Association! The system that Sharp, Clarkson and Wilberforce turned to garner support for the abolition of the slave trade was the 'brainchild' of a Unitarian! Had Jebb not died in 1786, I am certain he would be better remembered and would have taken a leading role in abolition.

At the same time as Cartwright was gathering a circle of metropolitan radicals around him, in Yorkshire the Rev. Christopher Wyvill embarked on a similar crusade by forming the Yorkshire Association.

The aim of the Yorkshire County Association, like Cartwright's Society, was to petition Parliament to complain about the expensive war and incompetent government, demand Parliamentary reform, including annual general elections, providing an extra 100 county MPs (who would be more independent of the government than borough MPs) and an expansion of the electoral franchise. Despite the criticism from the establishment, supporters included John Baynes, Sir Robert Bernard, Newcome Cappe the Unitarian minister of St Saviour Gate Chapel York, John Fountayne, Sir James Grant, Thomas Brand Hollis, Sir James Innes-Ker, John Lee, Gamaliel Lloyd, George Montagu, 4th Duke of Manchester, Charles Stanhope and William Johnson Temple. Another important supporter was the Rev. Thomas Zouch, vicar of Sandal, brother of Henry Zouch[24] and a local magistrate sitting with Pemberton Milnes. As the leading Whig magnate in Yorkshire, Milnes was crucial to the formation of the Association: where he led, the other Whigs would follow.[25] Jack Milnes was a key personality. In a letter from June 1780 he reports that in concert with Benjamin Heywood what he had achieved: 'though we had the Insinuations of a Powerful Adverse Party, and the Prejudice of the People to surmount, yet our Success was beyond our expectations'. Taking advantage of the crowds of people attending the weekly market in Huddersfield they had obtained signatures from many of the surrounding villages – three-quarters of those approached had agreed to sign the petition. He commented further: 'Had I more time don't doubt getting a great majority of the freeholders in this part, but in this manufacturing county, the houses are wide from each other so makes it very tedious.'[26] Others from the Milnes family took an active part in raising the petition, as well as funding candidates in the 1780 general election. James Milnes senior[27] and his son, James Milnes Junior (1755–1805) were likewise members of the Yorkshire Association and funded the election expenses of Henry Duncombe.[28] Their co-religionist and Westgate Chapel man Robert Lumb also subscribed to cover the costs of the 1780 election and the Association's candidates.[29] The 1780 election returned Henry Duncombe against Lascelles for the Tories, and perhaps more importantly, William Wilberforce was elected as an MP, on the 'Yorkshire Association Ticket'.

The Association slipped into decline after the election and the Gordon Riots, and a new petition was raised in 1782 arguing for an increased electoral franchise: the extended Milnes family worked tirelessly for the cause and attracted 1,500 signatures.[30] The Milnes family, with Jack at the helm, had helped instigate the first mass petitions across the West Riding – the way had been shown in rallying public opinion to a cause. The Yorkshire Association was the first step on the ladder for cementing Whig leadership into a unified political force, and engraining the idea of mass petitioning to Parliament in support of political objectives, which of course still happens today. Yet it was not to last; by 1785 the Yorkshire Association was no more.

The 'Zong massacre' of 1781 helped focus public opinion: the mass killing of more than 130 enslaved Africans by the crew of the British slave ship Zong on and in the days following 29 November 1781. The trial in 1783 was heard before Lord Justice Mansfield with the rough-spoken Yorkshireman John Lee (1733–93), the Attorney General, appearing for the defence against the insurance company: the ship and its owners sought compensation for the loss of the slaves and their investment in them. Lee argued that the slaves had 'perished just as a Cargo of Goods perished' and were jettisoned for the greater good, to save the ship. Lee had taken as his mistress for a time Hannah Milnes[31] – sister of Sir Robert Shore Milnes and Jack Milnes – and was a Unitarian attending Mill Hill and Essex Street Chapels. He was personal friends with Rev. Dr Priestley, Rev. William Turner and Rev. Lindsay. Did he, Lee, believe that the slaves were just cargo and not people? Legally that was what the law said: alas we do not have any other writings by Lee to understand if this is what he himself actually thought. His legal argument invoked the concept of chattel slavery and became notorious in abolitionist circles; I earnestly hope it cannot be taken as his personal view. Appearing for the insurers against the ship owners was Sergeant Samuel Heywood (1753–1828). He also a Unitarian lawyer, attending Essex Street Chapel, and was a personal friend of the Rev. Lindsay. He had been educated at Warrington Academy, and thence studied at Trinity Hall Cambridge, though his faith meant he could not graduate with a degree and had to pay a fine rather than receive the sacrament in order to practice as a lawyer. He was the eldest son of Benjamin Heywood and Phoebe Ogden, and a noted opponent of the Test and Corporation Acts and 'High Church' aspects of Anglicanism. His daughter Ann married Rev. Richard Astley and had a fine memorial brass at Northgate End Chapel Halifax. Samuel Heywood argued he 'appear as council for millions of mankind and the cause of Humanity in general . . . to say that wantonly or by ignorance a man may throw 132 lives overboard is a proposition that shocks humanity'. Despite Granville Sharp's efforts, no member of the crew was prosecuted for murder. In the immediate aftermath,

Sharp sent an account of the massacre to William Dillwyn, a Quaker, who had asked to see evidence that was critical of the slave trade. The London Yearly Meeting of the Society of Friends decided shortly after to begin campaigning against slavery, and a petition signed by 273 Quakers was submitted to Parliament in July 1783. Out of the great crime that the *Zong* massacre was, came a heightened awareness of slavery. Abolition as a movement was now moving forward like never before and firmly placed in the public sphere.[32]

Thanks to Granville Sharp, David Hartley, John Cartwright, Thomas Day and Josiah Wedgewood, abolition was in both the public and political spheres, and a solid plan had been formulated on how best to bring it about. Yet ironically, despite the dramatic gesture of Hartley and the work of Granville Sharp, abolitionism in the public mind is linked to one man, William Wilberforce MP.

Enter Wilberforce

William Wilberforce was born on 24 August 1759 in Hull, the son of a wealthy merchant. The abolitionist Thomas Clarkson had an enormous influence on him. He studied at Cambridge University where he began a lasting friendship with the future prime minister, William Pitt the Younger. Initially a Whig in politics, he championed political and economic reform. He joined the Yorkshire Association at New Year 1780, and stood in the general election of that year on the Society's cause against the sitting MP David Hartley. In the election, Jack Milnes and his uncle Pemberton financed the campaign and Jack appears to have canvassed for Hartley. All three men were staunch critics of the American War and the Government as well as the Test and Corporation Acts, and in favour of Catholic emancipation.[33] It was Hartley's support for the 1778 Catholic Relief Act and religious tolerance that cost him the 1780 general election: Lord George Gordon, a powerful and extreme Protestant, set up the Protestant Association in 1780, demanding the repeal of the Catholic Relief Act. He spread fears of 'Popery' and royal absolutism. Gordon sparked the riots on 2 June which left nearly 300 dead after a week-long rampage through London. In Bristol and Hull, the mob, whipped into anti-Catholic and anti-Whig fury, virtually destroyed the Catholic chapel in the town and damaged other buildings associated with Whig politicians. Hartley remained a critic of Wyvill all his life, and would negotiate the Treaty of Paris which ended the war with America.

On the back of anti-Catholic mob violence and loyalist pro-war sentiments in Hull, it was a forgone conclusion that Wilberforce was elected as MP on 11 September 1780. However distasteful Wilberforce's electioneering seems to us, 'fear of the other' got him into Parliament. Four years later Wilberforce with his cousin Samuel Thornton – Dick Milnes's brother-in-law – successfully contested Hull, on a joint interest. They were elected on 31 March 1784. Wilberforce, however, abandoned Hull in favour sitting for Yorkshire from 7 April 1784. Wilberforce now had a friend in a high place with the fall of Charles James Fox: his schoolfriend William Pitt was now prime minister.

In the winter in 1785, Wilberforce underwent a religious transformation: he was a nominal Anglican in order to attend university, he had heard John Newton preach and by 1784 is reported to have attended a Unitarian chapel in London. Following a tour of Europe, he became a committed evangelical Anglican, declaring 'God Almighty has set before me two great objects, the suppression of the slave trade and the reformation of manners'.[34] On 13 March 1787, during a dinner involving several important figures amongst the Clapham Sect of Evangelical Anglicans based at Holy Trinity Clapham – including Dick Milnes's brother-in-law Samuel Thornton who had married his sister Elizabeth – Wilberforce agreed to bring the issue to Parliament. His Christian faith prompted him to become interested in social reform, particularly the improvement of factory conditions in Britain. Wilberforce became the political front for the Society for the Abolition of the Slave Trade.

Chapter 14

Abolition Round 1

In late 1787 the Society for the Abolition of the Slave Trade, with Wilberforce at the helm, began a national campaign to raise petitions against the slave trade. Unitarians backed the Society in spite of being ostracised because of their faith and faced with open opposition from Granville Sharp for their religious beliefs.[1] In 1788 the Rev. Theophilus Lindsay, titular head of the denomination, hoped that the campaigning being done by Unitarians against the slave trade would help soften the hatred towards them from Granville Sharp and others in the national body working for abolition.[2] Unitarians across the country flocked to the cause: Rev. Dr Priestley, Josiah Wedgewood, Thomas Walker of Manchester, Rev. Dr Richard Price, Rev. John Disney, Rev. Joseph Towers, Capel Loft and the Rev. Andrew Kippis were members; indeed the Society was a veritable who's who of Unitarian radicals. Indeed, Kippis urged from his London pulpit that moves 'for abolishing the infamous traffic in slaves . . . be prosecuted with ardour'.[3] From the pulpit at Hackney, The Rev. Thomas Belsham (1750–1829) thundered:

> And though it has been admitted as a principle, that Christians might make slaves of unbelievers, and upon this ground a state of servitude was introduced far more horrible than the world ever witnessed before, a more enlightened system of Christianity, and a more enlarged view of Christian principles, have already given a powerful check to this enormous abuse, and will, no doubt, ultimately abolish it all together.[4]

The same sentiment was echoed by the doyen of the Unitarian radical clergy, the Rev. Dr Richard Price, who declared 'The negro trade cannot be censured in language too severe. It is shocking to humanity, cruel, wicked and diabolical.' He urged the abolition of chattel slavery as quickly as circumstances would allow.[5] A leading member of Price's congregation was Mary Wollstonecraft, who directly compared the experience of enslaved Africans to that of women. In her *Vindication of the Rights of Women* (1792), she asked, 'Is sugar always to be produced by vital blood? Is one half of the human species, like the poor African slaves, to be subject to prejudices that brutalise them, when principles would be a surer guard, only to sweeten the cup of man? Is not this indirectly to deny woman reason?' During the 1790s, women were actively encouraged to boycott slave-produced goods such as sugar and rum to add economic weight to the abolitionist campaign.

Sitting in the same pews was Benjamin Vaughan (1751–1835). In June 1789 he wrote to Thomas Jefferson about the slave trade: 'I do not think, and do not hope the trade will last many years for civilised nations.'[6] The Rev. Dr Priestley from his pulpit in Birmingham conjoined the ideals of the Revolution in France – the call for liberty and equality – with the cause of freeing slaves:

> . . . you will consider all mankind as brethren, and neighbours, entitled to every good office that it may be in your power to render them. As men, and as Christians, observant of the instructions of our great master in my text, we would interest ourselves not only for our relations, and particular friends – not only for our countrymen, & not only for Europeans, but for the distressed inhabitants of Asia, Africa, or America; and not only for Christians, but for Jews, Mahometans, and Infidels.
>
> And as we ought to feel for our fellow-men, we ought, to the utmost extent of our influence, to exert ourselves, to relieve their distress. Does not, then, the case of the African Negroes, who have long been unjustly en-slaved, and have been made to suffer numberless miseries, the least of which is mere servitude, in our West Indies, deserve our companion, and loudly call for our friendly interposition in their favour? And surely, they are not the less in titled to it because their oppressors are our countrymen, and because we have derived, or have imagined that we have derived, benefit from their oppression.[7]

William Belsham (1752–1827), the Whig politician and friend of Charles James Fox, began his career as an author by publishing *Essays, Philosophical, Historical, and Literary* in 1789 which rapidly spread throughout Whig circles in London. He was the brother of Rev. Thomas

Belsham and the brother-in-law of Rev. Kenrick. In his polemic against slavery he thundered:

> I mean to offer only a few remarks on the pleas which are usually advanced in defence or extenuation of this outrage against the common rights of humanity . . . it is alleged, that the Negroes are an 'inferior and subordinate' race of men, and it is, therefore, allowable to treat them as such, without incurring the imputation of cruelty and 'injustice.' What! to borrow the language of Shylock, 'Hath not a Negroe eyes, hands, organs, dimensions, senses, affections, passions? fed with the same food, hurt with the same weapons, subject to the same diseases, healed by the same means, warmed and cooled by the same Winter and Summer that a Christian is?' Say, ye profound Philosophers, ye enlightened Sages, who inhabit the shores of Mersey and of Avon, by what medium of proof have you discovered and ascertained the intellectual inferiority of this devoted race?[8]

Rev. John Yates (1755–1826), we are told by a diarist, preached an anti-slavery sermon in Liverpool, championing the 'equality of mankind' which apparently caused great offence to the slave owners in his congregation.[9] When the Unitarian Chapel on Kaye Street in Liverpool was opened in September 1791, Yates gave an impromptu sermon on the enormous cruelty of the slave trade.[10] Virtually all the leading inhabitants of the town, including the mayors, town councillors and MPs, invested in the slave trade and profited from it. The prosperity and growth of the town was closely connected with its involvement with slavery. To oppose slavery was a major risk, yet Unitarians did stand up for what was right. Yates in a letter of 1795 states:

> We do not, like the religious society with whom you are now connected, refuse to let slave-merchants be called members of our society, because we think we have no right to do so; but it is well known that the body of Dissenters of which I am a member think the carrying of Africans from their native country and selling them for slaves in another is a most iniquitous business; and I have reason to rejoice that some of our society have abandoned it; and others have declined any connection with us, who we have reason to believe would have attended our place of worship had they not been under apprehension of hearing the subject touched upon.[11]

How typical this was of Unitarians we have no idea. Yet we note that Yates broke his own rules. In 1801 the great patron of abolitionism in Liverpool purchased a 25 per cent stake in a West Indian merchant company, France, Fletcher Yates & Co, which imported slave-produced goods like sugar, rum, logwood etc, to get a trade for his son John Brooke Yates (1780–1855), who went on to be a major slave owner and at abolition received over £42,000 in compensation for 2,287 slaves![12] His younger brother John Ashton Yates (1781–1863) at abolition owned fifty-six slaves.[13] The Rev. Yates must clearly have known his sons were slave owners, and the business he had a share in owned slaves. Clearly it was morally wrong to be a slave trader, yet acceptable to be a slave owner. In this regard he was no different to the Vaughan family who were slave-owning abolitionists. The Yates's were in business with another Unitarian family, the Croppers. John Cropper (1773–1855) and his brother Nathaniel Bassnet Cropper were awarded compensation for three estates on St Vincent (two as mortgagee, one as joint owner), and with James France France awarded the bulk of the compensation for the enslaved people in Clarendon, Jamaica as trustees of Thomas France (probably his brother-in-law): the other part of the compensation in this Jamaica award went to Samuel Poole. In December 1815 James France France, John Cropper and Jonathan Brooks were identified as executors of Thomas France in an announcement by them and the partners in Fletcher, France Yates & Co. (Thomas Fletcher, Joseph Brooks Yates, Samuel Poole junior and John Henry Mathews) of the dissolution of the partnership by virtue of Thomas France's death the previous January, and the continuation of the business by Fletcher, Yates and Poole.[14]

In Yates's congregation, as well as slave owners we find William Roscoe, MP for Liverpool 1806–07 and an ardent abolitionist.[15] Roscoe was in business with his co-religionist Thomas Fletcher (1767–1850) as Fletcher, Roscoe & Co, bankers. Fletcher had a two-fifths stake in Fletcher, Yates & Co mentioned above. The bank failed in 1833: 'Among Thomas Fletcher's assets were a one-fourth interest in a mortgage for £5,636 7s 10d on a coffee plantation called Friendship Hall, Portland Jamaica with seventy slaves thereon, and one-fourth of a mortgage for £16,000 on a moiety of a sugar estate called Fellowship Hall, St Mary's Jamaica, and of the fifty slaves on the estate.'[16] Roscoe's granddaughter Margaret would marry Henry Robertson Sandbach (1807–95) in 1833; he was a major slave owner![17]

At nearby Gateacre Unitarian Chapel, the minister the Rev. William Shepherd joined the Society for the Suppression of the Slave Trade in 1788, the membership of which was just eight, these being: William

Roscoe, William Rathbone, Dr Binns, Daniel Daulby, William Wallace, Reverend John Yates and an anonymous subscriber generally thought to have been Scottish physician and Wallace's son-in-law Dr James Currie.[18] Yet we note 13,500 signatures were collected in the town against the abolition of the slave trade.[19] This was led by Colonel Banastre Tarleton, and sought to upset any bill on regulating the slave trade.[20] Thomas Fletcher and the Croppers were the authors of several letters to the *Liverpool Mercury* in 1823 defending themselves, unsuccessfully, against the charge of being pro-slavery.

In Bristol, Rev. John Prior Estlin took up the cause, and the Bristol Abolition Committee was founded at Lewins Mead Unitarian Chapel by the Rev. Thomas Wright. The first open meeting in Bristol on the abolition of the slave trade occurred in 1788, in the medieval guildhall (now demolished). They drafted a petition against the slave trade which was signed by, among others, Alderman John Harris, George Daubeny (Merchant Venturer and one-time mayor), Josiah Tucker (by then the Dean of Gloucester), the Dean of Bristol, the Baptist minister Rev. Caleb Evans and the radical minister of Lewin's Mead congregation, Rev. John Prior Estlin.[21] The Rev. Estlin also made addressed his congregation on the subject from the pulpit, a congregation which contained the Bright, Collard and Castle families – all slave owners. Here was a man not afraid to court the wrath of his congregation.

In Norwich, the former minister to Warrington Academy, Rev. William Enfield, thundered from the pulpit at Octagon Chapel that the emancipation of slaves 'was a universal obligation'.[22] The call for abolition in Newcastle was taken up by the Rev. William Turner Jnr, son of Rev. William Turner of Wakefield, the Unitarian minister of Hanover Square chapel. William Turner Jnr was the chairman and leading figure of the local abolitionist committee. Thomas Clarkson himself notes that the Newcastle committee was established in October 1787:

> The people could not bear the facts, which had been disclosed to them by the Abridgement of the Evidence. They were not satisfied, many of them, with the mere abstinence from sugar; but began to form committees to correspond with that of London. The first of these appeared at Newcastle upon Tyne, so early as the month of October. It consisted of the reverend William Turner as chairman, and of Robert Ormston, William Batson, Henry Taylor, Ralph Bainbridge, George Brown, Hadwen Bragg, David Sutton, Anthony Clapham, George Richardson, and Edward Prowit. It received a valuable addition afterwards by the admission

of many others. The second was established at Nottingham. The reverend Jeremiah Bigsby became the president, and the reverend G. Walker and J. Smith, and Mess. Dennison, Evans, Watson, Hart, Storer, Bott, Hawkesley, Pennington, Wright, Frith, Hall, and Wakefield, the committee. The third was formed at Glasgow, under the patronage of David Dale, Scott Moncrieff, Robert Graham, professor Millar, and others. Other committees started up in their turn. At length public meetings began to take place, and after this petition to be sent to Parliament; and these so generally, that there was not a day for three months, Sundays excepted, in which five or six were not resolved upon in some places or other in the kingdom.[23]

As Clarkson notes, Rev. George Walker MA FRS (1734–1807) supported the campaign to end the slave trade. Walker was minister of High Pavement chapel in Nottingham: he was both an energetic abolitionist and exponent of political reform. His uncle, Thomas Walker, had been minister at Mill Hill 1748–63. George studied at the University of Glasgow but could not graduate because of his heterodox faith: Newcome Cappe was a classmate. In conjunction with Rev. Gilbert Wakefield, who was in Nottingham from 1784 to 1790, he formed a literary club, meeting weekly at the members' houses. Nottingham was a focus of political opinion, which Walker led both by special sermons and by drafting petitions and addresses sent forward by the town in favour of the independence of the United States and the advocacy of Parliamentary and other reforms. His book *The Dissenter's Plea* (Birmingham, 1790), was reckoned by Charles James Fox to be the most important publication on the subject. He was so ardent in the cause of abolition, that he even wrote to a friend in Yarmouth, 120 miles away, to ask 'why has not Yarmouth joined the national voice in the cause of human liberty? . . . It is not too late to come in for your share of the honour.' We note Walker was thanked by Olaudah Equiano for his warm hospitality and invited him to his wedding. Walker, a radical agitator since the time of John Wilkes, was strongly sympathetic to the French Revolution. He served on the Nottingham abolition committee from 1788 to 1792, and organised a peace petition in 1790 to prevent war with France.[24]

In Exeter, Samuel Milford, took a leading part in the local committee, as did the Unitarian minister James Manning and Thomas Sparkes, who was an active campaigner throughout the county. History records 1,000 people signed the 1788 petition to abolish the slave trade from Exeter which was a Unitarian and Quaker initiative.[25]

Unitarian networks bolstered the campaign across the county. Thomas Clarkson, upon visiting Manchester in autumn 1787, was delighted to find an active abolitionist society already in existence. The society was led by Dr Thomas Percival, a member of Cross Street Unitarian Chapel. In the congregation could be found the notable local radicals Thomas Cooper and Thomas Walker. Other families at Cross Street in favour of abolition included the Rigby, Grimshaw, Hardman and Mathers. Manchester was 'a nest of abolition'.[26] Yet many slave-trading and slave-owning families met at Cross Street. The Hibberts were members along with the Bayley, Phillips, Greg, Robinson and Digges families: all were related through marriage, and all alas involved in slavery. Robert Hibbert (1686–1762) married Margaret Tetlow. The marriage of their children cemented the family's place in Unitarian Manchester merchant society:

> Sarah Hibbert married Samuel Bayley, who was nephew of Robert Digges, chapel trustee.
> Esther Hibbert (1714–72) married Thomas Digges, son of Robert Digges.
> Elizabeth Hibbert (1725–97) married Nathaniel Philips.
> Margaret Hibbert (1736–?) married Samuel Robinson.[27]

The Bayley and Digges families were involved in slavery. The great uncle of John Digges Bayley (1781–1848) was John Digges who owned Booth Hall Plantation. It was John Digges who passed the plantation to the Bayley family around 1787. At abolition John Digges Bayley owned 120 slaves on Ashley estate, Jamaica and received £2,429 18s 10d in compensation.[28] The Digges were linked through marriage to the Shores of Sheffield. Nathaniel Philips and his brother Thomas Philips (1728–1811) were Manchester cotton merchants. Thomas's son George (1766–1847) was very active in the Manchester Literary and Philosophical Society and the Portico Library, as well as in radical politics. He counted John Ferriar, Thomas Walker and Thomas Cooper amongst his closest friends. In 1792 he published *The Necessity of a Speedy and Effectual Reform in Parliament, a plea for universal suffrage*, including the right of women to vote. Yet, in spite of all his good works, the family was pro-slavery and with his business partner, Samuel Boddington, he owned slave plantations on Jamaica.[29]

The Manchester petition of 1787 amassed 11,000 signatures by December, representing 20–30 per cent of the adult population.[30] As Seymour Drescher points out, abolitionism in Manchester grew out of an eighteenth-century culture of 'improving' clubs and political societies.[31] Indeed, the Manchester Abolitionists Society had almost identical membership with a radical group based in the city. Thomas Cooper, along with James Watt Jnr and Walker were all members of the Manchester Constitutional Society – a branch of the London Society for Constitutional Information headed by none other than Major John Cartwright! Thomas Cooper was connected with the Jacobin Club, and had published his own reply to Edmund Burke's reflections on the French Revolution. Burke (1729–97) was a hugely influential Anglo-Irish politician, orator and political thinker, notable for his strong support for the American Revolution and his fierce opposition to the French Revolution. He expressed his hostility in *Reflections on the Revolution in France* (1790). Burke emphasised the dangers of mob rule, fearing that the Revolution's fervour was destroying French society, favouring national tradition over 'the horrible consequences flowing from the French idea of the Rights of Man'. Unlike the Rev. Dr Richard Price and Thomas Paine, Burke denied that a majority of 'the people' had, or ought to have, the final say in politics and alter society at their pleasure. Stating that 'People had rights, but also duties, and these duties were not voluntary. Also, the people could not overthrow morality derived from God.' When Fox called for a repeal of laws against Unitarians, Burke claimed that Unitarians were dedicated to the destruction of the Church of England and creating a state modelled on the French Revolution based on merit. He appealed to the British virtues of continuity, tradition, rank and property and opposed the Revolution and any notion of democracy to the end of his life. His is credited as the founder of Conservatism in English politics. His work sparked an intense debate on fundamental questions in politics fought out in over 300 publications – including Thomas Paine's *The Rights of Man*, Mary Wollstonecraft's *Vindication of the Rights of Man* and James Mackintosh's *Vindiciae Gallicae* – and spilling over into novels, poetry, popular songs and caricature. The controversy gave renewed energy to metropolitan and provincial reform societies, and fuelled the emergence of new associations, some organised by ordinary working people who declined the patronage and control of the wealthy. Thomas Hardy's London Corresponding Society, formed early in 1792, spent five evenings discussing whether they 'as treadesman [sic] shopkeepers and mechanics', had any right to seek Parliamentary reform. Like many thousands across the country, eager to partake in the Revolution Thomas Cooper and James Watt Jnr arrived in Paris in April 1792, and took part in the procession on the Champ de Mars, with Cooper carrying a bust of Algernon Sidney and Watts carrying the British flag.[32] Here they would have met Jack Milnes, the Woodsworths and of course Mary Wollstonecraft! However, abolitionism's links to political reform and support for the French Revolution was to have a major detrimental effect on any hope of reform and abolition.

The virtual Unitarian monopoly of the printing firm Joseph Johnson, of St Paul's Church Yard London, created a print culture of abolitionist and libertarian material that helped change the world. Unitarian-edited reviews included *The Analytical Review*, published by Johnson and founded by Thomas Christie,[33] *The Monthly Review*, founded by Ralph Griffiths and *The Critical Review*, and *The New Annual Register* owned and edited by the Rev. Andrew Kippis, as well as the *Sheffield Register* edited by Joseph Gales, the *Cambridge Intelligencer*, edited by Benjamin Flower[34] (a member of the extended Milnes family through marriage), the *Leeds Mercury* of Edward Baines, the *Wakefield Star* of Milnes and Lumb edited by Martin Naylor and lastly the *New Annual Register*, Rev. Joseph Towers whose sobriquet was 'pamphleteer', Rev. Dr Priestley and many other influential ministers, dominated the popular press for the cause of religious toleration and abolitionism. The success of abolitionism and the creation of organised reformist associations across the country can, in part, only be attributed to the dominance of Unitarians amongst the progressive enlightenment element of Britain's cultural elites.[35]

Within months of the formation of the London society urging for abolition in March 1787, the call had been taken up nationwide, led in the most part by Unitarians as we have seen. Relevant to Yorkshire, we note that the Manchester Society held a general meeting on 27 December 1787 whereby the society sent to every mayor and magistrate in Cheshire, Yorkshire and Lancashire a petition to agitate for abolition of the slave trade. From this came a flood of support in Yorkshire.

Chapter 15

Yorkshire for Abolition

As the leading Whig magistrate of the county, Pemberton Milnes backed the call for raising committees in January 1788.[1] Subscriptions rapidly appeared across Yorkshire. The Dean of Middleham in North Yorkshire preached that abolition of the slave trade:

> . . . would be materially and beneficial because the numbers would be increased by a melioration of the system of slavery; – the merchant, equally beneficial, because the planter, doing all the work without the addition of new slaves, would find himself in a better condition to discharge his British debts; – to the British nation it would be beneficial, because the planter, cultivating sugar cane at a lower price can afford to bring his goods cheaper to market; – it would give proof to America that we are, like her, friends to liberty; – to all the world it would prove our equity and humanity; – to nations yet unborn, it would transmit liberty and happiness . . .[2]

Was he calling for the abandonment of slavery or for planters to 'breed' their own slaves? Likely the latter: opposition to the slave trade did not always equate with opposition to slavery. It was perfectly 'moral and just' at the time to support the institution of slavery, attend church or chapel on a Sunday and sign petitions against the slave trade. This was not a clear-cut issue: abolitionism did not mean emancipation. We must be aware of this. Only in exceptional circumstances did those calling for abolition of the slave trade call for the abolition of slavery. These were two distinct issues; the ending of the slave trade did not guarantee the end of slavery. We are wise to remember that slave owners could be abolitionists, and in the morality of the era, see no hypocrisy in their action. It is all too easy to condemn slave owners as racist, those who profited from slavery as racist and all abolitionists who did not call for emancipation as racists. In our era we are too quick to apply modern judgements to the past. Was the Dean of Middleham racist? To many in 2020 yes, he is, as he supported the institution of slavery. So where does this leave his abolitionist stance? The economic argument he made is clear enough: planters breed their own slaves at no cost to them = an increase in slaves = increase in productivity = reduction in prices = happy consumer. This was the primary economic argument deployed at the time against the slave trade; one of economics. It ended 'a great evil' and replaced it with another.

Halifax

The involvement of Northgate End congregation, led by the Rev. John Ralph till his death in 1795, and the abolition of slave trade is notable. The Unitarian Edwards family seem to have taken the lead in local affairs along with Law and Thomas Atkinson. Oddly, the Edwards were Tories and not connected to the wool trade. The Atkinsons were Whigs and close friends with Jack Milnes in Wakefield. It was the Edwards family who drew Wilberforce to Halifax. John Goodchild reports the congregation here organised an anti-slavery petition in 1788.[3] This would make perfect sense, given the personalities involved.

Kingston Upon Hull

In the home of Wilberforce, one of the most vocal opponents of the slave trade was the Rev. John Beatson. He was a Baptist minister with very Unitarian sentiments and ideals. Born in Beeston, Leeds in 1743, he was educated at Leeds Grammar School. He shifted from Anglicanism to Congregationalism, then to Baptist theology and latterly Unitarianism 'affording the utmost countenance to Free Inquiry'.[4] Indeed in 1778 he states that 'it be an advantage to enjoy the liberty of worshipping God according to the dictates of your conscience without any to make you afraid'.[5] Indeed, Beatson's 1778 sermon was based squarely on the idealism of Marat:

> . . . when the Iron hand of tyranny is stretched out to destroy, where there is a direct, and avowed check on civil and religious liberty, when the happiness of a people, which is the great end of government, is likely to be subverted, and considerable breaches are already made in it, when, in short, the state of things is such; that the probable consequence of resistance appear more eligible to the wiser and worthier part of a nation, than

the probable consequences of submission, few I imagine will be found to condemn it either as impolitic or unjust.[6]

Such was the man who took a leading part in abolitionism in Hull: a man from the same mould as Turner and Cappe. In 1789 he delivered a sermon on abolition to the Unitarian congregation at Bowl Alley Chapel.[7] The congregation had been founded in 1680 by the Rev. Samuel Charles MA of Corpus Christi College Cambridge, who had been ejected from his living at Mickleover in Derbyshire in 1661. The Briggs family of Westgate and Northgate End originated from his congregation.[8] Beatson declared to them:

> My intention in addressing you at present is – to plead the cause of humanity and justice – to turn your attention to a practice, which, I conceive to be directly subversive of those principles . . . the practice I allude to, is that part of British commerce, which consists in buying and selling the human species; a practice, in my view, so repugnant to every idea of compassion and justice.[9]

And:

> . . . are we not under obligation to exercise the offices of kindness, independent of complexion, language, country, religion, or any other tye than that strongest of all relations – one common nature? That I am a MAN possessed of the feelings of a man, capable of partaking of the pleasures of a man and liable to the miseries indicent to man, is a sufficient reason in itself, to entitle me to the regard of my fellow-men. That another is a MAN, possessed of the same pleasures, capable of enjoying the same pleasures and liable to the same miseries as myself – thou he should be a different complexion or language or country or religion or even all these united, – yet that he is a man, is sufficient reason why I should behave to him in a friendly manner. I may add, that, if he be a man involved in calamity, there needs no other reason why he should be object of my compassionate regards.[10]

In conclusion:

> . . . as our liberty and prosperity has increased at home, has not our national power been increasingly exerted abroad; and that not

for the protection of freedom, not for the relief of the oppressed, not to do good to men, either with regards to their temporal and eternal interests – but rather to spread desolation and misery in all the three great continents of Africa, Asia and America? Have we not acted thus at the expence of justice, mercy, national honour and every principle that we ought to hold sacred as men, Britons and Christians? How astonishing, that those who are just and benevolent and jealous of the rights of men being invaded at home – whose government and laws are the admiration and envy of other nations, should pay little or no regard to any of those principles, in the commercial transactions they have with others! . . . Abolish, then, so infamous, so destructive a commerce. No longer enslave an unoffending people. Inform the inhabitants of Africa that you have done them an injury, that you have violated the law of nations, and you will no longer persist in such a procedure. Inform the unhappy slaves in various islands, that the injury you have done them is irreparable; but that you are willing to make every compensation within your power. That you will put them under equal protection of the Law, provide means for them to raise them to the enjoyment of freedom.[11]

The committee to organise a petition to Parliament was headed by the Rev. Thomas Clarke, brother-in-law of Wilberforce, but it did not come into being till 1792. No petition was seemingly forthcoming in 1788 and it was the Rev. Clarke who set the 1792 petition in motion.[12] Presumably, with Wilberforce as the spokesman for abolition, Hull people relied on 'their man' to get the message across rather than form a committee. Clarke thundered from his pulpit: 'Why is the Slave-Dealer in Africa to be stigmatized with every Opprobrium, whilst the Ravager of INDIA is honoured and applauded? Why are we so tremblingly alive to the Sufferings of Aliens, so insensible to the Hardships which our own Countrymen sustain, by the Rigours of an Impress?'[13]

Leeds

Voices had been raised against the slave trade long before Wilberforce became involved. On 20 December 1768, the *Leeds Intelligencer* newspaper, edited by its founder Griffith Wright, ran a two-column article against the slave trade: 'A trade by which many thousands of innocent people are brought under the greatest anxiety and suffering, by being violently rent from their native country, in the most cruel manner, and brought to our colonies, to be employed in hard labour.'[14] The article carried onto say that the trade was 'a great evil sin' and that the argument that the slaves had a better life as slaves than in their own countries was false because 'the Negroes are generally a sensible, humane and social people, and that their capacity is as good, and as capable of improvement as that of the Whites'. The author judged slavery to be racist, a crime against man and religion. This was the first glimmer of abolitionism in Yorkshire.

Leeds Quakers were instrumental in establishing the abolitionist movement in the town along with the dominant Anglicans. The editor and owner of the Tory *Leeds Intelligencer*, Thomas Wright (the son of Griffith Wright, appointed editor in 1785), remarked in February 1788 that:

> The idea of abolishing the slave trade does honour to the age, and to that description of men, with whom the design originated. It will meet with powerful opposition, and among the arguments for its continuance, will be urged, that –
>
> 1. The plantations in the West Indies cannot be worked without an annual supply of slaves from Africa.
> 2. As the males in our Islands are ten to one more than the female, a sufficient supply cannot be expected by marriages.

> To combat this necessity, the promoters of the abolition of slavery have procured the fullest testimony, that, by humane treatment the present race of negroes in the West Indies will increase sufficiently for every purpose of labour. – These friends to humanity, have documents properly authenticated to prove, that in adjoining estates, where severity had greatly reduced the numbers in one plantation, a kind and benevolent treatment had multiplied them in a far greater degree, on the other – And we have reason to believe, that they are also prepared to shew, that in this horrid traffic, not less than two fifths of the British seamen employed are sacrificed in the prosecution of it, from the various effects of climate, – contagion – and those hardships which they must unavoidably experience.
>
> The philanthropists are prepared to demonstrate, by specimens of African produce, the great impolicy of Africa herself in exporting those labourers who might be profitably employed in cultivating articles of valuable barter, for European or other manufacturers. – These specimens bear strong testimony in favour of opinions long since advanced by the Dean of Gloucester,

to shew the general disadvantage arising from the slave trade; – who among other arguments for the abolition of it, strongly urges the manifest differences in the quantity of labour voluntarily performed by one hired; in opposition to that which is enforced under slavish apprehension of punishment for neglect.

It is hoped, that an attempt to overturn a prejudice so deeply rooted will meet with that candour and support from the public at large, which so meritorious an undertaking deserves.[15]

Wright seems to drift between arguing for full abolition of slavery and the same time as arguing for retention of slavery and, to quote zoological terminology, to 'create a captive breeding programme of slaves' which is without a doubt in modern eyes is deeply and systematically racist.

In the same edition, Wright printed the following advertisement:

Slave Trade

Leeds, January 24th, 1788

At a GENERAL MEETING of the inhabitants of this Town and Neighbourhood, held at the Rotation-Office, WILLIAM HEY, Esq; Mayor of this Borough in the chair.

It was resolved,

1st That the African Slave Trade is a direct violation of those principles of humanity to which all Mankind are, by nature, equally entitled.

2d, That this is cruel, oppressive, and high reproachful to Christian people.

3d, That it is the opinion of this meeting that an application to Parliament, in behalf of these distressed sufferers is expedient.

A Petition being produced by a committee appointed by the meeting for the purpose of drawing it up.

4th. That the petition now offered be approved; and that Henry Duncombe and William Wilberforce Esqrs be requested to present the said petition to the House of Commons.

5th, That these resolutions be published in Leeds and York Newspapers; the St James's Chronicle; and the London Packet.

6th, The thanks of this meeting be given to the Chairman.

William Hey, Chairman.

NB Subscriptions for promoting the purpose of these resolutions, will be received by Joshua Walker MD and Mr Benjamin Kaye in Leeds.[16]

William Hey was a leading member of Leeds civic society and helped found the Leeds Club as well as the Leeds Philosophical and Literary Society.[17]

The *Leeds Intelligencer* reported:

> The meeting at the rotation-offices in this town, on Thursday last, was very numerously attended, and the petition respecting the abolition of the slave trade unanimously agreed to.
>
> Henry Duncombe Esq has subscribed 20 guineas towards defraying the expence of presenting a petition to Parliament for the abolition of the slave trade.[18]

The petition read:

> Your petitioners, sensibly feel, and deeply lament the calamities under which the Africa slaves have long laboured.
>
> That they consider a traffic in the human species as in the highest degree oppressive and unjust. That they are not convinced that it is founded in necessity – the only plea, which they can apprehend, can be plausibly offered in excuse of a trade so repugnant to the natural rights of mankind.
>
> That, relying in the justice and humanity of Parliament, and that Christian philanthropy which hath of late diffused itself these realms, they humbly solicit the attention of the honourable House of Commons towards the abolition of this inhuman commerce.[19]

Wright remarked at the end of February that the abolition of the slave trade occupied the attention of every friend of humanity, and drew parallels with abolition and the work of Laurence Sterne (1713–68).[20] Sterne was a harsh critic of slavery. Joseph Wright of Derby in 1774 painted 'The Captive' inspired by Sterne's 1768 book *A Sentimental Journey* and again in 1778, which was purchased by Jack Milnes of Wakefield, who commissioned a series of just twenty engravings. Clearly Sterne's anti-slavery rhetoric inspired Milnes and Wright!

By March 1788, the Leeds papers reported that a Petition for Liverpool had been signed by 13,500 people and from Manchester, 3,000 had signed.[21] The Leeds Petition was lodged at the Rotation Office and was able to be signed from ten till four on Tuesdays, Wednesdays and Thursdays. Subscriptions were collected for the London Committee by Dr Walker, Benjamin Kaye – a Quaker flax dresser – and at the Old and New Banks.[22] Dr Joshua Walker Esq. was the leading Quaker in Leeds.[23]

Thomas Wright suggested in his newspaper that women ought to take up the cause of abolitionism:

> It must give the friends of humanity great satisfaction to hear, that the French nation interests itself more and more in favour of the oppressed Africans and that in particularly the Marchioness de Fayette and Madame Necker exert themselves much in distributing Clarkson's excellent treatise on the impolicy of the slave trade – How desirable is it that the English ladies would follow such excellent examples; for surely there never was a cause which so loudly and so feelingly called upon the humane and the pious for their assistance![24]

The Rev. William Wood, who had succeeded Rev. Dr Priestley as minister at Mill Hill, proclaimed from his pulpit at Mill Hill:

> Civil Liberty is, in every view, a valuable possession. The natural feelings of the human heart revolt at the idea of slavery. If all mankind were wise and good, they would all have a right to act as they please; no one would be entitled, in any respect, to control another; and all might pursue their own desires, without detriment to any of their brethren.[25]

The Unitarian involvement with abolition in Leeds was liminal, and centred around Mill Hill Chapel. Rev. William preached on 4 July 1781:

> When all bear a similar relation to the Almighty, when all are entirely dependent, and all continually obliged, who can lay any particular claim to a superiority, or dare to interfere with privileges which have precisely the same origin with their own . . . What are the distinctions of European, Asian, African, or American, when set in competition with the feelings of universal humanity? Is our good will to be bounded by rivers, mountains and seas? Would a man have been entitled to our benevolence, if he had been born on this side of a small navigable strait, and may we regard him as an enemy, because his parents happened to reside on the other? Is a whole race of men to be made slaves at pleasure, because they have a black complexion and woolly hair? May the banks of the Ganges be lawfully made the

156

scene of continual rapine, merely because their inhabitants are peaceable and rich? Is it a good reason for depriving a people of their country, that they prefer hunting to agriculture, and had rather roam at large in a forest than live confined in a city? And are contiguous nations to be considered as natural and perpetual enemies, purely because they are neighbours, and find an interest in exporting to distant climes the same natural productions and manufactures . . . We remind you that, however temporary misunderstandings may sometimes interrupt the intercourse of nations, or the wicked ambition of Princes plunge their subjects and neighbours in the miseries of war, all the inhabitants of the earth sustain a mutual fraternal character which neither themselves nor any human power can ever dissolve. We assert that if you are capable of wishing the destruction of an enemy, and of rejoicing when he is deprived of the comforts of life, you are strangers to the influence of the gospel principles, and are Christians only in name.[26]

Yet, for whatever reason, he backed away from supporting abolitionism and/or Wilberforce. The Rev. Charles Wellbeloved reports about the Rev. Wood that in 1790:

He was indefatigable in the ablest exertions to establish the right of those with whom he was connected, to a perfect immunity from all civil restrictions in their peaceable dissent from the established church, and to assist in wiping away a stain which has too long defaced the character of a nation admired and envied for the freedom of its government. Several excellent papers were composed by him upon this occasion, of which the reply to a letter addressed to the Committee by Mr. Wilberforce, assigning some very extraordinary reasons for his opposition to the repeal; and a declaration signed by himself, and four other Dissenting Ministers of Leeds, occasioned by the remarks of the Clergy of that parish upon the resolutions passed at a Meeting of Dissenters held at Wakefield, are particularly deserving of remembrance. He attended in London as secretary with the delegates from the West Riding of Yorkshire, at the time of the last debate upon the subject in the House of Commons, when Mr. Fox's motion 'having to encounter the full weight of ministerial influence, was consequently negatived by a very great majority.'[27]

157

Ironically, we have the Unitarian-hating Wilberforce appealing to Unitarians for support: either his hatred was not yet fully formed, or he was prepared to 'do a pact with the devil' to get his bill passed. Wakefield, as Wellbeloved remarks, under Turner's indefatigable leadership, backed abolition of the slave trade, Wood did not, and, it seems, positively opposed abolition, along with, we assume, Call Lane congregation. This was a complete *volte face*! We do not know what we he said of course: the options are he was more concerned over the Test and Corporation Acts being repealed or congregational and familial pressure led to opposition. The good Rev. Wood was not unique. Not one public utterance was made by any clergy in Leeds against the slave trade: Leeds, dominated by its Tory merchants, was led by the press and not the clergy. Leeds merchants were heavily integrated into the slave economy; the great men at church and chapel were plantation owners and had a lot to lose. Slavery slipped from the news in summer 1788 and did not re-appear until 1791.

Malton

Despite the upsurge in abolitionist ideals, many fought against abolition. In Malton, 'a letter was read out from the great proprietor of the town to the people convened there for the purpose of petitioning, dissuading his tenants from such a measure'![28] Presumably this was William Fitzwilliam, the 4th Earl Fitzwilliam, who succeeded his uncle Charles Watson Wentworth, 2nd Marquis of Rockingham, in 1782. We also note that Earl Fitzwilliam, according to the Tory *Leeds Intelligencer*, voted against the abolition of the slave trade.[29] Despite being the de facto leader of the Northern Whigs and radicals, Fitzwilliam's blocking of abolition leaves a 'nasty taste in one's mouth'. Malton took no part in petitioning Parliament to end the slave trade!

Rotherham

In Rotherham, where a Unitarian congregation had met since 1662 and its chapel dated from 1704, a petition against slavery was raised in 1788:

On Monday a meeting was held at Rotherham which was numerously attended for the purpose of taking into consideration the African Slave Trade, when it was unanimously resolved to petition Parliament for the abolition of this traffic in the human species.

The approbation already given in different parts of the Kingdom, to the noble attempts now making for the abolition of slavery, must afford the sincerest pleasure to everyone who wishes to promoted the interests of freedom, humanity, and the Christian religion. The large and populous towns of Manchester, Birmingham and Leeds, have already distinguished themselves in subscribing for the support of the cause with a zeal and promptitude which does them honour.[30]

Rotherham was home to the Unitarian Walker family, who founded Rotherham Independent College. Samuel Walker sat on the Rotherham committee and knew both Samuel Shore, of Upper Chapel, Sheffield, and James Wilkinson, both of whom sat on the Sheffield Committee. Samuel had converted to Methodism by 1760, but others of the family remained Unitarians until the early nineteenth century. Jonathan, Samuel, Joshua and Joseph Walker all subscribed to the *Life of Olaudah Equiano*.[31] Ripon corporation organised a petition against slavery in 1788 headed by the Anglican clergy.[32] Scarborough also submitted a petition the same year.[33]

Sheffield

As in Wakefield, political reform and abolitionism in Sheffield were 'joined at the hip'. Like Wakefield, Sheffield had an active Unitarian community at Upper Chapel, the oldest Dissenting place of worship in the town, and at the time, the sole Unitarian one. Sheffield was home to Joseph Gales and Samuel Shore. Joseph Gales was a newspaperman – he ran the *Sheffield Register*. Through his pages he championed the writings of Thomas Paine and the abolition of slavery.

The first move in establishing an anti-slave trade committee in Sheffield can be found in the pages of Gales's newspaper. On 12 January 1788 he thundered:

We hear the town and county of Huntingdon are preparing a petition to Parliament for the abolition of that inhuman commerce, the slave trade, a practice which in whatever relation we consider ourselves, whether as men, as Britons or as Christians, is a scandal of these civilised, enlightened times; a disgrace to our excellent constitution, and a national stigma on the people of England. We hope that we have the honour of this Liberal age, this truly humane, generous Christian example will be followed unanimously, by all the other counties throughout the Kingdom, in applying to Parliament for the relief of a much injured race of men, who are not only despoiled, in defiance of the laws of God and nature, of the common rights of humanity, but even degraded below the condition of the brute creation.[34]

Gales's editorial had an immediate response. A meeting was held at the Cutlers' Hall, Sheffield on 16 January 1788 to discuss slavery and the slave trade. The meeting agreed to raise a petition to send to Parliament, that a committee was to be formed to manage the petition and the expenses in sending the petition to London. The meeting was chaired by the Rev. James Wilkinson, vicar of Sheffield.[35]

Others on the committee were the bankers John and William Shore, Mr Tudor, Mr Watkinson (master cutler) and a Dr Sutcliffe. Copies of the petition for people to sign were set up at the Tontine Inn, the Cutlers' Hall, and John and William Shore's bank. [36] In his editorial Gales commented:

The Superior dignity of English feelings is never so nobly enviced as when agitated by any question of humanity; how admirably just and equitable is the spirit with which so many opulent towns have taken up the subject of the slave trade . . . not only Manchester and Sheffield, but Shrewsbury, York, Northampton and indeed almost every inland town in England have resorted to the standard set up for the abolition of slavery – the main scope of the above benevolent undertaking is at one to annihilate the slave trade, and to place those who are in bondage on the foot of hired servants.[37]

Gales reported:

. . . the situation of the African Slave Trade: a traffic which upon the face of it appears to contradict the clearest rules of justice, which in its commencement subjects human beings, sprung from the same origin, equally entitled to the common rights of humanity with your petitions, to be comes as much the objects of purchase and sale as the various articles produced by bodily labour or mental ingenuity; which is a trade so circumstances as must in its consequences, naturally tends to increase, to a very great degree the evils that flow from war and oppression, through many populous districts of a wide extended continent.[38]

The petition read in part:

> In thus endeavouring to rescue thousands of their innocent and unoffending Fellow-Creatures (innocent and unoffending at least to the Natives of this Country) from the miseries that are the necessary attendants upon such a commerce, your petitioners are, as men, influenced by the feelings of humanity; as members of a free community, by the true principles of just and equal liberty; and as Christians, by a desire to act consistently with the Spirit of that most excellent religion, which does not confine good will and benevolent actions to a small part of the globe, or to any particular description, or complexion of men, but extends them to the whole human race.
>
> Your Petitioners therefore, humbly solicit this honourable house to proceed to a full and thorough investigation of this important subject: and if the most weighty and urgent reasons cannot be opposed to those advanced by your petitioners; and if those who are more immediately concerned in the question, cannot prove the Slave Trade from Africa to be agreeable to the dictates of humanity, conformable to just ideas of Liberty, and consistent with the precepts of religion, that then this honourable house will take such steps as in their wisdom may be deemed necessary, for the abolition of that inhuman and disgraceful traffic.[39]

Samuel Shore was elected chairman of 'The committee for managing the petition and subscription in Sheffield for the abolition of the slave trade' and by 16 February had gathered nearly 2,000 signatures. In addition, the committee had sent 100 guineas to the London society.[40]

A war of words erupted in the pages of Gales's newspaper. Joseph Gales championed abolition and received what we would call today 'hate mail', with many letters expressing deeply racist views.[41] In retaliation to the racist diatribes supporting slavery, one writer commented that the slave trade was a 'violation of every principle of liberty, justice, and humanity'.[42] Another argued that transportation was actually a force for good, as it gave 'brutes' a use in society and introduced laws for them to live by and asserted that 'apologists have not yet denied that the negroes are deprived for their liberty'! The writer is basically suggesting that slavery was imagined by 'left wing do-gooders' and that instead as the 'negroes' all shared the same rights, that 'equality of property among the subjects of a state is a public blessing'![43] Right-wing white exceptionalism was alive and well in Sheffield in 1788 alongside more humanitarian idealism. An anonymous letter sent to Gales reads in part:

> Can any human being have a right to drag his unoffending fellow creating from his native country and all his dear relative connections; compel him into his service, and there, retaining him by violence, feed him, work him, and correct him, at his sole will and pleasure? If this query cannot be answered directly in the affirmative, then the dispute seems at one terminated: for it is presumed no one can have the effrontery to take up his pen in vindication of the present practice of slavery, upon a plea of avaricious necessity . . .[44]

Clearly, Gales was not alone in Sheffield in condemning slavery. In endeavouring to be even-handed, and perhaps to show the pro-slave trade lobby to be bigots, Gales printed a letter in his paper from William Senhouse (1741–1800) a slave owner. Due to the influence of his patron, Sir James Lowther, MP for Carlisle, Senhouse had been appointed Surveyor General of the Customs in Barbados and the Windward and Leeward Islands. He held the post from 30 May 1770 until 1787, when the office was abolished. In 1787 he paid £18,000 for The Grove Plantation in St Philip's.[45] William's brother Joseph (1743–1829), was Collector of Customs on Dominica from 1771 to 1779 when became Sir James Lowther's political manager at Carlisle, elected mayor of the city and again through Lowther's influence received a knighthood. Joseph established Lowther Hall Plantation, valued in 1776 at £11,607 15s in Dominican currency.[46] William Senhouse wrote thusly to Gales:

> I have information from good authority, although they did not come so immediately under my own personal observation, have a strong tendency to prove, that if negro slaves be well fed, properly clothed, comfortably lodged, not overworked and duly taken care of when sick (Which I can affirm has been the case with those above mentioned) the owners by humanity

will in a few years be amply rewarded by a valuable increase in his property, and will need no further supply in the manner no so justly condemned. And I am warranted in this idea by the uncommon proportion of fine healthy children of both sexes upon these two plantations . . . the present is an age of liberality, and these unhappy people have in some degree benefited by the general improvement in the manners of mankind. But it is nevertheless to be apprehended, that humanity, even when aided by so powerful an auxiliary as self-interest, too frequently gives way, and in sordid minds, to cruelty and oppression . . . your laudable efforts, terminate where they will, cannot fail of benefitting the unfortunate race of men . . . by forcing them to examine into their own particular conduct, necessarily improve the good in the management of their slaves, and I sincerely hope will make the bad better.[47]

Basically, Senhouse, like the Dean of Middleham, was arguing for 'breeding' more slaves, which was a fairly common response to the abolition of the slave trade. He talks of liberty – no doubt for white middle-class persons – yet would deny freedom to this 'unfortunate race of men'. Racial stereotyping alive and well: not seeing people of colour as equal to himself, and deserving of freedom, is undeniably racist. This is likely to have been the predominant view at the time, which makes Gales and Shore's demand for emancipation in 1788 so remarkable! In May 1791 Gales argued that:

It has been asserted that the faculties of blacks are inferior – very inferior to that of men of another complexion. Perhaps it may be so; but let it be recollected that all animals are more or less sagacious, in proportion as they are removed from the tyranny of others. Naturalists assert, that in natural liberty an Elephant is a citizen, and the beaver an architect; but when the tyrant man intrudes on their community, their spirit is broken, they feel anxious only for safety, and their intellects suffer an equal diminution with their freedom.[48]

Gales was arguing against racial stereotyping. In his newspaper and elsewhere the pressure for boycotting sugar from slave plantations gained momentum. Many abolitionists were also campaigning for reform. Joseph Priestley, Thomas Paine and William Smith had all visited

Revolutionary France. Samuel Shore's brother-in-law had strong links to the new French government. The ideas of a more equal society were understandably exciting to many in Britain.

Wakefield

Acting on the call from Manchester, a meeting was held at the Moot Hall on Westgate, Wakefield chaired by Thomas Lang, a leading Unitarian. The petition read:

> Wakefield, 28th February 1788.
> At a meeting held this day, in consequence of Notice given to the inhabitants and Neighbourhood of Wakefield, at the Moot Hall for the purpose of taking into consideration the propriety of petitioning Parliament for the regulation and in due time abolition of the Slave trade.
> Thomas Lang, in the Chair,
> Resolved, that this meeting unanimously approve the petition now offered on this subject, and that the members of the County be requested to present the same to the House of Commons and the promote the objects thereof.
> That these resolutions be published in the York and Leeds Newspapers.
> That the thanks of this meeting be given to the Chairman.
> T. Lang, Chairman.

> To the Honourable Commons of Great Britain, in Parliament Assembled.
> The petition of the Inhabitants of Wakefield and its Neighbourhood, in the West-Riding of the County of York,
> Humbly Sheweth,
> That your petitioners, excited by the example of so many of their fellow subjects, have taken into their serious consideration the nature and effects of the trade carried on upon the coasts of Africa for the purchasing of Negro slaves, and cannot help regarding it with Abhorrence, as contrary to every amiable sentiment of humanity, as violating the plainest principles of equity, and the rights of human nature, as irreconcilable to the spirit and precepts of the Christian religion. We are shocked at the destructions, defilations and miseries brought on the

wretched natives by the wars and ravages which this detestable commerce is said to occasion.

We lament the miseries and oppressions which they suffer who are reduced to bondage in the British Colonies. We therefore earnestly request this honourable House to take these subjects into more mature consideration, and adopt such measures as shall appear most effectual for the relief of those already in captivity, and eventually to put a total end to a traffic which hath been too long a disgrace to our country and our religion. And your petitions will very pray &c.[49]

Lang and the petition were seemingly calling for improved living conditions for slaves, an end to the slave trade and, reading between the lines, an end to slavery. One can see here the influence of the Rev. Turner in the wording of the petition. The Lang family attended Westgate Chapel. Thomas Lang is recorded as renting pews 19 and 20 for £1 4s 0d a quarter in 1788.[50] The baptismal register reports several children of Obadiah Lang, his son, were baptised in the chapel. James Lang, son of Obadiah, married Priscilla Burrell, daughter of William Burrell who owned a dye works and a steam-powered mill in Thornes. The Burrell family were leading members of Wakefield's merchant class and Westgate Chapel. Thomas Lang himself died on 13 April 1803 aged 69. In death he lies alongside William Burrell and Martha Johnstone, the first wife of Rev. Thomas Johnstone. Thomas shares his grave with his daughter Esther, who died on 4 February 1833 aged 79. Both are interred in Westgate Chapel yard, where their gravestones can be found today.

York

Abolitionism in York was dominated by the Quaker community. John Woolman, was born into the farming family of Quaker Samuel Woolman near Mount Holly in New Jersey. He was moved by his faith and spoke persuasively to slave owners about the evils of slave ownership and was often able to convince them, without causing offence, to release their slaves. At this time, he also wrote two essays 'On Keeping Negroes'. They were later published in 1754 and 1762 respectively. Initially he was concerned about the inhumane treatment of Native Americans and then turned to campaigning against the brutality of the slave trade. In 1772 Woolman journeyed to England, visited York and help spread the anti-slavery message. Woolman died in York the same year from smallpox and is buried in Bishophill.

As well as having thriving Quaker and Anglican communities, York was and is home to those of heterodox faith. St Saviour Gate Unitarian Chapel in York was home to the Rev. Newcome Cappe (1733–1800), a firebrand radical and leading voice for change. He was born in Leeds, West Yorkshire, the eldest son of the Rev. Joseph Cappe, minister of the Nonconformist congregation at Mill Hill Chapel in the city. Newcome had risen to national prominence with his 1757 sermon praising Frederick the Great.[51] In 1776, he lambasted the government for the war with America, which pushed him back into the political spotlight.[52] Cappe went further, arguing that any policy of colonial conquest was immoral:

> Why may it not be good for Britain, gradually detached both from the Western and the Eastern world, to confine her attention to her own fields and seas? Let either the wisdom of man, or the wrath of heaven, in some mode or other, suppress the luxury that renders such connections useful, that renders such connections necessary, and from that moment they will have become, of necessary superfluous, and of useful noxious. Without them, being a better, we might also be a happier people.
>
> Why should it not be good, on what ground stands the doubt that it is good for her, that America should be governed by her own people and her own laws? Whoever is at all acquainted with the principles of the human nature, or the history of the human kind, cannot hesitate a moment to confess that, in respect of all the most valuable interests of men, many governments are far preferable to few. In wide extended empires the strain of law, in respect both of its requisitions and its sanctions, must be severe, and the execution of it must be rigorous; and yet, notwithstanding this, no severity of the one, and no rigor of the other, can preserve the distant regions of the empire from anarchies, usurpations, tumults, violences, oppressions, and disorders of every kind. The natural consequence of such inevitable disorders abroad, will be jealousies at home; and when rebellion abroad and suspicion at home decide the temper of the government, what must be the character, the condition, and the expectations of the subjects?[53]

Newcome Cappe's central position in York's political scene was bolstered in the 1780s with the election of a co-religionist and radical firebrand as MP. The city elected in 1784 a Unitarian MP: a self-made man who ousted the 'the old aristocracy'. Richard 'Dick' Milnes (1759–1804), son of Robert Milnes and Joyce Slater, a Unitarian, contested York in the Yorkshire Association's interest. Lord Galway was elected first member with 538 votes, and Milnes won as second member polling 514.[54] His acceptance speech was published in the *York Courant*:

> At the earliest opportunity to return to you my sincere and hearty thanks for the high honour you have thus conferred upon me, in electing me one of your representatives in Parliament – I can at present only profess my intended purpose to serve you with fidelity and diligence and to attend to your instructions and adopt as the rule of my Parliamentary conduct.[55]

In his maiden speech on 24 May 1784 he declared opinion in Yorkshire to be 'clearly and decidedly' in favour of Pitt – 'The conduct of the late ministers was held in execration'. A clear reference to the coalition government of Fox.

To commemorate the election of Dick Milnes as MP, the first of half-a-dozen Milnes to be so elected, on 22 April 1784 his cousin James Milnes Jnr (1755–1805) organised at the Strafford Arms Hotel Wakefield a meeting and banquet to celebrate the 'independency of the freeholders over the aristocracy'. James was president of the assembly, with Major General Anthony Loftus Tottenham as vice president.[56] Dick's childhood friend and cousin Jack Milnes, perhaps mocking Fox's failure, on Friday 30 April 1784 created a regional spectacle by launching a hot air balloon from his garden carrying a painted Fox hung by its neck beneath the basket. The balloon landed near Melton Mowbray at 14:45, having taken off at 12:06. This was no doubt the first hot air balloon ever launched in Wakefield.[57] The 1784 election was a watershed moment for the family: Pemberton Milnes told Fitzwilliam that politically he was now 'in opposition to all the rest of my near relations'. In the same letter, Pemberton reassured Rockingham that his Nottinghamshire interest and vote were at the disposal of the Duke of Portland.[58] Dick also noted the rupture in the family in a letter to Walter Spencer Stanhope dated 11 April 1784:

> Newland Park. I received the favour of Your letter this morning and lament that I am so situated as not to be able to have the small interest which we have at Hull operate to Your advantage. The little interest that I have at Hull arising not from Personal

acquaintance but Mercantile connections and our house being so exceedingly divided upon Political principles deprives me of the opportunity of gratifying my wishes upon this occasion I can only say it will give me great pleasure to hear of Your success.[59]

In the winter of 1785, Dick and Lord Galway gave 120 chaldrons of coal to the freemen of York – no doubt a way of thanking them for electing them as MPs![60] At the general meeting of York Corporation in February 1785, Milnes and Lord Galway gave £50 as their joint subscription for improvements to Little Blake Street.[61]

As an MP Dick worked tirelessly in seeking religious liberty and above all else the repeal of the Test and Corporation Acts and political reform, speaking the following words at the count meeting of 1785: 'I recommended to them not to rely on any Minister, however well disposed, but to place their confidence only in that which could not deceive them, and must be lasting—a Reformation of Parliament.'[62] Dick petitioned Parliament in 1787 and again in 1790 for the repeal of the Test and Corporation Acts. The petition stated 'we are forbidden by the first principles of our dissent to deny to any of our Fellow subjects that Liberty which we claim for ourselves'.[63] Alas, not all of his contemporaries felt the same: but his words ring as true today as they did over 200 years ago. Dick's uncle Pemberton signed the petition, along with his kinsman Samuel Shore of Sheffield, his brother-in-law Samuel Thornton, and his nephew John Pemberton Heywood, who was the Yorkshire delegate in London. Pitt voted in favour of retention. As well as religious freedom, he sought the end of the slave trade.

In 1788 with Unitarians making a stand against the slave trade, Newcome Cappe, minister at St Saviour Gate, was prompted by Rev. Dr Priestley to do something about slavery:

To Rev. NEWCOME CAPPE.
Dear Sir,
Birmingham, Jan. 23, 1788. It is now a long time since I have heard anything from you, but I take the opportunity of my being one of our Committee of Correspondence for abolishing the Slave Trade, to give you a few lines. I hope indeed something has been already done in York, from which place a petition to Parliament would have a good effect. We are zealous and unanimous here, and next Sunday, previous to a town's meeting, we all preach on the subject, (churches and meeting-houses alike,) not to collect money, but to give information to

such as may have been inattentive to the subject. I inclose one circular letter and a few tracts, though no doubt you have seen them.[64]

We wonder what kept the good Rev. Cappe from speaking out? The only utterance he made against slavery was made soon after the prompting from 'Gunpowder Joe':[65]

> . . . refuse those wicked practices, that worthless company, those criminal indulgences, that shameful slavery, which our comfort, which our dignity in this world, as well as our eternal interests, call upon us to refuse? What mighty sacrifice is this to make; what mighty price is this to pay for all the precious promises of God?[66]

Unitarians in York, despite having a Unitarian MP, were on the edge of the city's emerging abolitionist movement. William Mordaunt Milner, as Lord Mayor of York, soon to be MP, was party to the Quaker organisers of the anti-slavery committee in York and sponsored on the committee's behalf the publication of Rev. William Mason's anti-slavery sermon that he had preached in the Cathedral of St Peter on 27 January 1788:

> But were I to enter the lists against those, and, to the reproach of human nature itself, some there are who vindicate what they call the SLAVE TRADE, and who, by the very term they use, do enough to make every benevolent breast receive their arguments with detestation . . . Those of my hearers, who are least versed in their sacred pages, must have learned from them this plain, yet important truth, that they ought to do to others as they would wish others should do to them; and they must be ignorant indeed if they do not deduce from that divine rule this direct consequence, that as they would not themselves wish to be NEGRO Slaves, so they ought to wish, and, as far as possible, endeavour to free every Negro from the bonds of slavery.[67]

In York, it seems religious differences upset any cohesive action. The Anglican-Quaker committee seeming were ignorant of, or simply ignored, Cappe and the Unitarians. Yet it was Milnes and not Milner who was integral to our story. Indeed, on 3 November 1788 William Wilberforce visited Dick at Fryston and stopped the night, where he talked about slavery with Rachel Milnes.[68] This placed the Milnes four-square in the abolitionist camp. Be that as it may, Unitarians in York played little part in abolition and the Anglican-Quaker petition was presented to Parliament by Dick Milnes's co-MP Lord Galway.[69] Sir Robert Monkton-Arundell, 4th Viscount Galway (1752–1810), was a leading Whig politician, and an unlikely champion of abolition. He would marry Dick's niece Mary Bridgette Milnes, the only daughter and heir of Pemberton Milnes, in 1803. The marriage clearly was one to strengthen the Milnes's family position. Galway had firstly married Elizabeth Mathew, the daughter of Daniel Mathew of Felix Hall, Essex and Mary Bryam, on 1 March 1779. She died on 19 November 1801. The couple's second daughter, Henrietta, would marry Robert Pemberton Milnes, Dick Milnes's heir, on 22 August 1808. By the time of his second marriage Galway was a virtually bankrupt alcoholic. Lord Auckland had reported to Grenville from The Hague on 26 May 1792, informing him that:

> Lord Galway has been here in a state of continued intoxication, which must soon put an end to him. His understanding (such as it was) is quite gone; he lives in the streets, and is incessantly in quarrels with the lower people. He came to me at two o'clock in the morning to desire protection against a Jew whom he had taken by the beard, and by whom in return he had been treated with an unchristian severity. His servants had requested me to have him by some means sent back to his friends in England; luckily the want of money (for he spent £150 here in two days) has forced him back.[70]

Despite this, he was elected MP for Pontefract in 1796, a seat he held till 1802. Galway died on 23 July 1810. Mary Bridgette had been married firstly to Peter Auriol Hey Drummond, Colonel of the West Riding Militia, son of the Archbishop of York, who had died in 1799 falling down the staircase of the family home, Bawtry Hall, whilst drunk.

At the 1790 general election, Dick Milnes was re-elected, and the only subject on which Dick voted with Pitt in the ensuing Parliament was the abolition of the slave trade. So passionate was he about abolition, that the slave trade was the subject of his only known speech, made on 19 April 1791, censuring Lord Sheffield:

> Mr. Milnes declared, that he adopted all those expressions against the Slave Trade which were thought so harsh by the Noble Lord; and insinuated that his opinion had been turned by his being Member for Bristol. He quoted a passage from Lord Sheffield's

Pamphlet, and insisted, that the separation of families there complained of by the Noble Lord, ought to affect his mind as a crying evil in the West Indies, as well as in Africa, and that he ought on his own grounds, as stated in his Pamphlet, to take the contrary side of the question.[71]

At the election of 1796, Milner and Milnes, united in their opposition to the war, were returned unopposed, though it was thought that, had a third man stood, Milnes would have been defeated.[72] He again voted for abolition on 15 March 1796. In Parliament he was a consistent voter in favour of Fox. Dick voted against the suspension of habeas corpus on 16 and 17 May 1794, voted against the war on 30 May 1794, 24 March and 27 May 1795, was in the minority on the Prince of Wales's debts on 1 June 1795, and supported Grey's critical motion on the cost of war on 10 March 1796. This was not steady constant opposition, but his health may have impeded him from doing more – he was increasingly obese, with mobility problems. Despite this, he had gained the uncritical support of Rev. Theophilus Lindsay who remarked 10 June 1794 to Rev. William Turner of Newcastle: 'Mr R Milnes left town the middle of last week, a real patriot he.'[73] Dick wrote on 7 June 1796 to Wyvill: 'The present Parliament I think will do more in favour of a Parliamentary reform by disgusting the people than anything that has happened for some time. The contractors, money jobbers and clerks in office form the greatest part of the new Members.'[74]

Despite ill health, likely to be gout as he died, judging by his burial vault, morbidly obese, Milnes's re-election in 1796 was again unopposed. In his address (19 May) he stated:

> The same principle that induced me in the year 1784 to resist the measures that I then thought dangerous to the State, has lately occasioned me to oppose the system that has produced and maintained the present calamitous war . . . I shall strictly adhere to the line of independent conduct I have hitherto observed . . . I would not lay myself under obligations to any political men.[75]

Since joining the Yorkshire Association and the Society for Constitutional Information, Dick had been an ardent reformist and abolitionist, who sought real political change. He was enough of a realist to realise that whilst the country was at war with France, all the Pitt administration had to do was to wave the flag, shout 'God save the King' and any chance of reform was crushed immediately by public outrage. Little has changed, alas, in politics.

Dick retired from politics due to his failing health in 1802, claiming never to have given a vote in Parliament 'but from the conviction of his mind, that it was right'.[76] By this stage in his life, he could barely walk and was morbidly obese, and in his place, Earl Fitzwilliam put up his nephew Lawrence Dundas. Indeed, his brother-in-law Samuel Thornton wrote on 10 November 1797, 'I fear poor Richard Milnes will hardly ever get on his legs again'. Dick Milnes died on 2 June 1804 and lies beneath Westgate Chapel. His death was seemingly slow, as Lindsey records to Belsham on 6 August 1804: 'Fryston without its late owner would unavoidably occasion painful and melancholy sensations. We rejoice that the widow and the fatherless are supported, they were gradually weaned, and Mrs Milnes has a calm steady mind and & will we hope use her power well, or she will revolt her hitherto over indulged sons, who had a proper self-government to learn.'[77] Clearly Dick spoiled his children: his second son Richard Rodes Milnes was an alcoholic and gambler but he and his mother were astute enough to manage the family business for nearly 30 years, as we noted earlier.[78]

Quaker leadership and activism dominated the abolitionist movement in the city, none more so than William Tuke, Thomas Priestman (York Quaker and member of the first executive committee of The Retreat) and Lindley Murray (a Quaker who had settled in York after leaving New England, an abolitionist also known as 'the father of English Grammar') who urged members of the Society of Friends to vote to ensure the return of William Wilberforce as MP for Yorkshire, based upon his opposition to the slave trade. Sadly, we note the county-wide petition from York was raised too late to be considered as part of the evidence in support of the bill in Parliament, and had to be presented in February 1789.[79]

Chapter 16

Abolition Round 2

On the strength of the support from the petitions gathered in Yorkshire and nationwide, Wilberforce moved for abolition in a vote taken in the House of Commons on 12 May 1789. The Commons asked for time to assess the evidence gathered against the trade rather than make a rash and sudden judgement, which stalled the bill. The ensuing scrutiny of evidence by the House kept him working 'like a negro' and, a second vote after being delayed until 18 April 1791, when he raised a vote to prevent the further importation of slaves into the West Indies, which was defeated by 163 votes to 88. Voting in favour of abolition was Dick Milnes, MP for York. Charles James Fox, the Whig leader and champion of abolition – a vitally important man in Parliament – declared:

> . . . if they did not by the vote of that night mark to all mankind their abhorrence of a practice so enormous, so savage, so repugnant to all laws, human and divine, it would be more scandalous and more defaming in the eyes of the country and of the world than any vote which any House of Commons had ever given. He desired them seriously to reflect, before they gave their votes, what they were about to do that evening. If they voted that the slave-trade should not be abolished, they would, by their vote that night, give a Parliamentary sanction to rapine, robbery, and murder; for a system of rapine, robbery, and murder, the slave-trade had now most clearly been proved to be . . .[1]

Fox was known to both James and Dick Milnes – indeed the latter helped Fox financially during his two periods of bankruptcy. It was Fox who would lay the groundwork to pass the bill to abolish slavery shortly before his premature death in 1806. Despite the bill failing, Clarkson, Sharp and Wilberforce began another nationwide petition: one was raised in Huddersfield on 7 February 1792.[2]

The campaign for abolition had been championed across the West Riding by Olaudah Equiano, who had spoken in Halifax, Huddersfield and Sheffield. Born a slave in 1745, he purchased his freedom in 1766. As a freedman in London, Equiano supported the British abolitionist movement. He was part of the Sons of Africa, an abolitionist group composed of Africans living in Britain, and he was active among leaders of the anti-slave trade movement in the 1780s. He published his autobiography, *The Interesting Narrative of the Life of Olaudah Equiano*, in 1789, which depicted the horrors of slavery. About his public speaking in Yorkshire, the following letter in the *Leeds Mercury* notes support from Leeds and further afield:

Leeds, April 16th.
Having received particular marks of kindness from Mr Law Atkinson and family of Huddersfield, and many Gentlemen and Ladies, & C of and near this town who have purchased my genuine and interesting narrative: I beg to offer them my warmest thanks; and also to the friends of humanity here, on behalf of my much oppressed countrymen, whose case calls aloud for re-dress – May this year bear record of acts worthy of a British Senate, and you have satisfaction of seeing the completion of the work you have so humanely assisted in: – Tis now the duty of everyone, who is a friend to religion and humanity, to assist the different committees engaged in this pious work. Those who can feel for the distress of their own countrymen, will also commiserate the case of the poor Africans. Since that it does not often all to the lot of individuals to contribute to so important a moral and religious duty, as that of putting an end to a practice, which may without exaggeration, be styled one of the greatest evils now existing on the earth, it may be hoped, that each one will now use his utmost endeavours for that purpose. The Wise Man saith – 'Righteousness exalteth a nation, but sin is a reproach to any people'.[3]

The *Mercury* was a Whig newspaper, and remarkably this letter does not appear to have been reported or printed in the pagers of the Tory *Leeds Intelligencer*, which fully backed abolition!

Barnsley

Barnsley does not seem to have raised a petition against the slave trade in 1788, but in February 1792 a committee was formed to organise and petition 'for relief from cruelty and oppression occasioned by the slave trade to the suffering Negroes'. The Barnsley committee was headed by Francis Edmunds and the petition was lodged at the White Bear Inn 'to be signed by those who are inclined to countenance this act of humanity'.[4]

Bradford

In Bradford, the meeting was chaired by the Rev. John Crosse, the vicar. The petition read in part: '. . . by united opinions (however different to one another in other respects) of men of the greatest abilities, that the African slave trade is contrary to the primary laws of nature, is founded on the greatest injustice; it is attended with the greatest cruelty and barbarity and can never be excused. . .'.[5] No petition had been sent in 1788.

Halifax

A prominent member of the congregation at Northgate End Unitarian Chapel was Law Atkinson (1759–1835), who was the son of Joseph Atkinson (1732–1803). Law Atkinson was a subscriber to the London Committee for the Abolition of the Slave Trade and subscribed to 100 copies of Olaudah Equiano's book. He married for a second time, to his co-religionist Elizabeth Edwards on 30 July 1795, first cousin of William Edwards of Halifax. Elizabeth's father John Edwards resided at Pye Nest, a large classical mansion designed by John Carr of York, where Wilberforce would lodge in 1806.[6]

Olaudah Equiano, the great anti-slavery campaigner, had spoken in Elland and Huddersfield in spring 1791. Sadly, he received abusive comments because of the colour of his skin. Among those rushing to his defence were Law Atkinson and his wife Susannah. She wrote in a letter of 29 March 1791, 'It is I believe necessary that we should meet these rebuffs'. A 'Miss Haigh' and 'Cousin Tinkler' also sent their support against the racist abuse Equiano had received.[7] The 'Miss Haigh' mentioned we assume is Agnes Haigh who married Dr Disney Alexander of Halifax, who went onto become a Chartist, abolitionist and Unitarian attending Northgate End and later Westgate Chapel. Dr Alexander went on to marry William Edwards's daughter Mary as his second wife. We note a Miss Elizabeth Tinkler married John Cartwright of Halifax, merchant, in 1800 at Huddersfield Parish Church.[8] John Cartwright (1777–1854) was a JP and merchant, while his father, John Cartwright (1747–94) was a mercer and woollen draper in Halifax.

A second petition against the slave trade was sent in 1792, this time headed and managed by Anglicans. The Rev. Dr Henry William Coulthurst, the vicar of Halifax, chaired the Committee for Abolition of the Slave Trade, which called for 'a reciprocal trade' with Africa to be established trading goods and not people as the trade in people was 'barbarous and unjust' and 'cannot even be justified upon the principles of Commercial Advantage'.[9] Yet Coulthurst argued:

> . . . such importation tends to encourage a spirit of inhumanity in the planter, as the hopes of constant supplied from Africa render him too indifferent to the welfare and comfort of the Negroes already in his possession, and may be the indirect cause of the great barbarities exercised against the Negroes . . . that by the humane treatment and a well-regulated police the population of Negroes in the West Indies might be sufficiently upheld and preserved without said importations from Africa, and by improvements in the mode of agriculture, estates to all intents and purposes be equally as beneficial as at present . . .[10]

Basically, Coulthurst was arguing for 'captive breeding' of slaves coupled with better treatment, but given the amount of money to be made from plantations, he held back from suggesting emancipation. Indeed, he had much to gain from such a 'captive breeding programme': it would save him money buying slaves! After all, his father had a large sugar plantation to run, which no doubt hugely influenced his views! With little to no investment he could increase his number of slaves without the trouble of paying for them; literally free labour. The Rev. William Henry was born on a slave plantation: he knew all about the slave trade and the working conditions on plantations first hand. He and his brother inherited Grove Plantation on Demerara from their father Rev. Henry Coulthurst. In his will proved on 1 August 1792 the Rev. Henry left his house and specified enslaved people in Barbados to his wife Constantia for life and then to his daughter Margaret, and the rest of his estate, after two specific legacies to his oldest son and his daughter, equally to his sons William Henry, Mathew, William, Conrade and Tempest 'share and share alike'.[11] The Rev. William Henry inherited money and land rather than slaves from his brother Tempest when he died in 1816. The Rev. William Henry was a JP for the West Riding, and died at Heath Hall, Wakefield, whilst visiting his friend John Smyth in 1818. He is listed as a slave owner in 1817 – sixty-one females and fifty-six males on Demerara.[12]

Coulthurst was a man of his times: an evangelical, Tory High churchman. He opposed political reform and repeal of the Test and Corporation Acts (just like Wilberforce, who had a personal animosity for Unitarians) and was for war with France. He made money from slaves and saw no contradiction in his actions as a slave owner and a man of the cloth: although St Paul's New Testament Epistles don't condemn slavery, they argue that enslaved people must be treated fairly as brethren and at the same time called for slaves to 'obey their masters'. But while some clergymen used Christian scriptures to justify slavery, others were scouring the Bible to find references to help end the practice. The Unitarian poet Fanny Holcroft summed up this dichotomy of Christianity being for and against slavery in her poem of 1797 'The Negro':

TRANSPIERC'D with many a streaming wound, The Negro lay, invoking death:

His blood o'erflowe'd the reeking ground He, gasping, drew his languid breath.

His sable cheek was ghastly, cold; Convulsive groans their prison broke:

His eyes in fearful horror roll'd, while thus the wretch his anguish spoke:

'Accursed be the Christian race; Insatiate is their iron foul:

To hunt our sons, their fav'rite chace, they goad and lash without control.

'Torn from our frantic mother's breast, we bear our tyrant's galling chains;

Deny'd e'en death, that lulls to rest, The keenest woe, and fiercest pains.

From sun to sun the Negro toils; No smiles approve his trusty care;

And, when th' indignant mind recoils, His doom is whips, and black despair.

Yet Christians teach faith, hope, and love: Their God of mercy oft implore;

But can barbarian's mercy prove, or a benignant God adore?'

The abolition movement in Halifax waned till the 1806 general election thrust the subject back into the national psyche.

Leeds

Once more to the fore in Leeds was Thomas Wright, owner-editor of the *Leeds Intelligencer* and self-appointed spokesperson of the Evangelical Tories of Leeds. With surprising foresight, Thomas argued that even though Wilberforce's bill had failed 'the genie was out of the bottle' and abolition was now inevitable:

> . . . it is to be regretted that this question, however dictated by motives of humanity, should have been brought incautiously forward. The first object was to meliorate the condition of the slaves. For the event of the abolition, however desirable, a long train of preparation was necessary, the neglect of which it is to be feared may be productive of very serious consequences. A spirit of apprehension and distrust is excited among the planters, and the slaves whose minds are now agog with freedom, having once had that object proposed to them, are no longer to be satisfied with all that policy at present allows to be granted to them – a milder condition of servitude.[13]

Wright reported in December 1791 that in the light of Wilberforce's bill being defeated for the second time in 1791:

> The intention of the Methodists to promote a subscription towards forwarding the abolition of the Slave Trade may be eventually more productive that then opposite part are at present aware of; their subscriptions are usually, if not individually large, very general when inforced by their teaching, and 2,000,000 six pence's would make a very formidable sum coming from one quarter only.[14]

A meeting was held in Leeds on 17 February 1792:

> At a numerous and respectable meeting of the inhabitants of this Borough, held this day at the Rotation Office, to take into consideration the propriety of presenting a petition to the House of Commons for the Abolition of the Slave Trade.
> Wade Browne Esq. Mayor, in the Chair.

Resolved

That a petition be presented to the House of Commons by the inhabitants of this Borough, praying that Honourable House to reconsider their vote of the nineteenth of April last, respecting the Abolition of the Slave Trade, and to adopt such measures as in their wisdom may be seen best to prevent the further importation of Slaves into the British Colonies in the West Indies.

A petition to the purpose being read and approved,

Resolved

That the members of this County be requested to present the petition and to give it their earnest support.

Resolved,

That the thanks of this meeting be given to William Wilberforce Esq for his strenuous exertions in the case of justice and humanity; and to the Right Honourable William Pitt and the right Hon C J Fox and the other members of the House of Commons who co-operated with us.[15]

The Leeds petition stated:

That your petitioners are deeply affected, as men, by the wrongs which the Africans had long suffered from the inhuman commerce by the slave trade.

That they feel, as Englishmen, justly boasting the happiness of their unequalled freedom, the disgraceful inconsistency of being accessary to the slavery and destruction of nations, naturally and independent of, and unhostile to them.

That as Christians, they cannot but lament the invincible prejudices of these unenlightened heathens, against our common Christianity, which must arise in their minds from the cruelty and injustice of those Christian states who are the authors of their present misery.

Your petitioners, therefore beg leave humbly to request, that this honourable house will be pleased to reconsider their vote of the 19th of April last, respecting the abolition of this odious traffic; and to adopt such measures as in their wisdom may seem best to prevent further importation of slaves into the British Colonies in the West Indies.[16]

In printing the petition, Wright was publicly declaring that those who supported slavery and the slave trade had no right to call themselves Christian. This squarely aligned the cause of the Anglican Evangelicals and no doubt Quakers. Yet we note, Leeds was not universally supportive of abolition – we witnessed Rev. William Wood earlier, and no doubt the Glovers and Cadmans of Call Lane Unitarian Chapel with their local monopoly on slave produced tobacco, were against any changes to the status quo. By the 1820s the Cadmans had conformed and were good Anglicans. John Cadman (1724–97) had premises on Briggate in Leeds. Samuel Glover's children would also conform in the same period.

As tobacco wholesalers, the Glovers and Cadmans were an embedded part of the value-chains of the slave economy. The tobacco would have come into Yorkshire via Liverpool: tobacco production was directly link to the shipping of slaves from Africa to the Chesapeake, the back cargo being rum, sugar and tobacco. Slaves were captured in Africa, transported to the West Indies and then sold; the resulting profit was invested in the back cargo. Major tobacco traders often extended credit lines to their planters to finance slave voyages.[17]

Thomas printed the view of one objector in his newspaper, who argued the time was not right to campaign for abolition, that slave unrest and impending war meant that it should wait for some future time.[18] Despite this, Wright urged:

> As it is well understood that the Premier is favourable to the suppression of the African Slave trade and will exert himself on the occasion, provided he be convinced it is the general wish of the nation at large – the laudable design of petitioning Parliament upon the subject and making petitions as public as they may be, that they may act as a stimulus to others, cannot enough be commended. Such places, therefore, as mean to petition, have but little time left, as the great champion of the cause means to bring the business the twenty-ninth of this month. – Thus, conscious of the rectitude and importance of the cause: – Go and do ye likewise.[19]

Through his paper Wright argued for a boycott of sugar.[20] Remarkably for a Tory newspaper, Wright printed extracts from Thomas Paine's *Rights of Man* and argued for religious toleration:

Mr Paine, in the second part of his Rights of Man, gives this opinion of religion this concisely: 'Every religion is good that teaches man to be good; and I know of none that instructs him to be bad.' On this principle, civil governments should regulate their conduct respecting the several religions in a state; and ion this principle different sects should look with charity towards each other. It is time for men to pursue region as they do philosophy, with calmness and temper. They should not be all brandy, but like brandy and water.[21]

By referencing the highly controversial book by Paine and printing extracts, which was illegal at the time, Wright was courting controversy and imprisonment under the sedition laws. How Wright escape the censor and the magistrate we know not, unless he had 'friends in high places'. By 'brandy' we assume he means hot, and therefore the fire and brimstone of evangelical rhetoric, and water, we assume cool like Quakerism. However, as the 1790s drew on and the French revolution impacted British politics, the *Intelligencer* changed tack from one of almost Whiggish liberalism, to 'Church and King' denunciation of change and political reform, 'frothing at the bit' about the treason trials of 1794. Thomas Wright continued to print news about the slavery debate in Parliament, but the days of outspoken opposition to the state and calls for religious tolerance were gone.

Sheffield

Ever at the forefront of radical politics, Unitarian Joseph Gales announced in his paper the *Sheffield Register* on 20 August 1790 that he had published the *Life of Olaudah Equiano*. A week later Equiano himself was in Sheffield as a speaker, meeting with pro-abolition supporters. Gales encouraged locals to attend, then took to task London newspapers for their offensive language:

> The most pitiful thing we have lately seen, appeared in the London papers of last week, in the form of a petition from the '[pejorative simian terms] and other next of kin to the African Negroes,' attempting to prove them of the same species; and under the appearance of admiration, ridiculing the favourers of the abolition.
>
> Surely this unfortunate race is sufficiently degraded by being the objects of an iniquitous traffic, without being in every degree levelled with the beasts that perish.

With a little alteration, what Shakespeare says of a Jew may, with great propriety, be applied to the sable race – 'Hath not an African eyes, hands, organs and dimensions, senses, affections, passions? Fed with the same food, hurt by the same weapons, subject to the same diseases, healed by the same means, warmed and cooled by the same winter and summer as a European?' – Can this be denied? and yet there are people who are weak or base enough to affect disbelief.

Should any within the circle of our readers doubt the truth of this comparison, let them see GUSTAVUS VASA, the free African, now in Sheffield – his manners polished, his mind enlightened, and in every respect on a par with Europeans.[22]

Abolitionism in Sheffield merged with radical politics in winter 1790. In 1791 Samuel Shore, David Martin, Rev. James Montgomery,[23] and others founded the Sheffield Society for Constitutional Information, which, as in Manchester, was the regional branch of the London body headed by Major John Cartwright. Shore showed his moderation by wishing to remove any support of republicanism from an edited edition of the *Rights of Man*. Its spokesperson was, predictably, Joseph Gales. To support the aims of the society, Gales published a second newspaper, *The Patriot*, which Samuel Shore was keen to encourage. It was Shore who persuaded William Wilberforce to support the paper and to make it exempt from the recently-introduced newspaper tax; the tax was designed to push the price of newspapers beyond the reach of the 'common man' and reduce the circulation of anti-establishment ideas. *The Patriot* was an instant success with a readership of several thousand within weeks of first publication. The wealthy Rev. Benjamin Naylor, assistant minister at Upper Chapel, provided financial backing along with members of his congregation. Shore stated:

It is not the province of the Civil magistrates to direct, or to interfere with the religious opinions or practices of any members of the State, provided their conduct be not injurious to others.

That all the subjects of the State, conducting themselves in an equally peaceable Manner, are equally entitled not only to Protection in the possession of their civil rights, but also to any civil honours or emoluments, which are accessible to other subjects without any regard to their religion or practices.

Desiring nothing for ourselves but the same equal and liberal treatment, to which we think all other persons in a similar situation, are equally entitled, it is our earnest wish that an equal participation in all civil privileges may be obtained for Dissenters of every description, to whom nothing can be objected, besides their religious opinions or practices, and who can give that security for their Civil allegiance which the state ought to require.

That the protestant Dissenters of this country, have always had reason to complain of unjust treatment i.e. being disqualified to hold offices of Civil Trust or Power, though their behaviour has ever been peaceable, and loyal, and though they can even boast peculiar merit, as friends to the present government.

That it becomes Dissenters, as Men feeling their own disgraceful situation and the opprobrium which that reflects upon the country, to adopt every constitutional method of procuring the redress of their grievances and thus retrieve the honour of the nation.[24]

Shore no doubt had in the back of his mind the riots of the year before: celebrations of the French Revolution in Sheffield had taken a violent turn when many of the townspeople attacked the debtors' prison, letting the inmates out, and smashed the windows and furniture of the Duke of Norfolk's agent's house and then as the army presence increased went on the rampage at Broomhall, the home of the vicar James Wilkinson, smashing windows, furniture and books and attempting to set fire to the house. Having failed to do so they set fire to six of his hayricks. But the protest in Sheffield was not really about support for the French Revolution; it was poorest in society who had had 'lost out' with the Enclosure Acts, attacking those they deemed responsible for enclosing common land: the wealthy elites and magistrates, the Rev. Wilkinson also being the chief magistrate. This was in essence an anti-Tory, anti-capitalist riot. Anti-slavery had become bound up with the rising tide of Jacobinism in the town.[25] Jacobinism was a major influence in international politics. This new ideology attempted to marry the Rousseauist civic humanist focus on public virtue and political liberty, with the rational empiricism of the Enlightenment.[26]

The Society declared on 14 March 1792:

This Society, composed chiefly of the Manufacturers of Sheffield, began about Four Months ago, and is already increased to nearly TWO THOUSAND MEMBERS, and is daily increasing, exclusive of the adjacent Towns and Villages, who are forming themselves into similar Societies.

Considering, as we do, that the Want of Knowledge and Information in the general Mass of the People has exposed them to numberless Impositions and Abuses, the Exertions of this Society are directed to the Acquirement of useful Knowledge, and to spread the same as far as our Endeavours and Abilities can extend,

We declare that we have derived more true Knowledge from the Two Works of Mr. Thomas Paine, intituled 'Rights of Man,' Part the First and Second, than from any other Author or Subject. The Practice as well as the Principle of Government is laid down in those Works, in a Manner so clear, and irresistibly convincing that this Society do hereby resolve to give their thanks to Mr. Paine for his Two said Publications, intituled 'Rights of Man,' Part 1st and 2d. Also,

Resolved unanimously, That the Thanks of this Society be given to Mr. Paine, for the affectionate Concern he has shown in his Second Work in Behalf of the Poor, the Infant, and the Aged; who, notwithstanding the Opulence which blesses other Parts of the Community, are, by the grievous Weight of Taxes, rendered the miserable Victims of Poverty and Wretchedness.

Resolved unanimously, That this Society, disdaining to be considered either of a Ministerial or Opposition Party (Names of which we are tired, having been so often deceived by both) do ardently recommend it to all their Fellow Citizens, into whose Hands these Resolutions may come, to confer seriously and calmly with each other on the Subject alluded to, and to manifest to the World that the Spirit of true Liberty is a Spirit of Order and that to obtain Justice it is consistent that we be just ourselves.

Resolved, unanimously, that these Resolutions be printed, and that a Copy thereof be transmitted to the Society for Constitutional Information in London; requesting their Approbation for Twelve of our Friends to be entered into their Society, for the Purpose of establishing a Connection and a regular Communication with that, and all other similar societies in the Kingdom.

By Order of the Committee.[27]

The organisation actively promoted Thomas Paine's *Rights of Man* and other radical publications. By November 1792 both the London Revolutionary Society (in what proved to be its swansong) and the more plebeian associations had endorsed the French Republic and the demise of monarchical 'tyranny'. 'It is a maxim of mine', wrote one Scottish radical, 'that a king should be sacrificed to the nation once in a hundred years.' In a new wave of Gallic euphoria, French freedom was extolled as being 'far superior' to British; toasts were raised to 'the Virtue of Revolutions'. In London two radical societies burnt in effigy George III's brother-in-law, the Duke of Brunswick. Such demonstrations of radical solidarity were capped by a large-scale festival in Sheffield celebrating the French army's success at Valmy. Here, in the provincial mecca of radicalism, 5,000–6,000 supporters participated in a parade through the streets in which a banner was displayed condemning Burke's contempt for popular radicalism and the government's prosecution of Paine in mass rally on 15 October. Tom's 'Truth' had become 'Libel' at the hands of the ministry, the banner declared, and British liberty was now in peril. It was a defiant assertion of popular rights in the face of government censure. On 27 November, a procession marched through Sheffield. French republican banners were displayed, the tricolor cockade was distributed and the bells of the parish church pealed in support of the French Revolution.[28] But events in Sheffield would not turn out well, as our next chapter will show.

Wakefield

When in 1792 the call was made for a second mass petition, none came from Wakefield. In the highly-charged political situation for Unitarians following the Priestley riots (see the next chapter), speaking out against the government's policy of supporting the slave trade was not necessarily a good thing, as it could have drawn on the wrath of the mob. Yet the chapel's youthful assistant minister, the Rev. Thomas Johnstone, preached in in February 1792 that '. . . arising from equality of nature, the practice that has long prevailed among us, of extending our commerce to the human species, men who have never done us the smallest imaginable injury, must be utterly condemned'.[29]

The sermon was printed only for private distribution; thus, Johnstone was speaking to his own congregation and like-minded individuals. The Rev. Johnstone's preaching at Westgate at this time was so successful that the congregation enjoyed a period of rapid expansion.

In 1791 side galleries were erected in the chapel to accommodate the expanding congregation. Thomas Johnstone (1768–1856) was born at Stanstead in Essex in November 1768. His father was a Dissenting minister among the Independents; and the son, having determined to devote himself to the same calling, was sent to the Dissenting academy at Daventry, in Northamptonshire. The theological tutor at Daventry at this time was the Rev. Thomas Belsham, who would become a Unitarian of note. Johnstone studied under Belsham at Daventry and at the Unitarian Academy at Hackney taught by Andrew Kippis. After being a year at Hackney, he was invited to settle at Wakefield, as assistant to the Rev. William Turner in 1790. Clearly much was thought of the ambitious young man. He appointed minister at Westgate in 1792, a post he held till 1833. Johnstone's politics were very left wing, and he would be imprisoned for sedition.[30]

In September 1795 William Wilberforce arrived at Thornes House, where he dined and in the evening 'walked and talked – Jas Milnes rambling about religion and politics – good natured and well intentioned'.[31] Clearly Wilberforce's dislike of Unitarians was not yet as fully formed as it was to become in his public denunciation in 1797 in his book *A Practical View* we mentioned earlier.

James Milnes was the son of James Milnes Snr who had been a dominant local force in the Yorkshire Association and a prominent local supporter of Pitt. He had married Mary Anne Busk in February 1778. She was the eldest daughter of Hans Busk and had brought James a £150,000 dowry on their marriage. Mary Ann was baptised 24 January 1756 at Call Lane Arian Chapel in Leeds, and sister Rachel was baptised 22 February 1760, who went onto marry Dick Milnes.[32]

James Jnr showed rather different tendencies to his father and was an ardent Whig. In 1797 James was elected a corresponding member of the Manchester Literary and Philosophical Society, the leading scientific study society in the north of England.[33] James, unlike Dick and Jack, was very much part of the inner sanctum of the conservative side of the Whig party and on more than one occasion dined privately at Carlton House with the Prince of Wales.[34]

In London society, James Milnes and his wife held a marked degree of social influence. Mrs Milnes, at their flamboyant home on Piccadilly, hosted lavish 'routs' and balls. The press reported that 'Mrs Milnes commences her fashionable parties early in Easter week. Egremont House, after six months repair, is completed in its internal as well as external improvements.'[35] She held her second 'rout' a few days later, the press reporting on 20 April 1801 that 400 dined at Egremont, including the Prince of Wales, the Duchesses of Beaufort, Gordon, Bolton and Leeds, Viscounts Morpeth and Wentworth, Lord Portchester, Spencer and Harwood amongst others.[36] 'The Fashionable World' column in *The Morning Post and Gazetteer* reported on 8 June 1801 that 'Mrs Milnes would host a Rout at Egremont House'.[37] Clearly, Wilberforce was courting Milnes's influence in the campaign for abolition. The Milnes's social circle included the Prince of Wales, Prince William of Gloucester, Duchesses Beaufort, Buccleugh, Chambs, Bolton, Athol, Marchioness Salisbury, Hertford, Viscount Wentworth, Lords Harewood, Dundas, Generals Balfour and Bertie, Colonel Thornton, Mr Walpole – a veritable 'who's who' of London Society![38] From 1802 to his death in 1805 James sat as MP for Bletchingley in Surrey.[39]

The 1792 Bill

On the strength of the new petitions, Wilberforce went back to the house of Commons for a vote on abolition. His next bill for the abolition of the slave trade was heard on 2 April 1792: it was accompanied by Wilberforce giving a remarkable three-hour speech and he gained William Pitt's support. The bill was passed by 234 votes to 87. However, Henry Dundas's proposed amendment for gradual rather than immediate abolition was approved with 1 January 1796 as the date of the end of the slave trade. The bill was blocked in the Lords.[40]

The third person to speak in defence of the bill was the Unitarian Benjamin Vaughan who stated that, despite being the eldest son of a plantation owner and having control of a large plantation, he himself had never, and never would, own a slave, declaring 'I would sacrifice anything to a prudent termination of both evils, for all persons must with that neither had commenced' when referring to slavery and the slave trade. However, he went on to oppose the emancipation of negro slaves: as he feared not only a violent backlash against the former masters but also argued that the slaves lacked sufficient education to govern themselves, thus any change had to be gradual.[41] His radical left-wing politics led him back to Paris in June 1792, and upon his return to England he voted against the resumption of hostilities with France. Arrested in May 1794, he fled to France under Robespierre's protection, and was in America by 1795.[42] Vaughan was without doubt a complex man. In July 1792 his polemic *Concert to Princes* had this to say about slavery:

> Safe neither in property nor in person; denied the power of locomotion for their own purposes, but forced to abandon

their homes and families for the objects of power; dragged even into wars against their inclinations, there to provoke the revenge of an enemy, or to confirm their own slavery and that of other nations; their property and their labour pressed into the service of the despot or his subalterns, whenever it suits their purposes; no utterance allowed to any of their wrongs, each man being afraid even of his neighbour in private; these and a thousand similar circumstances, are so ordinary in despotic countries, as scarcely to excite notice: but madmen indeed are those, who are content to let such a lot become their own. [43]

His sympathies lay with freedom from the yoke of oppression, both it seems for those oppressed by a tyrannical state – England, those oppressed by war – France and Poland, and, we logically assume based on his speech in Parliament, African slaves. Yet Vaughan owned slaves and is today condemned as a racist slave owner, which has unfortunate connotations for Unitarians, despite his well-meaning intentions voting for the abolition of the slave trade. He was a man caught between his radical politics and commercial reality that made him extremely wealthy. As the Unitarian champion of the rights of man, Vaughan clearly felt trapped: on the one hand a Jacobin, the other a slave owner. Harsh criticism from the great MP and Unitarian Samuel Whitbread, who would have been otherwise a strong ally of Vaughan in the cause of political and religious liberty, must have stung. No doubt Vaughan's unease in the situation he found himself in, and unease with the slave trade, would have contributed to tensions amongst the slave-owning lobby. At Gravel Pit Lane, in addition to the Vaughan family we find Robert Lindsay, son-in-law of Ambrose Carter, a prosperous plantation owner who had a plantation on Jamaica – Barking Lodge was his property from 1817 to 1832 – where some of his children were born. His brother James Lindsay DD ran a school and preached at Newington Green. [44]

In response to the rejection of the bill, the Unitarian poet Anna Laetitia Barbauld published her 'Epistle to William Wilberforce Esq.' on the Rejection of the Bill for Abolishing the Slave Trade, which not only lamented the fate of the slaves, but warned of the cultural and social degeneration the British could expect if they did not abandon slavery. Anna was a prolific writer admired by Samuel Johnson and William Wordsworth and was the wife of the minister at Newington Green Unitarian Chapel. Also censuring the government was the Unitarian and former Anglican priest Rev. Gilbert Wakefield, who for a few months had held a curacy in Liverpool, and had busied himself to rouse public opinion against the slave trade, declared:

> Now I should be glad to know upon what grounds the House of Commons could vindicate their conduct in refusing to listen to so general and unanimous a requisition for the abolition of this traffic from all denominations and descriptions of people, as, I suppose, has seldom been displayed on any other occasion. I would put the question especially to those servile prevaricating wretches, who had grounded their most specious pretensions of opposition to the Coalition-Members, in a tone of whining supplication, upon a determination 'to listen in all cases to the instructions of their constituents.' What language will undertake to stigmatize such reptiles with suitable severity?
>
> As for Mr. Wilberforce, his exertions in this cause have, I dare say, been very laudable; but I must beg leave to withhold my general commendations from a man, who prevaricated on the question of the test-laws, and can support our Minister in every profligate and unconstitutional measure of his administration with unblushing uniformity.
>
> And it is most wonderful to me, how any man, endowed with the smallest portion of discernment, and capable of the feeblest exertions of the reasoning faculty, can allow Mr. Pitt the merit of sincerity on this subject. I know many will be shocked at the uncharitableness of this insinuation: but before these good admirers of the Minister allow scope to their indignation, I must entreat them, I must entreat Mr. Pitt himself, to answer one plain question. But it IS ANSWERED, by facts of indubitable evidence, and convincing beyond his oath, or the united oaths of all the interested and prejudiced votaries of this gentleman under heaven: 'Mr. Pitt! had you conceived the abolition of the slave-trade necessary to the preservation of your power and to the maintenance of your place, COULD YOU NOT HAVE CARRIED THAT MEASURE? Answer me.'[45]

The Rev. Wakefield's disgust at Parliament, Pitt and Wilberforce is plain to see. Wilberforce, frequently lauded as the 'conscience of the nation', was quite happy to deny justice to others, supporting the suspension of habeas corpus, and voting in favour of laws that clamped down on freedom of speech and expression.

Chapter 17

State-Sponsored Terror

T he wave of public meetings and petitions across the country in spring 1792 were the last for a generation. The popular groundswell of support for abolition and reform was a growing political force, bolstered with support from groups like the Revolution Society, the London Corresponding Society and the resurgent John Cartwright. It was now that real-world politics intervened.

At stake were conflicting visions of society: that of Marat where governance was for the benefit and happiness of the people, and where the government failed the people were empowered to overturn authority, or Burke's vision of a conservative society, with fixed rules, whereby everyone knew their place and reform was a danger to order and reason. Burke argued that unfettered individual freedom could not deliver social or personal well-being. This was an argument about the very soul and direction of the country: Marat's social idealism, or Burke's conservatism. The debate rapidly became an escalating battle of political rhetoric and mobilisation: of reform against conservatism. Tied to the demands for reform was the abolition of African slavery and of religious tests in public life, an increase in the electoral franchise, the ending of 'rotten boroughs' and questions about the very nature of government: all now coalesced into a heady mix of reformist radical politics. The fight for religious liberty, economic and political reform and that of slavery was intimately tied together. It was now that Wilberforce, an ardent Tory, joined the attack against reform. On 1 December 1792 the government issued a royal proclamation mobilising the militia to meet the 'radical invasion'. Earlier, on 20 November, John Reeves had announced the formation of a loyalist association, the Association for Preserving Liberty and Property against Republicans and Levellers, at the Crown and Anchor tavern in London, to counteract the groundswell of 'sedition' and encouraged like-minded souls to do the same. Within months his call, assisted by the government's press network, was answered by 1,500 local societies, creating a movement of prodigious proportions. Reeves was backed by Pitt and his government, who had conceived a programme of deliberate persecution of the voices of opposition. Reeves's populism for 'Church and King' and 'John Bull and England' stirred up public opposition to political reform and 'the other' i.e. Unitarians, Jews, Catholics, and nascent trade unionist ideas. Charles James Fox denounced the Association's publications and claimed that had they been printed earlier in the century they would have been prosecuted as treasonable Jacobite tracts due to their advocacy of the divine right of kings. In a speech on 10 December 1795, the Whig politician described the Association as a system designed to run the country through 'the infamy of spies and intrigues'. Reeves's project was pre-eminently a policing operation. A lawyer, former governor of Newfoundland and paymaster of the Westminster police magistrates, his natural disposition was to encourage the surveillance and prosecution of Painite radicals. This was to be achieved in three ways. In the first instance the loyalist associations sought to enforce public conformity to the campaign against republicanism by mobilising local authorities and employers against radical sympathisers, sometimes to the point of pressuring all local householders to declare their allegiance. This strategy was buttressed by a strict surveillance of taverns and alehouses, whose landlords were threatened with the loss of their licences if they permitted radical groups to meet on their premises. Judging by the number of loyalist declarations by the alehouse keepers themselves, this warning was taken very seriously. Thomas Hardy later recalled that the loyalists 'overawed the publicans so much than none of them would admit us into their houses', forcing the London Corresponding Society to meet privately and continually to shift its rendezvous. Besides attempting to disrupt the activities of the radical societies by clamping down on public houses, the loyalist associations answered the government's call in May 1792 to sniff out sedition, corresponding with Whitehall on cases which seemed to merit Crown intervention, but also prosecuting some themselves. The creation of associations to co-ordinate and finance private prosecutions was not new; similar societies had been formed throughout the eighteenth century, sometimes in response to royal proclamations. But their extension into the political sphere was novel. The Friends of the Liberty of the Press, for example, claimed that such unauthorised sedition-hunting intruded upon private opinions and intimidated juries to acquiesce to the forces of reaction, thereby undermining any libertarian gains made by the Libel Act of 1792. The provincial press, in particular, was severely weakened, radical newspapers in the Midlands and North succumbing to either prosecution or intimidation.

Broadly speaking, loyalists hoped to close down radical space. Legal prosecutions or their threat were only part of this strategy. Equally important was the active propagation of loyalism. This was the birth of English nationalism, jingoism, xenophobia and above all else English exceptionalism, all of which still impact the modern world and current politics. William Roscoe, the Liverpool Unitarian and MP for Liverpool 1806–07, wrote to the Marquis of Lansdowne complaining bitterly of Pitt's alarmist legislation 'where every man is called upon to be a spy upon his brother', adding he believed that 'the present war is not a war against the French but a war of the English aristocracy against the friends of reform in this country'.[1] He was perfectly correct in his opinion.

Paralleling official legal actions against accused traitors were unofficial vigilante acts by private citizens and institutions against persons whose liberal expressions alarmed others. These are the 'unusual suspects' of this book. As in the McCarthyite witch-hunts in 1950s America, the victims of this unregulated 'hegemonic' blacklisting are found disproportionately in academic and cultural arenas. National religious and educational bodies purged liberals, and promising literary careers were nipped in the bud. The loss to British culture is immense, if inestimable. Both local and national issues stirred the passions of the rioters, from disagreements over public library book purchases, to controversies over Dissenters' attempts to gain full civil rights and their support of the French Revolution. One month before the riots, Joseph Priestley attempted to found a reform society, the Warwickshire Constitutional Society, which would have supported universal suffrage and short Parliaments. Although this effort failed, the efforts to establish such a society increased tensions in Birmingham. Priestley was in effect, endeavouring to emulate the Shores of Sheffield, Cartwright and Wyvill.

The riots started on 14 July 1791 with an attack on the Royal Hotel, Birmingham, the site of a banquet organised in sympathy with the French Revolution. Then, beginning with Priestley's church and home, the rioters attacked or burned four Dissenting chapels, twenty-seven houses, and several businesses. Many of them became intoxicated by liquor that they found while looting, or with which they were bribed to stop burning homes. A small core could not be bribed, however, and remained sober. The rioters burned not only the homes and chapels of Dissenters, but also the homes of people they associated with Dissenters, such as members of the scientific Lunar Society.

193

While the riots were not initiated by Pitt's administration, the national government was slow to respond to the Dissenters' pleas for help. Local Birmingham officials seem to have been involved in the planning of the riots, and they were later reluctant to prosecute any ringleaders. The industrialist James Watt wrote that the riots 'divided [Birmingham] into two parties who hate one another mortally'. After the riots, Joseph Priestley argued in his *An Appeal to the Public on the Subject of the Birmingham Riots* (1791) that this cooperation had not in fact been as amicable as generally believed. Priestley revealed that disputes over the local library, Sunday Schools and church attendance had divided Dissenters from Anglicans. The riots revealed that the Anglican gentry of Birmingham were not averse to using violence against Dissenters whom they viewed as potential revolutionaries. They had no qualms, either, about raising a potentially uncontrollable mob. The mob and populism were Pitt's target through the work of John Reeves. In defence of Priestley, the 77-year-old William Turner preached:

> The flames of religious bigotry were rekindled, in so extraordinary a manner, against the authors excellent friend. But may we not hope, that it is now too late for persecution ever more prevailingly to lift up its head, and that the horrors of 1791 are rather to be considered as among the last struggles of an expiring daemon, which is not long to be permitted to trouble the peaceful society of men?[2]

Edmund Burke said on 11 May 1792, when he dismissed calls to bring the evidence concerning the Priestley riots before the House of Commons, that the Unitarians were 'connected with the Revolution Society here, and the Club of the Jacobins in Paris, and adopted the same principles to the fullest extent'. Indeed, in his *Appeal* concerning the riots in Birmingham, Priestley confirmed this connection by noting that he had received messages of condolence not only from other Protestant Dissenting congregations, but also from six Jacobin clubs in France and three patriotic societies in England. It is hard, therefore, not argue that Westgate Chapel, and for a time Upper Chapel in Sheffield were not hotbeds of English Jacobinism and that Jacobin ideas had a powerfully transformative effect on elements of these congregations.

In Wakefield, under the Seditious Writings Act, both Rev. Thomas Johnstone and Robert Bakewell challenged the proclamation: Johnstone declared it impacted on the liberty of freedom of thought and expression. Both men were taken to York Assizes and imprisoned for their radical beliefs. The windows of the parsonage were smashed, as were those of the chapel and of nearby homes of members of the congregation. Pemberton Milnes was slandered as a 'feign designing son of Cromwell'. Violence would erupt again three short years later.[3]

The burning of Birmingham and Kingswood Unitarian chapels and the wholesale destruction of Priestley's house and that of William Smith was not isolated. Across the Pennines in Manchester, the target for the loyalist mobs was the radical newspaper the *Manchester Herald*, its premises being broken up by a 'Church and King' mob over three or four nights in December 1792 – the constables refused to act and indeed connived in the riot! Birch and Falkner, the printers of the radical newspaper, left for America in spring of 1793, and the last issue of the *Manchester Herald* appeared on 23 March 1793. At the same time that the *Manchester Herald* fell to the mob, Cross Street Chapel was attacked and was almost burnt to the ground for harbouring Revolutionary ideas. The 'Church and King Club of Manchester' on hearing that Cooper and Watts were in Paris, gathered in St Ann's Square, to welcome the proclamation against seditious writings and marched on Cross Street Chapel crying 'Down with the Rump' and 'Church and King'. Failing to gain entry, the mob endeavoured to set fire to the chapel. The mob made a similar attempt on Mosley Street Unitarian Chapel. Walker's warehouse was attacked in December 1792. Thomas Cooper fled to America.[4] This was an end to Unitarian involvement with abolition in Manchester, Birmingham and Wakefield. In Liverpool, the Literary and Philosophical Society, of which William Roscoe and William Rathbone were members, was silenced by anti-Jacobin violence.

Rioting was just the start: arrests followed. In September 1793 the English Unitarian Thomas Palmer (1747–1802), then minister at Dundee, was sentenced to seven years' transportation for sedition. This was to be the start of a government crackdown against reformers. The government went to war against its own people to keep the voice of dissent and reform silenced. What followed became known as the 'Treason Trials'. In early summer 1794 William Pitt rounded up and arrested his most vocal opponents. Over thirty radicals were arrested; three were tried for high treason: Thomas Hardy, John Horne Tooke and John Thelwall. We note with pride that Equiano was an active member of the radical London Corresponding Society, which campaigned to extend the vote to working men. In 1792 he lodged with the society's founder Thomas Hardy. In Birmingham, the Unitarian printer John Belcher was arrested, and so was John Thompson who was Rev. Dr Priestley's printer and book seller. In Leicester Richard Phillips, a member of Unitarian Great Meeting, editor of the *Leicester Herald* and the *Monthly Magazine* was gaoled for two years. The liberal press was closed down and its presses smashed by loyalist attacks. The *Anti-Jacobin Review* described Unitarianism as a 'virus' to be stamped out as nothing more than 'Jacobin insolence'.[5]

The summer of 1793 had seen rumours circulate in Manchester about Thomas Walker: an informer, Thomas Dunn, working for the chief magistrate the Rev. John Griffith 'reported' the words he had used against the king, and caused alarm that Walker was arming and training 'a small army'. On the basis of Dunn's testimony, Walker was arrested on 12 May 1794 and put on trial for treason. The jury heard testimony about the attack on Walker's warehouse, and his subsequent collecting of arms, which were later fired over the head of the crowd. Dunn on re-examination was found to be drunk, and his evidence on armed men was directly contradicted and Dunn himself was tried for perjury. Walker's radicalism cost him dear: the cotton and fustian business he ran failed as he was ostracised by the loyalist elites in Manchester.

At the same time as anti-Jacobin hysteria was reaching its apogee in Manchester, across the Pennines in Sheffield, Joseph Gales and Henry Redhead Yorke had published their radical address to Sheffield on 1 April 1794:

> 1st. That the people being the true and only source of government, the freedom of speaking and writing upon any subject, cannot be denied to the members of a free government, without offering the grossest insult to the majesty of the people. 2d. That, therefore the condemnation of citizens Muir, Palmer, Skirving, Maragot, and Gerrald to transportation, for exposing the corruptions of the British government, was an act better suited to the maxims of a despotic than a free government 3rd. That the Address which has now been read, be presented to the king, in behalf of the above persecuted patriots. 4th. That in every country where the people have no share in their government, taxation is tyranny. 5th. That therefore a government is tyrannical or free, in proportion as the people are equally or unequally represented. 6th. Convinced of this truth, it is the opinion of this meeting that the people ought to demand as a right, and not petition as a favour, for universal representation. 7th. That therefore we will petition the House of Commons no more on this subject. 8th. That the committee of the Sheffield Constitutional Society be desired to see that the above resolutions be carried into effect; and that they prepare an address to the British nation,

explanatory of the motives which have induced this meeting to adopt the resolution of no more petitioning the House of Commons on the subject of reform.[6]

Gales and Yorke surely must have known they were 'treading on thin ice' and would likely become the target for arrest; despite this, the pair organised a mass open-air meeting on Castle Hill, Sheffield for 'the Friends of Justice, Liberty and Humanity' on Monday 7 April 1794. Contemporary reports put attendance at between 10,000 and 12,000 – but that number was possibly inflated by Gales and his newspaper in order to enhance the political importance and impact of the Sheffield group. In an impassioned speech Yorke boldly declared:

> Citizens! I repeat my former assertion. Go on as you hitherto have done in the culture of reason. Disseminate through the whole of your country, that knowledge which is so necessary to Man's happiness, and which you have yourself acquired. Teach your children, and your countrymen, the sacred lesson of virtue, which are the foundations of all human polity. Teach them to respect themselves, and to love their country. Teach them to do unto all men, as they would that they should do unto them, and their love shall not be confined to their country, but to the whole human race. When such a revolution of sentiment, shall have dispersed the mists of prejudice; when by the incessant thundering's from the press, the meanest cottage of our country shall be enlightened, and the sun of Reason shall shine in its fullest meridian over us.[7]

Yorke's speech was met with rapturous applause. It is hardly surprising, given his turn of phrase, that out of the meeting came a call for the emancipation of slaves:

> That we feel ourselves not only ashamed, but indignant, that the British Government should be actively engaged in the traffic and slavery of human beings.
> That as no compromise can be made between freedom and tyranny, between virtue and vice, justice and injustice, we think it our duty not to confine ourselves to the mere abolition of the slave trade, which would be sacrificing a right to a convenience, but to petition for the total emancipation of the Negro slaves.

That the petition to the King now reads 'for the total and unqualified Abolition of Negro Slavery', is approved.[8]

Not just an end to the slave trade, but total emancipation of all slaves was demanded by the people of Sheffield. Sheffield, the radical city, dared to boldly declare for freedom of slaves: France had freed all her slaves earlier in the year, and the Jacobins of Yorkshire likewise campaigned for immediate abolition in England. This was one of the earliest calls for total abolition in the country, led by Unitarians. But after this burst of optimism dark clouds were on the horizon.

Gales and Yorke had dared to mount a campaign against the suspension of habeas corpus and openly flouted the Seditious Writings Act, claiming it was a direct infringement of civil liberties. Gales was now considered a dangerous man and was charged with treason. Ever since he acclaimed the victory of 'our French brethren over despots and despotism' in 1792, he was aware that he would not receive a fair trial, so Gales decided to flee the country. After publishing the last edition of the *Sheffield Register* on 27 June, 1794, Gales escaped to Germany and then America, financed by Samuel Shore. In 1795, he travelled to Philadelphia, Pennsylvania, where he worked as a printer, bookkeeper and as a journalist covering the United States Congress. He then established the *Independent Gazetteer* newspaper. He moved to Raleigh, North Carolina and in October 1799, published the first issue of his *Raleigh Register*. The Whig-supporting paper was influential throughout the state for the next 60 years. He died in 1841 and is buried in Raleigh's City Cemetery.

At the same time as Gales fled for his life, his future brother-in-law Henry Redhead Yorke left Sheffield hoping to join his brother in Switzerland. He too was a wanted man for advocating universal suffrage and an end to slavery. Yorke's intention was to fight for Republican France but he was caught in Hull and was imprisoned. His brother was killed in action fighting for the young republic. Yet this was not the end of Sheffield radicalism. With Joseph Gales arrested, James Montgomery, a radical Moravian minister, entered into partnership with the Rev. Benjamin Naylor who provided the financial backing for him to launch the *Iris* newspaper to replace the defunct *Register*. Naylor was editor of the new paper. He was more cautious than Gales had been, and publicly broke with Montgomery. Naylor, seeing the fate that befell Gales and Yorke, and then Montgomery who was arrested for 'seditious writing' in questioning the arrest of Gales and Yorke fell into line with Pitt and the 'Church and King Mob'.

The years 1794–5 were marked by low wages and high food prices. A hard winter and a disastrous harvest in 1795 resulted in grain prices rising rapidly. Cut off from imports of grain from Russian ports in the Baltic, prices rose from 52s a quarter in April to 80s by July, and then reached 150s a quarter by August! Food riots broke out. Radicalism was given fresh impetus with Montgomery being released from prison and buying out Naylor's share of the *Iris*. Montgomery, through the paper, threw his weight behind the clamour for peace, cheaper food and Parliamentary reform. The last great mass meeting of the era was organised by the Rev. James Montgomery on 4 August 1795 calling for peace, abolition of the Corn Laws and Parliamentary reform. Over 20,000 gathered to hear Montgomery speak. The local magistrates panicked, read the Riot Act in secret and authorised Colonel Athorpe, at the head of the Loyal Sheffield Volunteers, to open fire on the peaceful gathering if they did not disperse. From the heavily censored press reports, we know that Athorpe panicked and gave the orders to open fire: two people were killed and over fifty were wounded, many dying of their wounds later. The Rev. Montgomery lambasted Athorpe's conduct in print: Montgomery was arrested for speaking truth to power and was tried for sedition once more. He was faced with the stark choice of moderation or martyrdom. Athorpe faced no charges and the magistrates congratulated him for his conduct.[9]

State sanctioned terror was the order of the day. For liberals and radicals alike, things went from bad to worse. In 1795 the 'Gagging Acts' came into being:

1. The Treasonable Practices Act forbade the expression of views calculated to bring king or government into contempt.
2. The Seditious Meetings Act forbade assemblies of more than fifty persons without prior notice and gave the magistrates power to disperse the onlookers if seditious observations were being made.

Fox spoke ten times in the debate on the acts. He argued that, according to the principles of the proposed legislation, Pitt should have been transported a decade before in 1785, when he had been advocating Parliamentary reform. Despite these obvious double standards from the Tory Party, Parliament passed the acts. More repression and censorship followed. The Newspaper Publication Act of 1798 required that all printing presses were to be registered in order to prevent the publication of material that criticized the government.

Protesting the status quo was now illegal: and calling for the abolition of slavery was to question the status quo. Under the new legislation it was now illegal to censure the government's action in not passing legislation to pass the abolition of the slave trade bill![10] Broadly speaking, loyalist attacks and legislation hoped to close down radical space through 'the institution of a system of terror, almost as hideous in its features, almost as gigantic in its stature, and infinitely more pernicious in its tendency, than France ever knew'.[11]

Seeking to wrest abolitionism from any taint of association with reform, Jacobinism and the ideals of the French Revolution, Wilberforce openly attacked Unitarians for their 'disgusting religion, morals and politics'.[12] Wilberforce knew that if he was to gain government support from the Tory benches on which he sat, he had to isolate abolitionism from reform: in doing so he alienated the majority of the Whigs in Parliament and of course Unitarians. In response to Wilberforce's attack, from his prison cell, where he had been imprisoned under the 'Gagging Acts' for daring to criticise the government, the Unitarian minister Rev. Gilbert Wakefield spoke out against Wilberforce's theology as totally inconsistent with the New Testament.[13] The Duke of Grafton, a former prime minister who was sympathetic to Unitarianism and attended Essex Street Chapel, thought that Wilberforce laboured under 'great but involuntary errors' in theology. The Rev. Thomas Belsham began a campaign in print that criticised Wilberforce's denunciation of Unitarians. Belsham declared Wilberforce's deformed doctrine was 'inconsistent with reason, unfounded in Scripture, and injurious to morality'.[14] Belsham thundered:

> What right can Mr. W. have to invade the province of the Omniscient Judge, and to arraign his fellow-servants, and fellow-Christians, of 'moral depravity,' because they strictly adhere to, what they believe to be, the genuine doctrine of their common Master, and resolutely reject all opinions which in their judgment are unauthorized, and untrue, by whatever epithets they may be dignified, or by whomsoever they may be embraced, defended, or imposed?[15]

Wilberforce's underlying conservative inclinations and his vested interest in the existing social order led him to emphasise those aspects of Christianity that were conducive to stability rather than the more radical strands of Jesus' teaching, and repeat the arguments Burke made in his attack on the French Revolution. Wilberforce was no friend of reform, or non-evangelical Christians. He was a man loathed by political reformers and Unitarians. Indeed, Wilberforce's sons would write the Unitarian contribution to abolition out of history

Abolition outside of politics was stone dead. Yet it did come, as we shall explore in our next chapter, ironically with the death of Pitt!

Chapter 18

Abolition!

In the midst of the loyalist attacks and state repression, Wilberforce moved further consideration for the abolition of the slave trade on 26 February 1793. The motion was defeated by 61 votes to 53. Yet, undeterred and filled with dogged determination, on 14 May 1793 Wilberforce got leave to present a bill to limit temporarily, as a wartime measure, the importation of slaves into British colonies. The bill failed, but remarkably Wilberforce did succeed in a vote to suspend supply of slaves to foreign colonies in British ships, passed on 7 February 1794, but which was again blocked by the House of Lords. Voting in favour of the bill in the Commons were Dick Milnes and Benjamin Vaughan. Wilberforce presented another bill on 18 February 1796, and despite recent disturbances in the West Indies, he won the day by 26 votes for his motion to abolish the trade on 1 March 1797. Despite initial optimism, on the bill's second reading in the house, it failed 74 votes to 70 on 15 March. A new motion was presented on 15 May 1797 and was lost by 82 votes to 74 on first reading. Undeterred, Wilberforce again presented an abolition motion on 3 April 1798; unsurprisingly it was defeated by 87 votes to 83. Less than a year later the motion presented on 1 March 1799 was defeated by 84 votes to 54. Without support from the Whigs, who Wilberforce had done his best to alienate, the bill to abolish the slave trade could not pass due to insufficient support from both sides of the House. Yet despite Wilberforce's best efforts, slavery and the slave trade were never far from the lips of the radical Unitarian clergy. Rev. Johnstone proclaimed from the pulpit of Westgate Chapel in February 1801 that the distress caused to the country by the war with France coupled with famine was 'God's vengeance' for allowing the continuation of slavery:

There is one other body of men to whom I should peculiarly wish the question to be asked: Are there not with you, even with you, sins against the Lord your God? These are the hardened and the brutal traffickers in human flesh, the slave merchants, who, devoured with the thirst of gain, can tear from their native homes, from all the endearments of life, from all that intercourse, which love, which friendship, or the warm emotions of a parent's heart, can render sweet and attractive, thousands of their fellow-creatures, and doom them, for life, to slavery's galling labour. This is indeed, a crying sin against us; and while permitted to exist in so wanton a violation of humanity, as not to have even the plea of policy or profit in its favour, it must draw down upon us the divine wrath. While this horrid stain remains upon our national character, never shall we be at a loss to account for any combination of misfortunes which may rise against us; for, if it exist not at the immediately preceding cause of trouble, so wisely arranged are the events of Providence for the correction of vice, that sooner or later such a profligate and abandoned protraction of iniquity must be followed by ruin. What we have yet suffered from the evils of war, from ruined trade, or from failing harvests, are trifles to what we may expect from the Great Avenger of human blood. Were we, indeed, finally plunged into the ocean, and lost in the wide waste of overwhelming waters, to become a subject of vain inquiry to the future mariner, could the eye of enlightened humanity, as it read our infamy in the annals of past history, do any other than own the divine justice in the event? Should we not be pointed to by the instructive moralist of future generations, as an awful memento, that there is a God who judgeth in the earth, that there is a God who avengeth the violation of the sacred rights of man.[1]

Here he condemned the slave trade and made an oblique reference to Thomas Paine's most famous book! Paine's work was illegal: Johnstone was flirting with the very edges of the law in standing against slavery and for the rights of man!

No further motions on the slave trade were presented till 30 May 1804 when Wilberforce's motion on its first reading was passed by the Commons by 124 votes to 49. The motion passed its second reading on 27 June, but the Lords adjourned it on 2 July. A year later, Wilberforce's motion was defeated at its second reading on 8 February 1805, by 77 votes to 70.

With the death of William Pitt, on 21 January 1806, the king reluctantly called a new government, termed 'the Ministry of all the Talents'. Charles James Fox, the Whig leader, was now back in office as Foreign Secretary. Pitt's first cousin Lord William Grenville was Prime Minister. The Whigs were ascendant. Fox's goals were simple: first to abolish the slave trade and second to make peace with France. Fox informed Wilberforce that he would be introducing a bill to Parliament to abolish the slave trade. It was Fox and not Wilberforce who played a major role in the subsequent drafting of a bill and the canvassing of Parliamentary support. Wilberforce and the Tories had alienated the Whigs and reformists: Fox was the vital personality in 1806. At the bill's first reading, Fox obtained unqualified success in carrying the vote for the abolition of the slave trade on 10 June 1806. Fox's second great aim for the Parliament was to end the hated and costly war with France and make peace with Napoleon. But tragedy befell the nation when the great man died on 13 September 1806.[2] The Tories continued the war, against which the Whigs and radicals loudly protested, organising national peace petitions under the name of 'friends of the people', the name used by Marat for his radical newspaper in France. The government fell on 24 October 1806.

Slavery was now back at the forefront of the national conscience. What happened next with the fall of the 'Ministry of all the Talents' was a referendum on the slave trade. The 1806 general election ran from 29 October to 2 December 1806.

A key figure in regional politics was Jack Milnes. Having been in Revolutionary Paris in 1791–3, he had lived in Kent before returning to Paris in 1801, and settled in London in the course of 1802, before leaving England with his young family to live with his brother Sir Robert Shore Milnes in Canada. He returned to Yorkshire in spring 1806 and was now living in his cousin's house in Sheffield, Meersbrook Hall, as a single parent to three children following the death of his young wife. Because of his politics and open support for the French revolution he was ostracised by society at large as Lady Elizabeth Spencer Stanhope reports:

November 14 1808
Last Monday we met the Mills'[3] at Grange . . . We saw their Jack Mills, the Democrat, and his little boy who is christened Alfred Ankerstrom Mirabeau. Ankerstrom was the man who killed the King of Sweden; Mirabeau the chief author of the French Revolution. He was godfather to this boy. Before you re-instate the Bourbons, should you not extirpate this man?[4]

By now Jack was verging on bankruptcy: the fine mansion on Westgate in Wakefield, which included a 60ft-long picture gallery, was let to Robert Bakewell and he had recently sold the contents. Yet this did not stop him taking to the platform once again. Jack Milnes, Bob Bakewell and Thomas Lumb ran the campaign for Fawkes in the West Riding. Wilberforce was in Halifax in 1806, campaigning in the general election. His diary records:

On Friday, off with William Hey to Wakefield—met a mile off, and drawn by people into town to inn, where addressed the people in the marketplace—vast crowd, and dragged in carriage again to Naylor's, and thence to Dawson's. Letters, and off for Dewsbury, where dragged, and addressed again. Carriage broke and stopped. Called Mr. Pooley's. Heckmondwyke, dragged, and speechified again—dreadful roads. Reached Pye-nest, two miles beyond Halifax, (Edward's,) by a quarter past seven, evening —found party of fifteen or sixteen just sitting down to dinner, having waited for me. I grazed hard against loaded waggon when dark, going opposite directions. One inch nearer, had infallibly been broken, and probably overset. Providential; but astonishing not an accident of any kind to speak of since leaving Lyme; and I have borne little inclemencies of weather and fatigue, much beyond what I thought possible . . . Saturday, after breakfast large party of gentlemen came on horseback from Halifax to Pye-nest to convey me to town, though a very rainy morning. The horses drew me up the hill, and the people to Cloth Hall, about a mile. Much hurt on first entering to read account of Samuel Thornton's defeat. Some hissed, and kept crying, Fawkes for ever; I doubt not, from believing, not unreasonably, that some secret junction between Lascelles and me. (I have since found the hissers were the ringers, who had been, by a little foolish zeal of our friends, prevented ringing for Fawkes.) I walked 'round the Hall— immense concourse, and afterwards addressed the people from the steps. Then Col. Hutton descanted on Lascelles's merits, and asked why not also there. Edwards explained. They would chair me to the inn. One man threw something which hit me on the forehead, happily not hard, and I kept watching afterwards. Amazing squeeze, and a very awkward operation. Taken to the Talbot. Bad, especially going through the gorges of the gates and narrow streets. Wrote letters till dinner, and Mr. W. Lawson came in about three, and

206

told me report that Lascelles had resigned. Dinner, and we sent to W. Walker's for the letter, which written by Fawkes's brother. About eight o'clock I received a letter, express from Lascelles, to announce that he resigned. Dickey Walker, Thomas Atkinson, Mr. Whitacre, Edward W. Rawson, &c. &c. two rooms full; about sixty-five to seventy in all. Home, Pye-nest, and bed at ·one. Sunday. 59 Old church, Halifax. Dr. Coulthurst preached. Monday. Letters all morning, till with Edwards to Whitacre's, Wood Hall, near Huddersfield. Mr. Ratcliffe and party, supped and bed.[5]

On the back of Wilberforce's visit, Dr John Thomson re-founded the Halifax Committee for the Abolition of the Slave Trade. According to Unitarian historian John Goodchild M. Univ, Dr John Thomson (1781–1818) was a Methodist Unitarian who attended Northgate End Chapel, where Law Atkinson and the Edwards worshipped as we noted earlier. So beloved by the community in Halifax was Tomson that a large monument was erected to him in white marble, designed by Sir Francis Legatt Chantrey and paid for by public subscription. It stood in Northgate End chapel and was moved to Liverpool Museum when the building was demolished to make way for Halifax bus station in 1983 against much vocal opposition. Dr Thomson had trained in Edinburgh before moving to Halifax to succeed Dr Joseph Hulme as 'Halifax Physician' and was a founder of the Halifax Dispensary in 1807 along with Dr Coulthurst: the latter invested some of his wealth from slavery to improve the community of Halifax. Three of his hymns appeared in Robert Aspland's collection of Unitarian hymns in 1813. He died in Leeds of typhus aged 37. Thomson was a correspondent of the abolitionist minister Rev. Lant Carpenter.[6] Yet, we note, not a single petition was sent from Yorkshire in 1806 in support of abolition. Abolition made the newspapers, but it was now detached from the 'real world' with limited local-level campaigning. The issue was in the hands of Parliament, just as Wilberforce and his Tory colleagues had engineered in the 1790s.

As expected, in 1806 Wilberforce stood on an abolitionist platform, as did Fawkes whose cultivation of the West Riding clothing merchants and workers was so successful that of 9,056 promises for him, 6,582 were from the West Riding. This underlines the crucial role in Yorkshire elections of the cloth merchants, and above all of the three men from Wakefield. Lascelles, whose support from most of the landed gentry was unavailing, withdrew a week before the election, complaining afterwards of 'the common cause made against me by the clothiers, and the secret and matured arrangement with which I had to contend'. No doubt he was bitter at the Whig organisation across the county. The Whigs at the 1806 election had a thirty-seat majority over the Tories.[7]

It was now inevitable that the slave trade would be abolished: the Whig ascendancy and support for abolition made the outcome of any vote a forgone conclusion. At its second reading on 23 February 1807 the motion for the abolition of the slave trade was passed 83 votes to 16, and received the Royal Assent on 25 March 1807.[8] Despite open persecution nationally, William Smith was the vital link in the chain between Wilberforce and his evangelicals who were hostile to dissent and above all Unitarians and political reform, and the Dissenting Whigs in Parliament and society at large.

Smith worked hard at lobbying MPs during the final debates. He had appeared alongside Clarkson for over 20 years, but despite his pivotal role, Smith and the Unitarians remains little mentioned in traditional accounts of abolition – this perhaps stems from the way in which Smith's role was marginalised and disparaged in the *Life of Wilberforce* edited by his evangelical sons and Wilberforce's own crusade against Unitarians. William Smith's objectives in public life – Parliamentary reform, emancipation of religious dissenters from civil disabilities and the abolition of the slave trade – were not at the outset a party matter. Pitt's abandonment of the first two key issues ensured Smith's gradual conversion to Fox and the Whigs. As with most Whigs he was enthusiastic for the goals of the French Revolution, visiting Paris with Benjamin Vaughan before he resumed his seat in 1790. Perhaps due to Vaughan's influence, he converted to Unitarianism and publicly condemned Burke's reactionary and divisive politics. Smith was a vocal champion of abolition. Losing his seat in 1806, his only regret at being out of Parliament was missing the successful conclusion of the campaign for abolition of the slave trade, and was now obliged to observe from the gallery.[9]

With the fall of the Grenville-Fox ministry in April 1807 due to the recalcitrance of the king over Catholic emancipation, the nation went to the polls again. Fawkes withdrew and rather than allow Lascelles to retake the seat, Earl Fitzwilliam sponsored his son Lord Milton. The election was hugely costly: Fitzwilliam spoke of spending £150,000 and Lascelles relied on his Barbados slave plantations to finance his electioneering to the tune of £140,000. Wilberforce, who prided himself on the support of 'volunteers' against the 'others' rebuked such extravagance by spending a modest £28,000, enabling him to return half the £64,000 raised for him by subscription in Yorkshire and by his friends all over the country.[10]

The general election ran from 4 May until 9 June 1807. Milton's success over Lascelles was in part due to a central committee of nineteen gentlemen who supervised the work of local committees and sixty-seven attorneys were employed as agents. Of the committee, we find once again Thomas Lumb, Robert Bakewell and Jack Milnes, who canvassed the West Riding clothiers.[11] Jack's contribution was vital, as victory was centred around mobilising the vote of the clothiers and non-Anglicans as Jack Milnes commented in June 1807 to Earl Fitzwilliam:

> The dissenting ministers have had their reward from the liberal endeavours of the later administration and their names being recorded in the poll books for Lord Milton is enough for them; those men from principle and gratitude will be upon like occasions hearty in your Lordship's interest and indeed it will be an interest of some importance to preserve as the influence of the dissenting clergy has of late years become diffusedly great, as nearly one half of the clothing country have become dissenters of one denominations or another.[12]

The Tories could not believe the outcome, and the Tory-Church of England *Leeds Intelligencer* went as far as to denounce Lord Milton as being a Jacobin, and quite correctly, labelled his supporters as 'free thinkers, rabble rousers and Presbyterians'.[13] 'Presbyterian' was the cover-all term for Unitarian at the time, as was 'Protestant Dissenter'. The Leeds paper identified the 'power behind the throne' in the election. Elected as MP for Pontefract at the same time as Milton and Wilberforce was Dick Milnes's son, Robert Pemberton Milnes, relying on Fitzwilliam's encouragement and, more particularly, on the interest of his Whig connection by marriage, Viscount Galway. He was listed among the 'staunch friends' of the abolition of the slave trade.[14] It was this Parliament that enacted the legislation that brought the slave trade finally to an end.

It is too simplistic though to ascribe success solely to the Whig ascendancy. We must recall that slave plantation-owning MPs backed abolition. Why? The Dean of Middleham explains: 'It would immediately raise the value of the Negroes, whose numbers also would be increased,'[15] through, to be crude, 'growing your own'. We must also remember that it was perfectly possible to be against the slave trade and be a supporter of slavery: slavery was the bedrock on which the economy was built. The prevailing morality of the period did not question the institution of slavery: Revolutionary France had freed her slaves, so to suggest England did the same was tantamount to treason and dangerous Jacobinism! The losers were the slave-ship owners, the crews of these ships and the allied trades. No study has yet been made of the economic impact in Bristol and Liverpool of abolition and how the slave-trading companies adapted to the new world. The other huge losers were the slaves themselves. In 1807, the Trans-Atlantic Slave Trade Database records 120 voyages were made and 33,682 people were transported as slaves, over 4,000 never reaching their destination. The trade did not end that day, nor could it, as many dozens of ships were still at sea carrying their cargo of human beings. Remarkably, despite the new law, between 1808 and 1811 34 slave voyages were conducted by British slave traders, using ships registered in England to transport 8,978 slaves. It is a complete myth to believe that the slave trade ended in 1807, perhaps as many as 40,000 people were made slaves and transported to slave plantations after the official date of abolition.

Chapter 19

Yorkshire and the Abolition of Slavery

The slave trade was ended, yet slavery still lingered on. Real-world politics once again collided with abolition. The Napoleonic Wars still had eight years to run. Despite peace petitions across Yorkshire in 1807 to 1808, the war continued. With Napoleon's abdication in April 1814, peace descended on Europe for the first time in a generation. In summer 1814 Thomas Clarkson busied himself lobbying for an end to the slave trade in Europe. The Congress of Vienna abolished the slave trade in New Year 1815, and Napoleon outlawed slavery on 31 March 1815 after his return to power. Following the Battle of Waterloo – which witnessed the last great peace petition of the period which Wakefield man Benjamin Gaskell as MP for Maldon signed – radical politics did not re-awaken for two years. In New Year 1817 a county meeting for reform was held in York, but was publicly boycotted by Henry Duncombe[1] and James Archibald Stuart Wortley who would be the MP for Yorkshire 1818–26.[2] The Wakefield reformers were led by Dr Martin Naylor and the Rev. Thomas Johnstone. A town meeting was held on 20 January, and a petition was drawn up desiring annual Parliaments, universal suffrage and greater representation for manufacturing districts. It was sent to Parliament by Benjamin Gaskell, and had been signed by 4,400 people.[3] As ever, politics was polarised between reform and 'strong and stable': a second petition was sent from Wakefield led by the Tories arguing against universal suffrage as it would allow the 'lower orders' to participate in government, which would be 'the greatest delusion and error' noting 'Parliamentary reform as a curse'.[4] The petitioners were distancing themselves from any reprisals that could occur – indeed the theme of government repression appears in the petition, and the petitioners pledged themselves 'to use our utmost exertions for the maintenance of tranquillity and order' and accepted that the 'lower orders' sending petitions that spread sedition should be met with force. The petition was headed by John Henry Smyth of Heath,[5] MP for Cambridge University as well as by virtually all the Anglican clergy: Samuel Sharpe of Wakefield, William Wood of St Johns, Jeremiah Dixon of Woolley, J. Drake of Warmfield, John Taylor of Horbury and W. Brown of Sandal.[6] Thus, as in the 1790s the debate was Tory Anglicans against largely Unitarian Whigs. One pro-reform petition declared to Tories and Churchmen:

> . . . . you view with just pride, the naval and military trophies of your country abroad: but bitter and unavailing will be your regret, if, from your own mismanagement at home, your heroes shall have bled only that their children may inherit a country in slavery, its agriculture ruined and its commerce gone.
>
> At this moment, one fourth of the all the inhabitants of England are paupers or insolvent. How far do you expect this system to go? How long do you expect it to last?[7]

In order to stamp out dissent, Parliament re-enacted the hated 'Gagging Acts' and suspended habeas corpus on 4 March 1817 and this was not lifted until January 1818. The Seditious Meetings Act was passed and continued in force until 24 July 1818: it was designed to ensure that all reforming 'Societies and Clubs . . . should be utterly suppressed and prohibited as unlawful combinations and confederacies'. No meeting of more than fifty persons could be held without the prior consent of the magistrates. The government also banned and ordered the arrest of all printers of seditious and blasphemous materials. State repression once more silenced the reformists, until tensions broke out again in 1819. The Peterloo Massacre shocked the nation. Walter Ramsden Fawkes' speech at the Yorkshire meeting to protest against the proceedings at Peterloo was sufficiently inflammatory to be quoted in the House by Lord Castlereagh. In Wakefield Martin Willans,[8] a Unitarian attending Westgate Chapel, was elected chairman of the Wakefield Reformers meeting in September 1819 to denounce Peterloo. The meeting resolved in addition to universal suffrage, annual Parliaments, abolition of slavery that:

> That as usurpers of our rights, in order to retain their power, have proceeded to acts of violence against the people, and even incarcerated many individuals, we earnestly entreat our fellow countrymen to enter their personal protest against such

acts . . . that this meeting views with regret and indignation the unprovoked conduct of the Magistrates and the Yeomanry Cavalry of Manchester, for the wanton attack upon the peaceable people . . . to oppose and put down the destructive power of the Borough Proprietors and to stay the blood stained hand of violence and passion . . . that a reformed Parliament would be the means of breaking up factions of divisions: of lessening taxation; of increasing trade and commerce; restoring prosperity and happiness; of disbanding a standing army.[9]

At the close of the meeting a vote of thanks was given to Major Cartwright and Thomas Johnstone for calling the meeting. It was estimated by the press that about 7,000 attended.

The immediate effect of Peterloo was a crackdown on reform: the Pentrich rising, the March of the Blanketeers and the Spa Fields meeting, all serve to indicate the breadth, diversity and widespread geographical scale of the demand for economic and political reform in 1817–19. It also represented the scale of the harsh reaction by the state with the re-imposition of the 'Gagging Acts' and suspension of habeas corpus. The Seditious Meetings Act was voted back into law at the close of 1819. Sadly, such protests achieved little and had no impact on the speed of reform. As in 1792, it was crushed under the boot of Toryism for a decade. Slavery as part of the reformist agenda was also 'off the cards' as an issue due to vested interests in high places by the MPs members of the House of Lords and the clergy.

Throughout the period 1807–25, the abolition of slavery had taken second place to political reform, and it was not until 1823, thanks in part to the lifting of the various 'Gagging Acts', that any progress was made when the London Society for the Mitigation and Gradual Abolition of Slavery was formed. Slave rebellions in 1816 and 1822 helped bring slavery back into focus in the public imagination at large. Thomas Clarkson had begun campaigning again in 1823, and within a year 250 anti-slavery societies had been formed – many of these societies were exclusively formed of middle-class 'ladies'. Yet for many, slavery was acceptable. John Fray, a nominal Unitarian from Bank Street Chapel, Bolton, who emigrated to Jamaica as a plantation owner, commented:

I am candid to tell you they are far better off than any class of peasantry in your country – both as to food, labour and general comforts and this I avow to you in the very strongest and most ungratified terms. I may without being an advocate for the oppression of the slave – which oppression is really rare but sometimes occurs, when 'tis I assure you visited on the white delinquent in a very severe manner by fine, imprisonment or pillory – I may I say without being an advocate for oppression avow myself a friend to good order and feel deeply the necessity of keeping the negro in good habits – which experience shows can only be done by imposing restraints, we should feel rather disagreeable but as reliable improvement is making in all classes of slaves – this restraint like the later heritages of our old feudal system is any fact clearing away and better methods are daily coming into use.[10]

Whilst ever views such as this lingered, overcoming them would take more than placards and petitions. Inspired by Thomas Clarkson's efforts, slavery in Wakefield was dramatically thrust back into the limelight by a leading member of Westgate Chapel: Ann Hurst. At the beginning of May 1823, in her capacity as the temporary editor of the *Wakefield and Halifax Journal*, Mrs Hurst declared in her editorial that 'a false belief has very generally existed, that slavery had ceased, or is in a gradual state of abolition'.[11] She called for a petition to be raised and an anti-slavery committee formed, which was headed by the Rev. Thomas Johnstone and included Unitarians like Frederick Gotthard, the Willans family and the Gaskell brothers to name but a few: all were members of the Wakefield Reformers Association. As in the 1790s, abolition was 'joined at the hip' to political reform.

Ann Hurst had been baptised at Westgate Chapel by the Rev. William Turner on 15 March 1772, daughter of John Day. Day was an active member of the local Whig Association and subscribed to the Westgate Chapel Lending Library in 1768. He had paid pew rent since 1761. In 1798 Ann married Rowland Hurst I at St John the Baptist Parish Church Wakefield – it being illegal for Unitarians to marry in their own chapels until the 1830s. Rowland, following the death of Dr James Richardson in 1806, became postmaster of Wakefield. Richardson was physician to Wakefield Dispensary – an institution he and fellow Unitarians helped found in 1786. By trade Hurst ran a printing business from the post office premises on Wood Street, Wakefield. He bought out the *Wakefield Star* at New Year 1811. The newspaper had been a joint venture between Thomas Lumb and Jack Milnes to provide the town with its own newspaper, the first edition appearing on 1 March 1803. In Leeds, the Milnes family financed Edward Baines to run the *Leeds Mercury*. Baines went onto found the 'Bainestocracy' of Mill Hill Chapel:

he and his family dominated Leeds politics. The Milnes and the Lumbs sought to emulate Baines and provide a mouthpiece for the radical left. Active freemason and Anglican priest the Rev. Dr Martin Naylor was appointed the editor. Naylor was linked with the Milnes family through Whig politics and Freemasonry: Richard Slater Milnes was Provincial Grand Master of Yorkshire 1784 to 1804. Under the Hursts' ownership the paper became known as *The Wakefield and Halifax Journal and Yorkshire and Lancashire Advertiser*, the first edition being published on 1 March 1811. Martin Naylor remained as editor until 1832, the assistant editor, music and art critic being the Rev. Thomas Johnstone till his death. It was very much a Unitarian enterprise! Rowland Senior had converted to his wife's faith in the 1790s from the preaching and politics of the aforementioned Rev. Johnstone. Rowland I died in 1823 aged 48, and with his eldest son not yet in his majority, Mrs Hurst took over the running of the newspaper. Her son Rowland II would marry Marianne Johnstone in 1830, the daughter of the Rev. Thomas Johnstone. Using the pages of her newspaper and backed by the Wakefield reformers, in 1825 an anti-slavery petition was raised by Mrs Hurst, which called for immediate abolition. The petition was drafted by Wakefield lawyer Twistleton Haxby. Ann Hurst died in 1832, her son Rowland having taken over the newspaper two years earlier it becoming *The Wakefield and Halifax Journal*. Rowland sold the paper in 1833 to Thomas Nichols, it becoming *The Wakefield and West Riding Examiner* in 1849 and ceasing to exist in 1852 upon amalgamation with *The Wakefield Journal*. Ann Hurst died on 17 March 1832 was buried with her husband and four children in the Unitarian burial ground at Westgate End, Wakefield. Her mortal remains were moved to Wakefield municipal cemetery in the 1960s and placed in an unmarked mass grave with her husband, children, and over 200 co-religionists as well as the Rev. William Turner. As a pioneering business owner and editor, Mrs Hurst has been recognised with a blue plaque by Wakefield Civic Society working with 'Forgotten Women of Wakefield'. Rowland II would go onto be a leading light in Wakefield Whig politics and abolition and was named a Trustee of Westgate Chapel.

Returning to abolition, as a result of Thomas Clarkson's renewed efforts, in 1825 a London society for the abolition of slavery was formed, with regional associations formed rapidly afterwards, with Ladies' Associations being formed in Barnsley, Sheffield and later in Wakefield by the Rev. Carpenter of Northgate End Chapel. This was the start of a new nationwide movement that submitted hundreds of petitions from Yorkshire to Parliament to appeal for the abolition of slavery: women made a significant contribution. In Sheffield, two women collected 187,000 signatures in 1831. In Leeds some 6,000 crammed into the Coloured Cloth Hall to hear lectures against slavery. Between 1824 and 1831 it is reckoned some three million anti-slavery tracts were published, 500,000 in 1831 alone. Yet Parliament was unmoved on the subject. Despite the best efforts of Mrs Hurst and Westgate Chapel, it was not till the end of the 1820s when religious groups flocked to the cause. Through Edward Baines Junior of the *Leeds Mercury* and John Marshall – both Unitarians and members of Mill Hill – slavery became a hot topic in the election of 1826. Henry Brougham, another candidate, also backed abolition, and both were duly elected as MPs for Yorkshire. Dick Milnes's grandson, Marmaduke Wyvill MP, during his 1826 election campaign reaffirmed his support for reform and Catholic relief and declared himself an enemy of slavery, blamed 'excessive tax' as the 'primary cause' of distress and said that the Corn Laws had 'no other tendency than to oppress the working classes and render exorbitantly dear the prime necessity of life'. He presented a petition from the Catholics of York for their relief, 'the first that had been agreed to since the recommendation from the throne', on 24 February 1829 and presented a York anti-slavery petition on 11 May 1829. He voted for Jewish emancipation on 17 May 1830 and paired for abolition of the death penalty for forgery on 24 May 1830. He stood down as an MP in 1830.[12] The 1826 election was a foretaste of what was to come: reform and an end to slavery was solidly on the agenda. Unitarians in Parliament and in the pulpit championed both. In 1828, after 50 years of agitation, the Test and Corporation Acts were repealed. Unitarians at last nearly had the same rights as Anglicans.

The Chamber of Commerce in Leeds joined other similar bodies in 1827 in demanding free trade and an end to slavery. A significant step in bolstering the cause of abolitionism came with the formation of the Yorkshire Protestant Dissenters Association for the Abolition of Slavery in September 1829 in Leeds. The association argued that slavery had been approached as a political and not a religious question:

> That slavery is an evil of fearful magnitude, directly opposed to the well-being and happiness of man, the law of God, and the religion of Christ—the existence of which, especially in any part of the British dominions, we, as Christians, do most seriously deplore, and the entire extinction of which we feel ourselves called upon most strenuously to seek and promote, by all those means which the providence of God, and the laws and constitution of our own favoured and happy country have put into our power. That to us it does appear, that the various

religious denominations of this country, with perhaps one exception, have not yet applied themselves to the destruction of this great evil, in that determined manner, and with those systematic and energetic measures, which the magnitude of the evil itself, and of the powers banded together for its continuance, obviously and most imperatively demand.[13]

On doctrinal grounds, Unitarians were excluded. With 1,000 Non-conformist congregations in Yorkshire by 1830, the county was a major centre for abolition. In 1830 all four MPs for the county were abolitionists.

On 10 November 1830, under the chairmanship of the Rev. Dr Martin Naylor, the Wakefield Reformers Society organised a mass meeting calling for the abolition of slavery. The Rev. Thomas Johnstone sat on the platform alongside Joseph Gosnay, the Methodist Chief Constable.[14]

Emancipation, as was ever the case, was tied up with domestic 'slavery' through the lack of political representation and the legal status of non-Anglicans. Anti-government and anti-Tory agitation reached its peak with the blocking of the Reform Act. Between October 1830 and April 1831 Parliament received about 3,000 petitions on the question, the overwhelming majority being in favour. At the same time a comparable number were sent to Parliament calling for the abolition of slavery. In 1831, the House of Commons passed a Reform Bill, but the House of Lords, dominated by Tories, defeated it, the Duke of Wellington taking the lead in opposition, who overnight became the most hated man in the country. There followed riots and serious disturbances in London, Birmingham, Derby, Nottingham, Leicester, Yeovil, Sherborne, Exeter and Bristol. The riots in Bristol were some of the worst seen in England in the nineteenth century. They began when Sir Charles Weatherall, who was opposed to the Reform Bill, came to open the Assize Court. Public buildings and houses were set on fire, there was more than £300,000 of damage and twelve people died. Of 102 people arrested and tried, 31 were sentenced to death. Lieutenant Colonel Brereton, the commander of Crown forces in Bristol, was court-martialled.

There was a fear in government that unless there was some reform there might be a revolution instead. They looked to the July 1830 revolution in France, which overthrew King Charles X and replaced him with the more moderate King Louis-Philippe who agreed to a constitutional monarchy. In Britain, King William IV lost popularity for standing in the way of reform. Eventually he agreed to create new Whig peers, and when the House of Lords heard this, they passed the Reform Bill. 'Rotten boroughs' were removed and the new towns given the right to elect MPs, although constituencies were still of uneven size. However, only men who owned property worth at least £10 could vote, which cut out most of the working classes, and only men who could afford to pay to stand for election could be MPs. This reform did not go far enough to silence all protest, and it resulted in the 1866 Reform Act: universal suffrage did not come about until after the First World War!

With the passing of the Reform Act, Wakefield could return an MP. The 'Wakefield Reformers' chose Daniel Gaskell as their candidate. His brother had been an MP, and using the inheritance from his uncle James Milnes who died in 1805, he could afford to finance the campaign. Forty years after the Society of the Friends of the People was formed, and over 50 years since the Milnes family began its political agitation, the Reform Act of 1832 helped establish the Parliamentary reform that the Society had called for. It removed representation from fifty-six 'rotten boroughs' and lowered representation in areas with lower population from two to one. It also created sixty-seven new boroughs so areas with larger populations had representation in Parliament. It also allowed a wider range of men to vote by loosening the property and tax qualifications to the right to vote. In 1832 the Rev. Johnstone commented:

> Of the great struggles which have been made at different times to achieve this blessing, without feeling a glow of deepest veneration towards those who have distinguished themselves in this great cause. I recall, more especially, as belonging to Yorkshire, the names of Sir Geo Saville, that simple-minded warm-hearted patriot; the venerable Wyvill, of kindred soul to Major Cartwright and the eloquent Walter Fawkes, with many others who are deeply fixed in our memories. If I could call spirits from the vasty deep, or rather from a higher world, I would call them, and I do think, if they could, that they would come when they were called; but at any rate gentlemen, our imaginations can in some measure embody them, and as we think how such great and good men would cordially join in our triumph, so we can animate our hearts by the thought.[15]

Johnstone was directly linking the Reform Act with the Yorkshire Association and the Friends of the People. He lived through this tumultuous time, and faced gaol for his beliefs at one stage. He had known Wyvill, Cartwright and Fawkes personally as friends. Johnstone acted as spokesman for Gaskell.[16] He defended Gaskell against charges of wanting to disestablish the Church of England and not being a

Christian in order to discredit the reformist cause from Richard Dunn, an Anglican corn factor. Rev. Johnstone, in answering for Gaskell in saying he wished to see a reformed Church of England, free of abuse and the church rate abolished, almost sparked a riot and was defended in his views by the liberal Rev. Thomas Kilby of St John's and Rev. Dr Martin Naylor.[17] Hostility towards Unitarians would boil over in the 1830s and lead to the Dissenting Chapels Act of 1844, which finally gave Unitarians the same rights as congregants of the Church of England, university attendance excepted.

Yet what highlighted the matter of slavery and inequality the most to Parliament and the general public was the increasingly troubled Caribbean. Slaves no longer tolerated not being free and began to fight for their freedom. Revolt broke out six times in 1816, in 1821, on Demerara in 1823 and again in 1824 at Hanover on Jamaica. Wilberforce did his level best to steer abolitionism away from the slaves' own attempts at freedom. Orders in Council were passed in 1824 to ameliorate slavery: the end was in sight. The law allowed slaves to purchase their own freedom. Everything changed six years later.

The Baptist War of 1831–2 in Jamaica was a volcanic slave revolt, on a par with the uprising in St Domingo in 1792. It is estimated some 60,000 slaves revolted: 14 white plantation owners and 540 slaves were killed. The bloodshed resulted in an outcry in Britain. When the general election was called in August 1832, using the newly reformed franchise, abolitionists seized their moment. Black Lives Mattered: in the canvassing for the election candidates were pressed to declare their position: 200 MPs declared Black Lives Matter. Reform of Parliament made freedom inevitable for hundreds of thousands of slaves. In Wakefield Daniel Gaskell was elected the town's first MP: he squarely campaigned on the abolition of slavery.[18]

One of the first acts of the reformed Parliament was to abolish slavery. The Abolition of Slavery Bill was passed in August 1833: but it did not grant freedom. Slaves under the age of six were automatically freed, while those over the age of six were apprenticed to their masters for six years with little to no change in their working conditions and worked for no wage. The whole exercise to many, including Daniel Gaskell, of giving millions in compensation was a vast exercise in slave trading: freedom was bought and had not been given: each slave had a price on their head. Some £20 million was paid in compensation: the rich got richer, the slaves got nothing except more years of toil and labour. Lord Harewood, already astronomically wealthy, received £26,309 in compensation; not a penny went to the slaves themselves.

Some Yorkshire MPs were revolted by this idea: Daniel Gaskell MP for Wakefield, along with John Gully MP for Pontefract, voted in favour of reducing the compensation by £5 million and to pay the former slaves during 'their period of apprenticeship'. Sadly, neither motion passed.[19] The rich got richer, and kept their free labour for five more years. Gaskell was appalled by the slaves 'being sold out': did they not too deserve a share of the compensation?[20] Very few MPs agreed with him, alas. Finally, on 1 August 1838 full freedom to slaves was granted.

Yet slavery lingered on in America. In Leeds the Rev. Charles Wicksteed the minister at Mill Hill was a devoted servant of abolitionism. When Frederick Douglass – an escaped slave – and Henry Clarke Wright (1797–1870) spoke in Leeds in 1847, Wicksteed was the only minister of religion present! As was ever the case, unpopular in politics and religion, where a Unitarian went, the Trinitarians would not follow. Douglass and Wicksteed both spoke to the Anti-Slavery League at Leeds Music Hall.[21] Douglass pressed that whilst ever English churches were in union with the slave-owning denominations in America, then the English churches and chapels had no legitimate claim to be against slavery. Douglass proclaimed that Methodists hold Methodists in slavery, Baptists hold Baptists in slavery and the church in America and England had to be reformed or otherwise destroyed as they were the bulwarks of slavery. Garrison Lloyd Wright, the famous American journalist and abolitionist, also spoke. He argued that until these churches in favour of slavery had been revolutionised or destroyed, slavery and intolerance of blacks would persist. By implication Wicksteed commended that English Methodists, Presbyterians, Baptists and Independents by being in fellowship with slave-owning congregations, were partakers of their crimes. Wicksteed urged that it was the duty of the churches to disown these slave owners, and purge themselves of the guilt of supporting slave-owning ministers and congregations. The orthodox ministers in Leeds all agreed that Douglass, Garrison and Wicksteed had gone too far in arguing for a reform of the church and expulsion of slave owners, and ultimately concluded 'neither Garrison or Douglass, nor Wright have given any satisfactory proof to Christians and ministers of this country, that they hold the great doctrines of the gospel as held by the various orthodox denominations, and as embodied in orthodox creeds in this land . . . they have given no proof they believe in the Trinity'. By association with Wicksteed, they were 'damnable Unitarians'. Christian piety was only for other Christians, and the orthodox clergy would not and could not support Unitarians or any other non-orthodox body.[22] Clearly, the ministers of Leeds were a bigoted lot, the teachings of the Sermon on the Mount clearly had no bearing on them, or the parable of the Good Samaritan. Religious revivalism and evangelism had turned denomination against denomination in the fight to save souls; to declare to the world that their way was the only way; that their sect and their sect alone had the right answers; and that any deviation from the orthodox was to be cast out – thus, as was ever the case, Unitarians became a focal point of unity for the Methodists, Baptists, Anglicans, etc to rally together against!

Wicksteed was joined in his abolitionist crusade by the Rev. Russel Lant Carpenter, minister at Northgate End, and began a highly vocal campaign across the country. He encouraged the formation of abolitionist societies. He was joined by a Mrs Griffiths who promoted the formation of Ladies' Abolition Societies. The Rev. Edward Higginson at Bowl Alley in Hull was also a vocal champion of abolition and began agitation in Hull and Wakefield from 1848 when he was appointed minister at Westgate Chapel. From 1858, the communist, poet and Chartist Rev. John Goodwyn Barmby became minister at Westgate, Wakefield: he too had been a strident abolitionist since the 1840s and had met Frederick Douglass in London in 1847 and would do so again in Wakefield in 1860 whilst Douglass was hosted by the Carpenters in the parsonage at Northgate End along with Sarah Parker Remond. Both spoke in Wakefield at the long-demolished Corn Exchange.

Slavery was based on racism – racism still lingers today in the reaction against the Black Lives Matter movement. Slavery exists because we judge others to be inferior to ourselves. As soon as we lose sight of our humanity, we are able to treat people as things – 'the other'; from that stems slavery, racism and the great evil of nationalism. Abraham Lincoln ended slavery in America on 18 December 1865. Yet even in 2020 slavery is still a phenomenon. To change the world and bring about an end to real slavery – which still exists in many parts of the world – in the British Empire required courage, vision, and a faith that they were right. The French Revolutionary ideals of freedom, reason and tolerance, that all men are equal, inspired Unitarians to take a stand against those who sought to uphold slavery and the slave trade; who sought to limit access to justice by suspending habeas corpus; the limitation of free speech by censoring the press, organising book-burnings and arbitrary arrests; despite hostility and open persecution Unitarians took a stand for freedom of expression against those who sought to end protest; Unitarians took a stand for all those discriminated against on grounds of religion; Unitarians fought for an end to slavery. These men and women, in opposing the state, suffered heavily at the hands of the state and the nationalist mob, hell-bent on keeping the rich oligarchy in power come what may. History has judged that Unitarians were in the right, and that Pitt and the Tory Party of the 1790s were wrong. The modern world owes a debt to the French Revolution and not the ideals of Burke and Pitt, with their narrow ultra-nationalistic views. To conclude our book, we can do no better than to quote the Rev. John Goodwyn Barmby to provide our closing words:

That slavery should exist in any form is abhorrent to the free spirit: That discussion has commenced in earnest, and will never cease until the black is as free as the white, when they can again march onward together to further conquests on the moral battle-field of liberty. In the grand charter of creation, man is declared to be in the image of God. Man, as male and female, is created in the divine likeness. There is no difference made between the black and the white. There is no exception introduced between the image of God in ebony, and the image of God in ivory. Why, therefore, is man's law different to God's law! Why is there a superiority asserted of one race over another? Why is one bought and sold as a chattel by the other, and why are such purchases esteemed lawful by any portion of humanity? While slavery of the negroes exists, in the absolute mode it has manifested itself, in any part of the globe, these questions demand discussion, even in those countries which are not practically connected with their operation; as humanity is integral, and ever responsible for the action of any of the members of its entire body . . . There is a future promised in which the internal shall surpass the external, in which the soul shall be above body, and the light of the spirit above the colour of the face. There is, in the meantime, a book wide open before us. It is the volume of resent duty. It reads – 'Cain, what hast thou done with thy brother?' We have ill-treated and murdered the divine soul of our brother. That poor slave, that degraded negro is our brother. Let us bespeak him kindly; let us do him no wrong; let us pray the ever-living God to restore his spirit to life. Thus, may our sin be atoned for.[23]

Conclusion

Starting in the 1770s, Unitarians and English radicals had driven the message of reform. Despite imprisonment, their homes and churches being burned down, their printing presses smashed and having to flee for their lives, the Reform Act and the ending of the slave trade and slavery owed everything to their sacrifice.

In the West Riding, one man stands head and shoulders above others for his early radicalism: the Rev. William Turner. The 'political brains' behind the Yorkshire Association, a champion of American liberty since 1774, a passionate abolitionist, Turner had died in 1794; he was buried in Wakefield at Westgate End burial ground alongside his wife. In the 1960s the body of this forgotten abolitionist was exhumed when the graveyard was cleared to make way for a new bakery development. His body was unceremoniously dumped in an unmarked mass grave at Wakefield Municipal Cemetery. John Goodchild M. Univ rescued the good reverend's gravestone, so that it could be set up as a memorial to him in the grounds of the Orangery, Back Lane, Wakefield. At the time of writing, this stone tablet to an unsung abolitionist and political radical can no longer be found. It would be fitting indeed to commemorate his life once more, and that of Thomas Lumb, Robert Bakewell and Jack Milnes the Democrat: Jack and Thomas lie in the catacombs beneath Westgate Chapel. Turner's successor, the equally radical firebrand Rev. Thomas Johnstone, died in his sleep on 21 April 1856 in his 88th year at his daughter's house, Springfield Lodge, Outwood near Wakefield. He was buried in the catacombs beneath Westgate Chapel on 24 April 1856 by Rev. Edward Higginson, the minister of the chapel and a lifelong abolitionist. Johnstone's life was one of duty, driven by his deep religious and political convictions of compassion for his fellow man, seeking to free the oppressed. He is one of the unsung heroes of abolition. His determination to champion the cause for virtually the entirety of his life, despite imprisonment for his vocal support for political reform, marks him out as a good man. Tragically, he is unknown in his adopted home city of Wakefield, and his legacy forgotten. Hopefully, this book has reclaimed the legacy of Johnstone and others. Maybe one day we will see a blue plaque for him on the site of his home, Westgate Parsonage, that was wantonly demolished in the 1960s by Wakefield City Council. Dick Milnes, the abolitionist MP for York, died in 1804. Wilberforce wrote: 'Alas! At the very time I am writing I am expecting to hear of poor Dick Milnes's death. O my friend, let us be ready.'[1] He too lies beneath Westgate Chapel, forgotten by the City of York which he represented for 18 years.

At the same time, Wakefield, like other communities across Yorkshire, has a legacy of slave ownership that it needs to acknowledge. Grand civic buildings and mansions were paid for with the proceeds of slavery. The darkness at the heart of Yorkshire's history needs to be acknowledged. The Heywood family and others, through advantageous marriages, drew into Wakefield and Liverpool huge amounts of capital which allowed these towns to flourish on the back on slavery. This book has shone a light onto a darkness at the heart of Yorkshire. The institutions, churches and chapels that slavery money flowed into need to acknowledge the darker aspects of their past. The civic institutions bankrolled by slavery, the grand houses paid for from slavery that are now put to other uses, need to acknowledge that they are built from the toil, bondage and blood of slaves. Our museums are shamefully quiet in acknowledging the links of Yorkshire and the slave trade away from Hull and the Wilberforce Museum. In the city of Wakefield, a blue plaque was erected to Francis Ingram for his achievements in banking, and both Benjamin and John Pemberton Heywood boast blue plaques: all three fail to acknowledge the fact that these three men owed their fortunes to the sweat of slaves.

As we have seen in the first section of this book, Yorkshire played a leading role in the slave trade and the wider slave economy: Yorkshire men and women owned slaves, owned plantations and participated in the 'value-chains' of slavery. Yorkshire with its merchants made rich on the back of trade with America, got richer by investing in slave voyages and plantations. Men down on their luck became spectacularly wealthy by leaving Yorkshire and investing in slavery. The slave trade for many families was the 'golden ticket' out of mediocrity and relative poverty to the dizzying heights of wealth and prestige. It worked for the Lascelles and Dundas families, so too for the Heywoods, Staniforths, Denisons and many others. As a relatively easy way to make money very rapidly, the slave trade underpinned the shift in political power from the aristocracy to the 'merchant princes' of the eighteenth century who became the great families of the nineteenth century. The slave trade made a rich country richer; it allowed for a huge degree of social mobility. The value-chain economy of slavery allowed the Milnes family of Wakefield to rise from relative obscurity to becoming baronets and lords in four generations. The same story is repeated across the county and country. Without the massive financial stimulus of the compensation scheme at abolition of slavery, the burgeoning railway network may not have happened. By the late nineteenth century, many slave owners became recorded in history as 'West Indian Merchants' to make their role in slavery more obscure and perhaps also to expunge the stain of association with slavery.

The vast majority of the compensation money was invested in infrastructure and industry: new mechanised mills appeared in Lancashire; railways criss-crossed the country. The slave compensation scheme funded the industrialisation of Great Britain. The blood, sweat and tears of slaves made Britain the dominant economic and military superpower of the era: this is all too often overlooked or ignored. It allowed the rape and pillaging of half the globe. The ending of slavery in the British Empire meant that new sources of free or cheap labour were needed to fuel the ever-expanding capitalist economy: India became the target for exploitation.

Without the exploitation of workers and resources, capitalism does not work. Victorian laissez-faire economics allowed for the ever-increased use of bonded labour, i.e. slavery by another name at home in factories, through transportation of prisoners to colonies or through exploitation overseas. Slavery made the Empire and Great Britain. This darker, more sinister aspect of our past is often overlooked or ignored, and increasingly in the modern day, any critique of the homogenised past by certain elements of society results in derision and abuse as critical and evaluative historians are accused of 'changing history'. No longer can we homogenise the diversity of our past; the past is a story written by us all, and we ignore our diversity at our peril if we are to overcome the forces of exceptionalism and nationalism that led to world wars and lay directly behind the motives for slavery: racism. Seeing ourselves, white people, as superior to those of different ethnicity. This allows us to see fellow human beings as not like us, instead, we see them as things to be used and abused. We all human and have the same rights and responsibilities.

The same 'banality of evil' that allowed over a million men, women and children to be transported as slaves to provide cheap sugar, coffee, tobacco and rum, still exists with the desire for cheap clothing and other goods on the high street. The same conscious decisions to make money and to 'grab a bargain'; without thinking about the working conditions of the workers affects us all. We all want those clothes at bargain prices, made by workers who earn far less than the minimum wage, but expect of course that we receive the minimum wage or more for our labour: we refuse to accept for others what we benefit from ourselves as it would inconvenience us. The same process of greed and selfishness which lies at the heart of modern consumer society is exactly the same forces that drove the slave trade and the larger slave economy, which is sadly alive and well as I write. The same forces of exclusion which did not want to grant to Unitarians the same rights and privileges as members of the Church of England, that could only see an end to its own power in the words of Marat, Paine and the ideals of the French Revolution, silenced political debate. The Tory oligarchy, by invoking 'God save the King', 'Rule Britannia' and English exceptionalism appealed to the basest instincts of the mob – national pride and violence: through appeals to xenophobia for a decade or more, the government enacted the most repressive regime the country had then known at the expense of 'the other'. The same forces against 'the other' were against liberal, inclusive politics and nascent democracy and instead supported politics that was centred on dividing society, and ultimately still drives modern-day Tory politics. The vested interests of the rich, MPs, the lords of the land and established church in slavery and the slave trade, in keeping the vaunted legal status of Anglicanism, opposing political reform mean that abolition was doomed to fail from day one until the Whigs took office for the first time in a generation: abolition did come, but it took the death of William Pitt, the 'English tyrant', for it to happen.

Despite opposition, Yorkshire men and women stood up to slavery and helped bring about changes to the law that forbade slavery. Standing up and going against the status quo took courage. Yorkshire had brave men and women who stood up for what was right, and faced ostracisation, bankruptcy and exile. As Unitarians, perhaps the very fact that their faith was illegal, and had to fight for the same rights that others enjoyed made these men and women far more determined in their course of actions and drove them to be proactive in changing the world. I certainly think it was the case. They stood for a world that said no to discrimination on grounds of race, religion and increasingly gender – thanks to Mary Wollstonecraft and others! – against those, mostly Tories, who wanted to discriminate on grounds of race, religion and gender.

Between 1788 and 1792 Yorkshire merchant communities actively engaged in both sides of the debate; a debate that was part of a wider one on the vision for society and the nature of community: the conflicting visions of Burke and Richard Price. Britain, led by William Pitt, was fighting a war from 1791 to end democracy, however flawed, in France. Pitt created a country that said yes, we discriminate on religious grounds, that said yes, we want a state that denies justice to all by suspending habeas corpus, and yes, we do not want any opposition by closing down the printing presses; created a state which heavily censored what was printed, created a state that said yes, we do not want freedom of expression with the passing of the Seditious Writings Act, and the Seditious Meetings Act. Yet for some Pitt and his aims were laudable achievements.

Indeed, the prominence of Unitarianism in the growing middle class in Nottingham, Birmingham, Manchester, York, Bristol, Liverpool and Leeds, helps to explain why men of commerce decided not to support the slave trade. If Unitarians had not been prominent amongst the commercial class, with its heady combination of liberal Christian values, scientific rationalism and enlightenment ideas, the West Indian interest may well have had broader and more unified support. Unitarian communities, lobbying and wide spread popular print culture, provided fora in which tension between commercial and civic morality could be discussed, and solutions to tensions proposed.

Without Unitarian agitation from 1776, in print, pulpit and Parliament, the slave trade may not have been abolished. The traditional narrow focus on abolition from a religious standpoint centred on Quakers and Anglicans has written Unitarians and their place in abolition out of history. Abolition starts with Jean Paul Marat at Warrington Academy and the transmission of his ideas from pulpits across the country led to a generation of radicals who sought to change the world. The take-off of British Abolitionism in the 1780s in Yorkshire, Bristol and Manchester emerged from concerns about Religious freedom, political rights and national identify in the aftermath of the American Revolution made possible through Unitarian printing presses, pulpits, protests and agitation.

After 1794, Unitarians were increasingly 'squeezed out' of the debate on religious and political grounds: hated in politics, equally hated by mainstream Christians in religion, Unitarians were relegated to the sidelines as Methodism, Congregationalism and evangelical Anglicanism took over, and would never work with 'heretics'.

Traditional accounts of abolitionism as rooted in religion focused too narrowly on Quakerism and evangelical Anglicanism, are wrong. This is perhaps not surprising as in the last years of the 1790s witnessed

Unitarians, or Protestant Dissenters as they were then known, losing their leading position in religious Dissent and being relegated to the sidelines; marginalised on the grounds of both their politics and religion. Wilberforce, William Pitt, Edmund Burke and the Tory oligarchy contrived in this. The story of abolition has been homogenised to make Wilberforce a saint, the 'moral conscience' of England, and has literally 'airbrushed out' the vital contributions Unitarians made to abolition and political reform. It is fair to say that without Unitarians, Wilberforce and Clarkson would not have had the 'blueprints' for establishing a national network for abolitionists; without Unitarian support in Parliament, and through sermons, printed pamphlets and books, as well as their undeniable socio-economic importance in late eighteenth-century England, Wilberforce would have faced a nearly impossible task. The association by Burke, Pitt and Peel of Unitarians with the ideals of the French Revolution – which was certainly true – in order to raise the mob against them and reform, destroyed the Unitarian dominance of Dissent and radical politics for over 50 years. Unitarians never again would wield the influence that they had done as a concerted body after 1794 in Yorkshire or nationally. Tis truly said 'they also served'.

Yorkshire has much to be proud of in its Unitarian heritage in the campaign for the abolition of slavery. Yorkshire has a darker history too that needs to be acknowledged. Both legacies have been virtually forgotten and this book hopefully goes someway to redress the balance.

Notes

Introduction

1. Stange (1984), p. 39.

Chapter 1: Eighteenth-Century Yorkshire

1. John Goodchild. Heywood Family MSS Notes.
2. A director of the railway was John Gladstone, a major slave owner; deputy chairman was John Moss a banker and slave owner; the chairman was Charles Lawrence, a slave plantation owner who invested £60,000 in the railway. https://www.ucl.ac.uk/lbs/firm/view/1482498357
3. Smail (2001), p. 32.
4. Ibid., p. 51.
5. *The Leeds Mercury* – Tuesday 7 June 1774.
6. Maw (2010), pp. 766–7.
7. For a fuller description of Wakefield and the wool trade see Paul L. Dawson (2020), *Wakefield at Work*, Stroud: Amberley Publishing.
8. https://www.ucl.ac.uk/lbs/person/view/2146650005
9. https://www.ucl.ac.uk/lbs/person/view/2146665805

Chapter 2: The Slave Trade

1. Clarkson (1788), pp. 91–3.
2. Ibid., pp. 33–44.
3. Ramsay (1784), pp. 62–3.
4. Ibid., pp. 887–8.
5. Ibid., pp. 75–6.
6. Clarkson (1788), pp. 91–107.

Chapter 3: Yorkshire and Slavery

1. https://www.york.ac.uk/projects/harewoodslavery/about.html
2. https://www.slavevoyages.org/voyage/database#results Moulton
3. https://www.slavevoyages.org/voyage/database#results Barrett
4. https://www.historyofParliamentonline.org/volume/1820-1832/member/moulton-barrett-samuel-1787-1837
5. https://www.historyofParliamentonline.org/volume/1790-1820/member/chaloner-robert-1776-1842
6. https://www.ucl.ac.uk/lbs/person/view/2146649393
7. https://www.historyofParliamentonline.org/volume/1790-1820/member/adey-stephen-thurston-1801
8. https://www.ucl.ac.uk/lbs/person/view/2146633153
9. Dawson (2019), p. 117.
10. https://www.historyofParliamentonline.org/volume/1790-1820/member/wentworth-godfrey-wentworth-1773-1834
11. https://www.historyofParliamentonline.org/volume/1790-1820/member/chaloner-robert-1776-1842
12. https://www.ucl.ac.uk/lbs/person/view/45212
13. https://www.ucl.ac.uk/lbs/person/view/2146630501
14. https://www.historyofParliamentonline.org/volume/1790-1820/member/denison-william-joseph-1770-1849
15. https://www.historyofParliamentonline.org/volume/1790-1820/member/denison-william-joseph-1770-1849
16. https://www.ucl.ac.uk/lbs/person/view/1299826570
17. https://www.historyofParliamentonline.org/volume/1790-1820/member/duncombe-charles-1764-1841
18. https://www.ucl.ac.uk/lbs/person/view/-258646517
19. https://www.historyofParliamentonline.org/volume/1754-1790/member/rose-george-1744-1818
20. https://www.ucl.ac.uk/lbs/person/view/9681
21. https://www.ucl.ac.uk/lbs/person/view/2146651075
22. https://www.ucl.ac.uk/lbs/person/view/721746990
23. https://www.historyofParliamentonline.org/volume/1790-1820/member/dundas-hon-george-heneage-lawrence-1778-1834
24. https://www.ucl.ac.uk/lbs/person/view/2146649425
25. https://www.ucl.ac.uk/lbs/person/view/2146662605
26. http://www.historyofParliamentonline.org/volume/1820-1832/member/wilson-james-1830
27. https://www.ucl.ac.uk/lbs/person/view/2146644189

28. https://www.ucl.ac.uk/lbs/estate/view/3483
29. https://www.ucl.ac.uk/lbs/person/view/46372
30. https://www.ucl.ac.uk/lbs/person/view/22215
31. https://www.ucl.ac.uk/lbs/person/view/2146648589
32. https://www.ucl.ac.uk/lbs/person/view/2146647831
33. Munkhouse (1799), pp. 51–3.
34. The National Archives (hereafter TNA) PROB 11/1356/84 Will of Arthur Savage of Saint Marylebone, Middlesex 10 April 1801.
35. TNA PROB 11/1565/541 Will of Arthur Savage of City of London, 28 February 1815.
36. https://www.ucl.ac.uk/lbs/person/view/2146638079
37. TNA PROB 11/1793/168 Will of Faith Munkhouse, Widow of Pontefract, Yorkshire 26 December 1831.
38. TNA PROB 11/2228/89 Will of Edward Steer, Merchant of Wakefield, Yorkshire.
39. https://www.ucl.ac.uk/lbs/person/view/2146648955
40. https://www.ucl.ac.uk/lbs/claim/view/16418
41. https://www.ucl.ac.uk/lbs/person/view/2146630491
42. https://www.ucl.ac.uk/lbs/person/view/14732
43. https://www.ucl.ac.uk/lbs/person/view/43217
44. https://www.ucl.ac.uk/lbs/person/view/22453

Chapter 4: East Yorkshire Slave Owners and Traders

1. TNA; Office of Registry of Colonial Slaves and Slave Compensation Commission: Records; Class: T 71; Piece Number: 117.
2. https://www.ucl.ac.uk/lbs/person/view/22999
3. https://www.ucl.ac.uk/lbs/person/view/2146644187
4. https://www.ucl.ac.uk/lbs/person/view/17136
5. TNA PROB 11/1912/387 Will of Simon Taylor of Etton Hall near Beverley, Yorkshire 25 June 1839.
6. https://www.ucl.ac.uk/lbs/person/view/21590
7. TNA PROB 11/1937/208 Will of Stephen Denton of Beverley, Yorkshire 4 December 1840.
8. TNA PROB 11/1507/401 Will of Samuel Walter, Gentleman of Holmpton, Yorkshire East Riding 27 January 1810.
9. https://www.ucl.ac.uk/lbs/estates/Chancery Hall
10. East Riding of Yorkshire Archives. DDBC/15/80.
11. https://www.ucl.ac.uk/lbs/person/view/22768
12. https://www.ucl.ac.uk/lbs/person/view/19326

Chapter 5: West Yorkshire Slave Owners and Traders

1. https://www.ucl.ac.uk/lbs/person/view/17589
2. https://www.ucl.ac.uk/lbs/person/view/14177
3. A 'quadroon' was a person with one white grandparent and three black but can also be used as a coverall term for mixed race. The author Alexandre Dumas is one of the most famous quadroons, being the son of General Alexandre Dumas, a 'mulatto' or person with one white parent and one black. The 'Three Musketeers' were created by a person of colour!
4. https://www.ucl.ac.uk/lbs/person/view/22042
5. TNA PROB 11/1692/385 Will of Samuel Barrett of Park Hill, Yorkshire 9 December 1824.
6. https://www.ucl.ac.uk/lbs/person/view/2146641349
7. https://www.ucl.ac.uk/lbs/person/view/19861
8. James Gregory 'Historical perspectives on the transatlantic slave trade in Bradford, Yorkshire: Abolitionist activity c.1787 – 1865'.
9. Ancestry.com. England, Select Deaths and Burials, 1538-1991 [database on-line]. Provo, UT, USA: Ancestry.com Operations, Inc., 2014.
10. https://www.ucl.ac.uk/lbs/person/view/2146634506
11. https://quod.lib.umich.edu/c/clementsead/umich-wcl-M-1351goo ?id=navbarbrowselink;view=text
12. TNA IR 26/304/229 Abstract of Will of Thomas Staniforth, Esquire of Liverpool, Lancashire.
13. TNA PROB 11/1710/132 Will of Thomas Staniforth of Liverpool, Lancashire.
14. https://www.ucl.ac.uk/lbs/person/view/2146630481
15. https://www.ucl.ac.uk/lbs/person/view/27325
16. TNA; Kew, Surrey, England; General Register Office: Registers of Births, Marriages and Deaths surrendered to the Non-parochial Registers Commissions of 1837 and 1857; Class Number: RG 4; Piece Number: 3167.
17. https://www.ucl.ac.uk/lbs/person/view/29104
18. John Goodchild. Ingram family MSS Noyes.
19. John Goodchild Milnes and Torre family of Snydale MSS Notes.
20. TNA IR 26/425/849 Abstract of Administration of Benjamin Hammond, Yeoman of Pilley in the parish of Tankersley, Yorkshire. Proved in the Court of York. November 07 1803.
21. *Gore's Liverpool General Advertiser* – Thursday 28 May 1795.
22. *Gore's Liverpool General Advertiser* – Thursday 25 June 1795.

23. *Gore's Liverpool General Advertiser* – Thursday 24 September 1795.
24. TNA IR 26/304/70 Abstract of Will of Benjamin Hammond of Liverpool, Lancashire. Proved in the Court of Chester. May 20 1803.
25. TNA PROB 11/1556/92 Will of Elizabeth Hammond, Widow of Liverpool, Lancashire.
26. https://www.ucl.ac.uk/lbs/person/view/6635
27. https://www.ucl.ac.uk/lbs/person/view/21727
28. TNA Prerogative Court of Canterbury and Related Probate Jurisdictions: Will Registers; Class: PROB 11; Piece: 1512.
29. https://www.ucl.ac.uk/lbs/person/view/14164
30. https://www.ucl.ac.uk/lbs/person/view/2146639017
31. Wilson (1971), pp. 188–90.
32. https://www.ucl.ac.uk/lbs/person/view/10314
33. https://www.ucl.ac.uk/lbs/person/view/2146650641
34. https://www.ucl.ac.uk/lbs/person/view/45822
35. *Leeds Intelligencer* – Tuesday 8 November 1774.
36. Wilson (1971), pp. 186–90.
37. Cooper (1824).
38. TNA PROB 11/1886/418 Will of George Hibbert Oates, Planter of Jamaica 4 November 1837.
39. https://www.ucl.ac.uk/lbs/estate/view/2586
40. https://www.ucl.ac.uk/lbs/person/view/2146653641
41. TNA PROB 11/1987/116 Will of Hibbert Oates of Clarendon, Middlesex 13 October 1843.

Chapter 6: North Yorkshire Slave Owners and Traders

1   https://www.ucl.ac.uk/lbs/person/view/2146644399
2. https://www.ucl.ac.uk/lbs/person/view/2146630473
3. https://www.ucl.ac.uk/lbs/person/view/45217
4. https://www.ucl.ac.uk/lbs/person/view/44517
5. https://www.ucl.ac.uk/lbs/person/view/2146649653
6. https://www.ucl.ac.uk/lbs/person/view/15137
7. East Riding Archive Service. DDSA/1138.
8. https://www.ucl.ac.uk/lbs/person/view/2146635659
9. https://www.ucl.ac.uk/lbs/person/view/46278
10. Haggerty (2012), p. 80.
11. TNA PROB 11/1601/113 Will of Leonard Parkinson of Kinnersley, Herefordshire 10 February 1818.

Chapter 7: Wakefield, Capital of Slavery

1. https://www.visionofbritain.org.uk/travellers/Defoe/31
2. *Newcastle Chronicle* – Saturday 14 September 1771.
3. *Leeds Intelligencer* – Tuesday 22 September 1772.
4. https://www.historyofParliamentonline.org/volume/1754-1790/member/lowther-sir-james-1736-1802
5. *Leeds Intelligencer* – Tuesday 17 September 1782.
6. *Leeds Intelligencer* – Tuesday 12 September 1786.
7. https://www.ucl.ac.uk/lbs/person/view/2146645203
8. https://www.ucl.ac.uk/lbs/person/view/2146645205
9. *Leeds Intelligencer* – Tuesday 02 July 1771.
10. Dawson (2019), p. 57.
11. *Leeds Intelligencer* – Tuesday 17 February 1778.
12. https://www.ucl.ac.uk/lbs/person/view/2146640629
13. https://www.ucl.ac.uk/lbs/person/view/2146653827
14. https://www.ucl.ac.uk/lbs/person/view/2146651441
15. https://www.ucl.ac.uk/lbs/person/view/2146649653
16. https://www.ucl.ac.uk/lbs/estate/view/17295
17. https://www.ucl.ac.uk/lbs/estate/view/3166
18. https://www.ucl.ac.uk/lbs/person/view/2146650619
19. Ancestry.com. England, Select Marriages, 1538–1973 [database on-line]. Provo, UT, USA: Ancestry.com Operations, Inc., 2014.
20. https://www.ucl.ac.uk/lbs/person/view/16512
21. Site visit 12 September 2020.
22. Dawson (2019), p. 49.
23. Nicols (1831), pp. 354–429. This remarkable collection of letters deserves greater study.
24. London Metropolitan Archives. MS 11936/361/560711.
25. Ancestry.com. West Yorkshire, England, Select Land Tax Records, 1704-1932 [database on-line]. Provo, UT, USA: Ancestry.com Operations, Inc., 2014.
26. West Yorkshire Archive Service; Wakefield, Yorkshire, England; Yorkshire Parish Records; New Reference Number: WDP79/5.
27. https://www.ucl.ac.uk/lbs/person/view/2146645203
28. https://www.ucl.ac.uk/lbs/person/view/2146650623
29. https://www.ucl.ac.uk/lbs/person/view/2146632630
30. TNA PROB 11/1328/240 Will of Sarah Brisco, Wife of Wimpole Street Cavendish Square, Middlesex 23 August 1799.
31. https://www.historyofParliamentonline.org/volume/1790-1820/member/goulburn-henry-1784-1856

32. https://www.ucl.ac.uk/lbs/estate/view/7048
33. TNA; Kew, England; Prerogative Court of Canterbury and Related Probate Jurisdictions: Will Registers; Class: PROB 11; Piece: 1827.
34. https://api.Parliament.uk/historic-hansard/people/mr-musgrave-brisco/index.html
35. https://www.ucl.ac.uk/lbs/person/view/2146633329
36. https://www.historyofParliamentonline.org/volume/1790-1820/member/mitchell-william-1742-1823
37. Dawson (2019), pp. 115–16.
38. John Goodchild. Ingram family MSS notes.
39. *Leeds Intelligencer* – Monday 10 November 1806.
40. John Goodchild. Heywood family MSS notes.
41. https://www.ucl.ac.uk/lbs/person/view/9346
42. https://www.ucl.ac.uk/lbs/person/view/2146634716
43. West Yorkshire Archive Service; Wakefield, Yorkshire, England; New Reference Number: WDP20/1/4/1.
44. John Goodchild T N Ince MSS Notes.
45. https://www.ucl.ac.uk/lbs/person/view/2146652463
46. https://www.ucl.ac.uk/lbs/person/view/8060

Chapter 8: Kith and Kin

1. Dawson (2019), pp. 115–16.
2. https://www.ucl.ac.uk/lbs/person/view/2146659181
3. Sheffield City Archives. WWM/R58-4 Arthur Heywood to Rockingham 11 May 1766.
4. John Goodchild. Heywood family MSS notes.
5. Westgate Chapel Archive. Pew Rent and Subscription Book 1762–1803.
6. Haggerty (2012), pp. 80–1.
7. Dawson (2018), pp. 65–7.
8. John Goodchild. Heywood family MSS notes.
9. https://www.ucl.ac.uk/lbs/person/view/44880
10. https://www.ucl.ac.uk/lbs/person/view/19278
11. https://www.ucl.ac.uk/lbs/person/view/1311936591
12. https://www.ucl.ac.uk/lbs/person/view/15128
13. https://www.historyofParliamentonline.org/volume/1820-1832/member/birch-joseph-1755-1833
14. https://www.ucl.ac.uk/lbs/person/view/2725
15. https://www.ucl.ac.uk/lbs/person/view/15207
16. https://www.ucl.ac.uk/lbs/person/view/41207

17. https://www.historyofParliamentonline.org/volume/1820-1832/member/bright-henry-1784-1869
18. https://www.historyofParliamentonline.org/volume/1715-1754/member/johnson-sir-thomas-1664-1728
19. https://www.historyofParliamentonline.org/volume/1715-1754/member/gildart-richard-1671-1770
20. Sheffield City Archives. CM Marriage Settlement Richard Milnes Bridgett Pemberton 18 February 1717.
21. Sheffield City Archives. CM 1500a Will John Pemberton.
22. Sheffield City Archives. CM 1502 Will Richard Milnes.
23. TNA S SP 42/27/137 1744 Sept 19 Request from his majesty's agent at Kinsale for the escort by English troops of French prisoners landed at Cork (by the privateers 'Old Nol' and 'Thurloe'). See also TNA P 36/88/2/94 1746 Oct 20.
24. TNA HCA 32/96/13 HCA 32/96 – Ships captured as prizes.
25. Sheffield City Archives. Wentworth Woodhouse mun. R58-259-28.
26. Sheffield City Archives. Wentworth Woodhouse mun. R58-259-29.
27. John Goodchild Milnes family MSS Notes.
28. Sheffield City Archives. CM 1505. Wakefield Court Baron.
29. Sheffield City Archives. CM 1504. Receipt October 22 1757 signed John Tarleton.
30. Sheffield City Archives. CM 1506-2 Receipt July 5 1765 signed John Tarleton.
31. Minchinton et al (1984), pp. 30–1.
32. Rawley et al (2005), pp. 178–83.
33. https://www.historyofParliamentonline.org/volume/1790-1820/member/tarleton-banastre-1754-1833
34. https://www.ucl.ac.uk/lbs/person/view/2146632009
35. Sheffield City Archives. CM 1505 Indenture 1755 Milnes, Tarleton, Goodwin, Heywood.
36. John Goodchild John Milnes MSS.
37. *Wakefield Star* – 2 March 1810.
38. John Goodchild Collection. John Milnes.
39. York City Archives. Yorkshire Association Papers. WYV/1/39/50 Letter from John Milnes of Wakefield 18 April 1780.
40. https://www.ucl.ac.uk/lbs/person/view/2146648811
41. https://www.ucl.ac.uk/lbs/person/view/2146644163
42. *Leeds Intelligencer* – Tuesday 11 October 1774.
43. *The Leeds Mercury* – Tuesday 7 June 1774.
44. John Goodchild Collection. Pemberton Milnes MSS.

45. Ibid.
46. https://www.ucl.ac.uk/lbs/person/view/25792
47. TNA HCA 26/11/105.
48. https://www.ucl.ac.uk/lbs/person/view/2146642763
49. https://www.ucl.ac.uk/lbs/person/view/2146642761
50. TNA SP 78/303/50 Folio 114: Henry Haffey to Gill Slater, merchant of Liverpool, on arrival at Grenada, he found privateers, mainly French, taking British ships as prizes and selling slaves to Bingham. 'What admiral Young is doing God knows. It would be better if war were declared.' Date and place: 1777 Apr 12 Grenada.
51. TNA SP 78/302/150 Folio 334: Henry Haffey of St. Vincent to Gill Slater of Liverpool. Encloses a list of privateers at Martinique and St. Lucia in the last 15 days. The Congress agents issue blank commissions, prizes are taken into French ports and openly sold. He gives an example of this. Date and place: 1777 Mar 10 St Lucia.
52. https://www.ucl.ac.uk/lbs/person/view/2146642765
53. TNA PWLB 11/105 – St Vincent: MOUNT ALEXANDER and SHARPES plantations; PETIT BORDELS (formerly KLADERS), CHANTONES and WALLILABO estates. Release for a year of 36 acres by William Henry MASTERTON to Henry HAFFEY and Jacob RICHARDSON.
54. Sheffield City Archives. WWM/R58-4 Merchants of Sheffield to Rockingham, no date 1766.
55. Hall et al (2014), p. 204.
56. https://www.ucl.ac.uk/lbs/person/view/2146660215
57. https://www.ucl.ac.uk/lbs/person/view/44886
58. https://www.ucl.ac.uk/lbs/firm/view/-1928154154
59. Dawson (2019b), pp. 25–6.
60. John Goodchild. The Ossett Mill Company MSS Notes
61. https://www.historyofParliamentonline.org/volume/1754-1790/member/dawkins-henry-1728-1814
62. https://w https://www.ucl.ac.uk/lbs/person/view/19278ww.ucl.ac.uk/lbs/person/view/41819
63. https://www.cambridge.org/core/books/legacies-of-british-slaveownership/helping-to-make-britain-great/DD5B983DBBEDD4983933A0DFBE751A97/core-reader
64. John Goodchild. Milnes Gaskell of Thornes House MSS Notes.
65. https://www.ucl.ac.uk/lbs/person/view/8961
66. Dawson (2019), pp. 66–7.
67. https://www.ucl.ac.uk/lbs/person/view/2146631733

Chapter 9: Island Governance

1. https://www.ucl.ac.uk/lbs/person/view/722
2. https://www.ucl.ac.uk/lbs/person/view/2663
3. Site visit 15 August 2020.
4. https://www.slavevoyages.org/voyage/database#statistics Metcalf
5. https://www.ucl.ac.uk/lbs/person/view/41944
6. https://www.ucl.ac.uk/lbs/person/view/2146665403
7. Dawson (2018), p. 73.
8. Rebecca Hartkopf Schloss (2012), *Sweet Liberty: The final days of slavery in Martinique*. Philadelphia: Philadelphia University Press.
9. Dawson (2018), p. 73.
10. Site visit 15 August 2020.

Chapter 10: Yorkshire and the Slave Trade

1. Epstein (2007).

Chapter 11: Slaves in Yorkshire?

1. *Gentleman's Magazine*, October 1764, p. 493.
2. Paul L. Dawson 'Rachel and Mary' Lecture delivered on International Women's Day, March 2020 at Wakefield One, Burton Street Wakefield, detailing the lives of the Busck family of Leeds and Wakefield.
3. Ibid.
4. Sally Fairweather pers comm 3 September 2020.
5. https://www.africansinyorkshireproject.com/black-servants.html
6. Sidney Leslie Ollard and Philip Charles Walker (1928), *Archbishop Herring's Visitation Returns, 1743*, Vol. 1. Cambridge: Cambridge University Press, p. 105.
7. Ancestry.com. England, Select Marriages, 1538–1973 [database on-line]. Provo, UT, USA: Ancestry.com Operations, Inc., 2014.
8. https://www.africansinyorkshireproject.com/black-servants.html
9. Ancestry.com. England, Select Births and Christenings, 1538-1975 [database on-line]. Provo, UT, USA: Ancestry.com Operations, Inc., 2014.
10. Ibid.
11. Ancestry.com. England, Select Births and Christenings, 1538-1975 [database on-line]. Provo, UT, USA: Ancestry.com Operations, Inc., 2014.

12. Yorkshire Parish Register Section; Leeds, England, United Kingdom; Yorkshire: Rillington Parish Register, 1638-1812.
13. https://www.historyofParliamentonline.org/volume/1715-1754/member/st-quintin-sir-william-1662-1723
14. https://www.africansinyorkshireproject.com/black-servants.htmlw.york.ac.uk/borthwick/holdings/guides/research-guides/race/black-baptisms/carolina-letter/
15. John William Walker (1888), *The History of the Old Parish Church of All Saints Wakefield*. Wakefield: W. H. Milnes, p. 304.
16. https://www.ucl.ac.uk/lbs/estate/view/600
17. John Goodchild. Burneytops House MSS.
18. The National Archives of the UK (TNA); Kew, Surrey, England; Collection: Board of Stamps: Apprenticeship Books: Series IR 1; Class: IR 1; Piece: 44
19. R. C. Richardson (2010), *Household Servants in Early Modern England.* Manchester: University of Manchester Press, p. 67.
20. https://www.findmypast.co.uk
21. Kirklees Archives KCZ0016 – RAMSDEN OF BYRAM AND LONGLEY (DD/R) DD/RA/F/2b/52(1) Governor Wentworth to Lady Rockingham from Long Island 1 Dec 1776.
22. West Yorkshire Archive Service; Wakefield, Yorkshire, England; Yorkshire Parish Records; New Reference Number: WDP5/1/1/8.
23. https://www.findmypast.co.uk/
24. https://www.ucl.ac.uk/lbs/person/view/2146662171
25. https://www.findmypast.co.uk/
26. *The Yorkshire Archaeological Journal*, Vol. 77 (2005), p. 212.
27. Ancestry.com. England, Select Births and Christenings, 1538-1975 [database on-line]. Provo, UT, USA: Ancestry.com Operations, Inc., 2014.
28. https://www.historyofParliamentonline.org/volume/1660-1690/member/osborne-peregrine-1659-1729
29. https://www.york.ac.uk/borthwick/holdings/guides/research-guides/race/black-baptisms/wakefield-letter/#transcript
30. Walker (1888), p. 304.
31. https://www.ucl.ac.uk/lbs/estate/view/332
32. Levon et al (2014), p. 75. See also p. 15, p. 62 note 7 and p. 76 note 6.
33. http://www.biographi.ca/en/bio/prescott_robert_5E.html
34. https://www.ucl.ac.uk/lbs/person/view/2146665465
35. Ancestry.com. England, Select Births and Christenings, 1538-1975 [database on-line]. Provo, UT, USA: Ancestry.com Operations, Inc., 2014.

36. TNA, Prerogative Court of Canterbury and Related Probate Jurisdictions: Will Registers; Class: PROB 11; Piece: 933.
37. Hampshire Archives and Local Studies 23M93/E/B3 Account of James Leigh Perrot with Robert Wadeson, 1764-1766, c. 1766.
38. https://www.ucl.ac.uk/lbs/person/view/2146660413
39. https:/ Ancestry.com. Barbados, Select Baptisms, 1739-1891 [database on-line]. Provo, UT, USA: Ancestry.com Operations, Inc., 2014.
40. Ancestry.com. London, England, Clandestine Marriage and Baptism Registers, 1667-1754 [database on-line]. Provo, UT, USA: Ancestry. com Operations, Inc., 2013.
41. Ancestry.com. England, Select Marriages, 1538–1973 [database on-line]. Provo, UT, USA: Ancestry.com Operations, Inc., 2014.
42. Ancestry.com. Caribbean, English Settlers in Barbados, 1637-1800 [database on-line]. Provo, UT, USA: Ancestry.com Operations Inc, 2007.
43. TNA, Court of King's Bench: Plea Side: Affidavits of Due Execution of Articles of Clerkship, Series I; Class: KB 105; Piece: 1.
44. www.ucl.ac.uk/lbs/person/view/2146656037
45. Ancestry.com. England, Select Births and Christenings, 1538-1975 [database on-line]. Provo, UT, USA: Ancestry.com Operations, Inc., 2014.
46. Sheffield City Archives. Crewe Muniments.
47. https://www.findmypast.co.uk/
48. https://www.york.ac.uk/borthwick/holdings/guides/research-guides/race/black-baptisms/visitation-record-q9/
49. https://www.genuki.org.uk/big/eng/YKS/WRY/Darfield/DarfieldBaptisms1760-1769
50. Ancestry.com. England, Select Births and Christenings, 1538-1975 [database on-line]. Provo, UT, USA: Ancestry.com Operations, Inc., 2014.
51. *Williamson's Liverpool Advertiser and Mercantile Register* – 8 September 1758.
52. J.D. Ellis (2003), '"Distinguished in action": The Black Soldiers of the 4th Dragoons, 1715-1842', *The Chronicle: The Journal of The Queen's Royal Hussars Historical Society*, Vol. 1, No. 3.
53. Yorkshire Parish Register Section; Leeds, England, United Kingdom; Yorkshire: Allerton Mauleverer Parish Register, 1557-1812.
54. Ancestry.com. England, Select Births and Christenings, 1538–1975 [database on-line]. Provo, UT, USA: Ancestry.com Operations, Inc., 2014.
55. https://www.ucl.ac.uk/lbs/person/view/2146656213

56. Ancestry.com. England, Select Births and Christenings, 1538–1975 [database on-line]. Provo, UT, USA: Ancestry.com Operations, Inc., 2014.
57. Yorkshire Parish Register Section; Leeds, England, United Kingdom; Oswaldkirk, 1538-1837.
58. https://www.historyofParliamentonline.org/volume/1715-1754/member/thompson-edward-1696-1742
59. https://www.jerseyheritage.org/media/Learning/BoJ%20Heroes%20and%20Villains.pdf
60. *Yorkshire Archaeological Journal*, Vol. 6 (1881), p. 203.
61. Ibid.
62. https://www.ucl.ac.uk/lbs/person/view/2146650617

Chapter 12: Free Black People in Yorkshire

1. Surtees Society, *Register of the Freemen of the City of York from the City Records*, vol. I, no. 96 (1897) and vol. II, no. 102 (1900).
2. Sally Fairweather pers comm 3 September 2020.
3. https://www.findmypast.co.uk/
4. https://www.ucl.ac.uk/lbs/person/view/2146651053. Leonard Parkinson's son Richard married into the Lechmere family, who were also slave owners.
5. https://www.ucl.ac.uk/lbs/person/view/2146642461
6. https://www.ucl.ac.uk/lbs/person/view/43736
7. https://www.ancestry.co.uk/family-tree/person/tree/13274425/person/-95758103/Gallery?_phtarg=NNG349
8. TNA PROB 11/1770/111 Will of Henry Kirlew, Gentleman of Phoenix Park Parish of Westmorland, Island of Jamaica 22 April 1830.
9. https://www.findmypast.co.uk/transcript?id=GBPRS%2FD%2F814109054
10. Military-Genealogy.com, comp. UK, Waterloo Medal Roll, 1815 [database on-line]. Provo, UT, USA: Ancestry.com Operations, Inc., 2010.
11. Yorkshire Marriages. East Riding Archives & Local Studies Service. PE 46/22. Page 53. findmypast.co.uk
12. Ancestry.com. England, Select Births and Christenings, 1538-1975 [database on-line]. Provo, UT, USA: Ancestry.com Operations, Inc., 2014.
13. *Journal of the Society for Army Historical Research*, Vol. 82 (2004), p. 206.

14. Ancestry.com. England, Select Births and Christenings, 1538-1975 [database on-line]. Provo, UT, USA: Ancestry.com Operations, Inc., 2014.
15. Henry Clarkson (1889), *Memoires of Merry Wakefield*. Wakefield: W.H. Milnes, p. 19.
16. Sheffield City Archives. Wentworth Woodhouse Muniments, Y16. General correspondence relating to the militia and the volunteer corps.
17. https://www.ucl.ac.uk/lbs/person/view/2146645293
18. Ancestry.com. 1841 England Census [database on-line]. Provo, UT, USA: Ancestry.com Operations, Inc, 2010.
19. Ancestry.com. 1851 England Census [database on-line]. Provo, UT, USA: Ancestry.com Operations Inc, 2005.
20. https://www.ucl.ac.uk/lbs/person/view/2146635036
21. https://www.ucl.ac.uk/lbs/person/view/2146638489
22. https://www.ucl.ac.uk/lbs/person/view/13594
23. George Tierney PC (1761–1830) was an Anglo-Irish Whig politician. He joined the Whig Club in 1791, far more than the £1,000 which he apparently received from opposition funds. His subsequent activities as co-treasurer of the Association of the Friends of the People, for whose *Report on the State of the Parliamentary Representation* (1793) he was primarily responsible, gained him the friendship of Charles Grey and some notoriety as a devotee of French republican principles. In 1796, 'Citizen' Tierney, financed by public subscription, contested Southwark with a slogan of 'peace and reform against war and corruption'.
24. Richard Brinsley Butler Sheridan (1751–1816) was an Irish satirist, a playwright, poet, and long-term owner of the London Theatre Royal, Drury Lane. In 1780, Sheridan entered Parliament as the ally of Charles James Fox on the side of the American Colonists in the political debate of that year. He is said to have paid the burgesses of Stafford five guineas apiece to allow him to represent them. As a consequence, his first speech in Parliament was a defence against the charge of bribery. He was a supporter of the ideals of the French Revolution, and broke with Burke and the Portland Whigs over this.
25. https://www.ucl.ac.uk/lbs/person/view/10067
26. https://www.ucl.ac.uk/lbs/person/view/2146638489
27. Ancestry.com. 1851 England Census [database on-line]. Provo, UT, USA: Ancestry.com Operations Inc, 2005.
28. Site visit Beverley Minster.
29. https://www.ucl.ac.uk/lbs/person/view/2146638489

30. https://www.ucl.ac.uk/lbs/person/view/46243
31. Site visit 1 August 2020.
32. Ancestry.com. England, Select Births and Christenings, 1538-1975 [database on-line]. Provo, UT, USA: Ancestry.com Operations, Inc., 2014.
33. Ancestry.com. 1851 England Census [database on-line]. Provo, UT, USA: Ancestry.com Operations, Inc, 2010.
34. Ancestry.com. West Yorkshire, England, Church of England Births and Baptisms, 1813-1910 [database on-line]. Lehi, UT, USA: Ancestry.com Operations, Inc., 2011.
35. Ancestry.com. 1841 England Census [database on-line]. Provo, UT, USA: Ancestry.com Operations, Inc, 2010.
36. Ancestry.com. 1851 England Census [database on-line]. Provo, UT, USA: Ancestry.com Operations, Inc, 2010.
37. Ancestry.com. England, Select Deaths and Burials, 1538-1991 [database on-line]. Provo, UT, USA: Ancestry.com Operations, Inc., 2014.
38. TNA HO 42/31 – HO 42. Letters and papers. Folios 124-125. Letter from Reverend John Griffith, magistrate of Manchester, 14 June 1794.
39. TNA HO 42/31 – HO 42. Letters and papers. Folios 116-117. Letter from John Brookfield, solicitor, of Sheffield, 9 June 1794.
40. The National Archives of the UK (TNA); Kew, Surrey, England; Collection: Board of Stamps: Apprenticeship Books: Series IR 1; Class: IR 1; Piece: 28
41. Amanda Goodrich (2019), *Henry Redhead Yorke, Colonial Radical: Politics and Identity in the Atlantic World 1772-1813*. London: Routledge.
42. TNA PROB 11/1128/157 Will of Samuel Readhead or Redhead of City of London, 06 April 1785
43. TNA HO 42/31 – HO 42. Letters and papers. Folios 116-117. Letter from John Brookfield, solicitor, of Sheffield, 9 June 1794 .
44. Malcolm Chase, 'Wedderburn, Robert (1762–1835/6?), radical', [*Oxford Dictionary of National Biography*, online edn.] http://www.oxforddnb.com/view/article/47120?docPos=2

Chapter 13: The Road to Abolition

1. A. Smith (1761), p. 316.
2. Davis (1999), p. 269.
3. Sharp (1769), pp. 48–9.
4. Ibid., pp. 10–11.
5. Ibid., p. 14.

6. Sharp (1773).
7. To Benjamin Franklin from [David Hartley], 14 November 1775, Founders Online, National Archives, https://founders.archives.gov/documents/Franklin/01-22-02-0153. [Original source: *The Papers of Benjamin Franklin*, vol. 22, March 23, 1775, through October 27, 1776, ed. William B. Willcox. New Haven and London: Yale University Press, 1982, pp. 254–260.]
8. Hugh Thomas (1997), *The Slave Trade: The story of the Atlantic Slave Trade: 1440-1870*. New York: Simon & Schuster, p. 478.
9. A. Smith (1776).
10. Turner (1777), pp. 26–34.
11. Ibid., pp. 26–7.
12. Ibid., p. 28.
13. Ibid., p. 33.
14. Abraham Rees (1743–1825) was a Welsh Nonconformist minister, and compiler of *Rees's Cyclopædia*. His theology was of a mediating and transitional character; his doctrines had an evangelical flavour, though essentially of an Arian type, and inclining to those of Richard Price, and he held the tenet of a universal restoration. He was the last of the London Dissenting ministers who officiated in a wig.
15. Andrew Kippis (1725–95) was an English Nonconformist clergyman and biographer. From 1763 until 1784 he was classical and philological tutor at the Coward Trust's academy at Hoxton, and subsequently in the New College at Hackney, under Belsham, having adopted Unitarianism. Kippis was a voluminous writer. He contributed frequently to *The Gentleman's Magazine*, *The Monthly Review* and *The Library*; and he established the *New Annual Register*. He published sermons and pamphlets; and he prefaced a life to Nathaniel Lardner's works (1788). He wrote a life preface to Philip Doddridge's *Exposition of the New Testament* (1792).
16. Jonathan Shipley (1714–88) was a clergyman in the Church in Wales, also having held offices in the Church of England (including Dean of Winchester from 1760 to 1769), who became Bishop of Llandaff from January to September 1769 and Bishop of St Asaph from September 1769 until his death. He was much concerned with politics, and joined the Whig party in strong opposition to the policy of George III towards the American Colonies. In 1774, when the British Parliament were discussing punitive measures against the town of Boston after the Tea Party incident, Shipley was apparently the only Church of England bishop (who were legally constituted members of Parliament) who raised his voice in opposition. He

prepared a speech in protest of the proposed measures, but was not given the opportunity to present it. Therefore, he had it published, but due to the general feeling in England against the rebellious colonies, the speech had no impact at all. One can easily see why he would be drawn to Rev. William Turner. Shipley also maintained a strong friendship with the Philadelphia printer Benjamin Franklin, who stayed with Shipley in Winchester, and while there wrote much of his autobiography. In 1784, in a letter to Henry Laurens, Franklin called Shipley 'America's constant friend, the good Bishop of Asaph' In 1779, Shipley was the only bishop to advocate the abolition of all laws against Protestant dissenters i.e. Unitarians.

17. Dr William Rose (1719–86) was a Scottish schoolmaster and classical scholar.
18. Newcome Cappe (1733–1800), was an English unitarian divine.
19. Wood (1794), p. 44.
20. Richard Price (1776), *Observations on the Nature of Civil Liberty.* London: J. Johnson.
21. John Cartwright (1826), *The Life and Correspondence of Major Cartwright* Vol. 1. London: Henry Colburn, p. 66.
22. Sharp (1773).
23. John Jebb and John Disney (1787), *The Works Theological, Medical, Political and Miscellaneous of Dr John Jebb* Vol 2. London: J. Johnson, p. 462
24. York City Archives. Yorkshire Association Papers. WYV/1/37/71 Thomas Zouch 19 December 1779.
25. Ibid., WYV/1/37/71 Pemberton Milnes to Wyvill 5 December 1779.
26. Ibid., WYV/1/39/67 Letter from John Milnes of Wakefield 1 June 1780.
27. Sheffield City Archives. WWM/R139-20 James Milnes to Rockingham,12 September 1780.
28. York City Library. Yorkshire Association Papers. WYV/1/39/97 Letter from James Milnes Jnr 1 October 1780.
29. Ibid., WYV/1/39 uncatalogued letter Robert Lumb 2 October 1780.
30. York City Library. Yorkshire Association Papers. Collection of Signatures made by John Milnes of Wakefield; Collection of Signatures made by James Milnes of Wakefield.
31. Dawson (2019c), p. 22.
32. Walvin (2011).
33. Berkshire County Record Office Hartley MSS., D. EHy. 017/2/51 William Waller to David Hartley 27 May 1780.
34. Wilberforce (1843), Vol. 1, p. 94.

Chapter 14: Abolition Round 1

1. Ditchfield (2007), Vol. 1, p. 338.
2. Ibid., pp. 539–40.
3. Kippis (1788), p. 36.
4. John Goodchild Pers Comm. Notes on Thomas Belsham reference educated of Thomas Johnstone.
5. Richard Price (1784), *Observations on the importance of the American Revolution and the means of making it a benefit to the World*. London, J, Johnson, pp. 83–4.
6. To Thomas Jefferson from Benjamin Vaughan, [ca. 14 June 1789], Founders Online, National Archives, https://founders.archives.gov/documents/Jefferson/01-15-02-0187. [Original source: *The Papers of Thomas Jefferson*, Vol. 15, 27 March 1789–30 November 1789, ed. Julian P. Boyd. Princeton: Princeton University Press (1958), pp. 182–3.]
7. John Goodchild. Priestley MSS.
8. William Belsham (1789), *Essays Philosophical, Historical and Literary* Vol. 1. London: C. Dily, pp. 438–40.
9. Seckers (ed.) (2008), p. 50.
10. Thom (1854), p. 61.
11. *The Christian reformer; or, Unitarian magazine and review* ed. by Robert Aspland. John Goodchild Collection MSS notes.
12. https://www.ucl.ac.uk/lbs/person/view/21522
13. https://www.ucl.ac.uk/lbs/person/view/28769
14. https://www.ucl.ac.uk/lbs/person/view/42162
15. https://www.historyofParliamentonline.org/volume/1790-1820/member/roscoe-william-1753-1831
16. https://www.ucl.ac.uk/lbs/person/view/43542
17. https://www.ucl.ac.uk/lbs/person/view/8821
18. Brian Howman, 'Abolitionism in Liverpool' in Tibbles and Schwarz (2007), p. 279.
19. *Leeds Intelligencer* – Tuesday 11 March 1788.
20. *Sheffield Register, Yorkshire, Derbyshire, & Nottinghamshire Universal Advertiser* – Saturday 12 July 1788.
21. Dresser (2001), pp. 139–42.
22. Enfield (1788), p. 17.
23. Clarkson (1808), Vol. 2, p. 279.
24. John Goodchild. Nottingham High Pavement MSS.
25. http://www.tellingourstoriesexeter.org.uk/uploads/Documents/Stories%20to%20Publish/Exeter%20Abolitionists.pdf
26. Hunt (1977), p. 35.

27. Hall et al (2014), pp. 202–10.
28. https://www.ucl.ac.uk/lbs/person/view/45878
29. https://www.ucl.ac.uk/lbs/person/view/1844309632
30. Drescher (1987), p. 70.
31. Ibid., pp. 68–71.
32. Andrews (2003), p. 124.
33. Andrews (2003) p. 149 reports that Christie had travelled to France in 1789 with a letter of introduction from Rev. Dr Richard Price, and during his six-month sojourn met Mirabeau, Abbe Sieyès and Necker. He defended Price against Burke's attack with his publication *Letters on the Revolution in France*. Christie also met Rev. William Turner of Westgate Chapel.
34. Benjamin Flower (1755–1829) was an English radical journalist and political writer, and a vocal opponent of his country's involvement in the early stages of the Napoleonic Wars. From the early 1780s Flower belonged to the Society for Constitutional Information. In 1799 Flower was summoned before the House of Lords, for remarks made in the *Intelligencer* against Richard Watson, bishop of Llandaff, whose political conduct he had censured. After a short hearing he was adjudged guilty of a breach of privilege, and sentenced to six months in Newgate Prison and a fine.
35. Andrews (2003), pp. 149–57 provides context for Unitarian Jacobin journalists and publications.

Chapter 15: Yorkshire for Abolition

1. John Goodchild. Pemberton Milnes MSS.
2. *Sheffield Register, Yorkshire, Derbyshire, & Nottinghamshire Universal Advertiser* – Saturday 26 January 1788, p. 3.
3. John Goodchild. Northgate End MSS Notes.
4. John Beatson (1799), *The Divine Right of a Christian to Freedom of Enquiry and Practice in Religious Matters* 2nd Edition. London: T. Chapman, pp. iii–xii.
5. John Beatson (1778), *A Sermon preached February 27 1778*, p. 45.
6. Ibid., p. 25.
7. John Beatson (1789), *Compassion the Duty and Dignity of Man: And Cruelty the Disgrace of His Nature. A Sermon, occasioned by that Branch of British Commerce which Extends to the Human Species. Preached to a Congregation of Protestant Dissenters in Hull, January 21st, 1789. By John Beatson.*
8. John Goodchild. Hull Unitarian Chapel MSS Notes.

9. John Beatson (1789), p. 5.
10. Ibid., p. 12.
11. Ibid., pp. 55–6.
12. *York Courant* – 21 February 1792. Advertisement for a meeting in Kingston Upon Hull on 13 February 1792.
13. Thomas Clarke (1792), *A sermon on the injustice of the Slave Trade, preached February 12th 1792 in the Church of the Holy Trinity, Kingston-Upon-Hull*. Hull: J Feeraby, pp.18-19
14. *Leeds Intelligencer* – Tuesday 20 December 1768.
15. *Leeds Intelligencer* – Tuesday 05 February 1788.
16. Ibid.
17. William Hey (1736–1819) was an English surgeon, born in Pudsey. He was a surgeon at Leeds General Infirmary from its opening in a temporary building in 1776, and senior surgeon from 1773 to 1812. Hey served as mayor of Leeds in 1787–88 and 1802–03. In 1783 he was President of the Leeds Philosophical and Literary Society. He also founded the Leeds Club. In March, 1775 he was elected a Fellow of the Royal Society. He gave his name to Hey's amputation (a tarso-metatarsal amputation), Hey's internal derangement (dislocation of the semilunar cartilages of the knee joint), Hey's ligament (the semilunar lateral margin (falciform margin) of the fossa ovalis), and Hey's saw, used in skull surgery.
18. *Leeds Intelligencer* – Tuesday 29 January 1788.
19. *Leeds Intelligencer* – Tuesday 04 March 1788.
20. *Leeds Intelligencer* – Tuesday 26 February 1788.
21. *Leeds Intelligencer* – Tuesday 11 March 1788.
22. *Leeds Intelligencer* – Tuesday 12 February 1788.
23. Richard Vickerman Taylor (1865), *The biographia Leodiensis*, Leeds: John Hamer, pp. 264–6.
24. *Leeds Intelligencer* – Tuesday 12 January 1790.
25. John Goodchild. Rev. William Wood MSS.
26. John Goodchild. Rev. William Wood MSS. Sermon delivered to Assembly of Protestant Dissenting Ministers at Bradford 4 July 1781.
27. Charles Wellbeloved (1809), *Memories of the life and writings of the late Rev. W Wood FLS and minister of the Protestant Dissenting Chapel at Mill Hill in Leeds*, London: J. Johnson, pp. 62–3.
28. J.R. Oldfield (1998), *Popular Politics and the British Anti-Slavery*, London: Routledge, p. 108.
29. *Leeds Intelligencer* – Monday 18 May 1807.
30. *Leeds Intelligencer* – Tuesday 05 February 1788.

31. John Goodchild Rotherham Unitarian Chapel MSS Notes.
32. *Sheffield Register, Yorkshire, Derbyshire, & Nottinghamshire Universal Advertiser* – Saturday 16 February 1788.
33. *Sheffield Register, Yorkshire, Derbyshire, & Nottinghamshire Universal Advertiser* – Saturday 23 February 1788.
34. *Sheffield Register, Yorkshire, Derbyshire, & Nottinghamshire Universal Advertiser* – Saturday 12 January 1788.
35. *Sheffield Register, Yorkshire, Derbyshire, & Nottinghamshire Universal Advertiser* – Saturday 19 January 1788.
36. *Sheffield Register, Yorkshire, Derbyshire, & Nottinghamshire Universal Advertiser* – Saturday 26 January 1788.
37. John Goodchild pers com. Shore MSS.
38. *Sheffield Register, Yorkshire, Derbyshire, & Nottinghamshire Universal Advertiser* – Saturday 26 January 1788.
39. John Goodchild pers com. Shore MSS.
40. *Sheffield Register, Yorkshire, Derbyshire, & Nottinghamshire Universal Advertiser* – Saturday 16 February 1788.
41. *Sheffield Register, Yorkshire, Derbyshire, & Nottinghamshire Universal Advertiser* – Saturday 02 February 1788.
42. *Sheffield Register, Yorkshire, Derbyshire, & Nottinghamshire Universal Advertiser* – Saturday 16 February 1788.
43. *Sheffield Register, Yorkshire, Derbyshire, & Nottinghamshire Universal Advertiser* – Saturday 22 March 1788.
44. *Sheffield Register, Yorkshire, Derbyshire, & Nottinghamshire Universal Advertiser* – Saturday 01 March 1788.
45. https://www.ucl.ac.uk/lbs/person/view/2146645567
46. https://www.ucl.ac.uk/lbs/person/view/2146654247
47. *Sheffield Register, Yorkshire, Derbyshire, & Nottinghamshire Universal Advertiser* – Saturday 06 June 1789.
48. *Sheffield Register, Yorkshire, Derbyshire, & Nottinghamshire Universal Advertiser* – Friday 06 May 1791.
49. *Leeds Intelligencer* – Tuesday 11 March 1788.
50. Westgate Chapel Archive. Pew Rent Register 1768–1803.
51. Cappe (1757).
52. Cappe (1777).
53. Cappe (1784), pp. 22–3.
54. *Leeds Intelligencer* – Tuesday 06 April 1784.
55. *York Courant* – 13 April 1784.
56. *Leeds Intelligencer* – Tuesday 22 April 1784.
57. *Leeds Intelligencer* – Tuesday 04 May 1784.

58. Ibid. WW F43-34 Letter from Pemberton Milnes, Wakefield, to Fitzwilliam 24 February 1784.
59. Sheffield City Archives. WW F34-31 Spencer Stanhope MSS., 60567/5.
60. *Leeds Intelligencer* – Tuesday 25 January 1785.
61. *Leeds Intelligencer* – Tuesday 15 February 1785.
62. Wyvill papers.
63. *Leeds Intelligencer* – Tuesday 05 January 1790.
64. John Goodchild. Newcome Cappe MSS.
65. Priestley earned this sobriquet from his 'Gunpowder Sermon' of 5 November 1785 in which he declared that rational Dissenters, i.e. Unitarians, were 'laying gunpowder, grain by grain under the old building of error and superstition' i.e. the Church establishment. In time a spark might ignite this gunpowder and produce 'an instantaneous explosion' so that the 'work of ages, may be overturned in a moment, and so effectually as the same foundation can never be built on again'.
66. John Goodchild. Newcome Cappe MSS.
67. William Mason (1788), *An occasional discourse preached in the Cathedral of St. Peter in York, January 27. J 788. on the subject of the African Slave-Trade*. York.
68. Wilberforce (1843), Vol. I, p. 189.
69. *Sheffield Register, Yorkshire, Derbyshire, & Nottinghamshire Universal Advertiser* – Saturday 09 February 1788.
70. https://www.historyofParliamentonline.org/volume/1790-1820/member/monckton-arundell-robert-1752-1810
71. Anon (1792), *The debate on a motion for the abolition of the slave-trade; in the House of Commons on Monday and Tuesday, April 18 and 19, 1791, reported in detail*. London: Printed by J. Phillips, p. 132.
72. Sheffield City Archives. Wentworth Woodhouse mun. F27/30; F34/203; F42/55; Fitzwilliam MSS, box 46, Milner to Fitzwilliam, 18 Nov. 1794; Add. 47569, f. 52; Morning Chron. 23, 26 May 1796.
73. Ditchfield (2007), Vol. II, p. 296.
74. *Morning Chronicle* – 23 May 1796; see also Wentworth Woodhouse mun. F34/204; N. Riding RO, Wyvill MSS ZFW7/2/104/19.
75. John Goodchild R S Rich MSS Notes.
76. Sheffield City Archives, Spencer Stanhope Mss, Thornton to W. Spencer Stanhope, 10 Nov. 1797; See Also Wyvill Mss 7/2/131/18; 7/2/134/18; Wyvill Papers, vi, pp. 167–72.
77. Ditchfield (2007), Vol. II, pp. 609–10.
78. Wilson (1971), p. 132.

79. House of Commons Journals, 5 February 1789. The petition was raised on 10 July 1788.

Chapter 16: Abolition Round 2

1. Charles James Fox (1853), *The Speeches of right Honourable Charles James Fox in the House of Common, 3rd Edition*. London: Ayclott & Co., p. 368.
2. *Leeds Intelligencer* – Monday 13 February 1792.
3. *Leeds Mercury* – 19 April 1791.
4. *Leeds Intelligencer* – Monday 12 March 1792.
5. *Leeds Intelligencer* – Monday 27 February 1792.
6. John Goodchild. Northgate End MSS Notes.
7. Olaudah Equiano (2003), *The Interesting Narrative and other writings*. London: Penguin Books, p. 355.
8. *The Monthly Magazine*, Issues 61–68, p. 372.
9. *Leeds Intelligencer* – Monday 27 February 1792.
10. Ibid.
11. TNA PROB 11/1222/2 Will of Henry Coulthurst, Mariner of Saint Michael Island of Barbados, West Indies.
12. https://www.ucl.ac.uk/lbs/person/view/2146634732
13. *Leeds Intelligencer* – Tuesday 08 November 1791.
14. *Leeds Intelligencer* – Tuesday 27 December 1791.
15. *Leeds Intelligencer* – Monday 20 February 1792.
16. *Leeds Intelligencer* – Monday 05 March 1792.
17. Richardson et al (2010), pp. 102–11.
18. *Leeds Intelligencer* – Monday 27 February 1792.
19. *Leeds Intelligencer* – Monday 12 March 1792.
20. *Leeds Intelligencer* – Monday 30 January 1792.
21. *Leeds Intelligencer* – Monday 19 March 1792.
22. *Sheffield Register* – 27 August 1790.
23. James Montgomery (1771–1854) was a Scottish-born hymn writer, poet and editor. His writings reflected concern for humanitarian causes such as the abolition of slavery and the exploitation of child chimney sweeps. He was raised in and theologically trained by the Moravian Church.
24. John Goodchild pers com. Shore MSS.
25. Stevenson (1989).
26. For more on the philosophical origins of Jacobin thought, see Gregory Dart (1999), *Rousseau, Robespierre, and English Romanticism*. Cambridge and New York: Cambridge University Press, pp. 1–19.

27. https://www.marxists.org/history/england/britdem/events/ sheffield.htm
28. Horgan (2016), p. 141.
29. John Goodchild Collection. 'Sermon on the good Samaritan delivered to the Congregation of Protestant Dissenters gathered at Westgate Chapel Wakefield by Rev. Thomas Johnstone', MSS notes February 1792.
30. John Goodchild pers comm.
31. Wilberforce (1843), Vol. II, p. 107.
32. TNA RG4/ 3674 Call Lane Arian Independent Chapel Baptisms 1695-1778. See also TNA GR4 /3723 Call Lane Independent Chapel, Baptisms 1778-1835.
33. John Goodchild Collection. James Milnes MSS Notes.
34. *The Morning Post and Gazetteer* – Wednesday 23 June 1802.
35. *The Morning Post and Gazetteer* – Wednesday 1 April 1801.
36. *The Morning Post and Gazetteer* – Monday 20 April 1801.
37. *The Morning Post and Gazetteer* – Monday 8 June 1801.
38. *The Leeds Intelligencer* – Monday 19 April 1802.
39. https://www.historyofParliamentonline.org/volume/1790-1820/ member/milnes-james-1755-1805
40. https://www.historyofParliamentonline.org/volume/1790-1820/ member/wilberforce-william-1759-1833
41. The Debates on a motion for the abolition of the Slave Trade, in the House of Commons, on Monday 2nd April, 1792, pp. 56-63. See also ibid. p. 73.
42. https://www.historyofParliamentonline.org/volume/1790-1820/ member/vaughan-benjamin-1751-1835
43. Vaughan (1793), p. 46.
44. https://www.ucl.ac.uk/lbs/person/view/2146653505
45. Wakefield (1792), pp. 188–1.

Chapter 17: State-Sponsored Terror

1. https://www.historyofParliamentonline.org/volume/1790-1820/ member/roscoe-william-1753-1831
2. Turner (1792), p. 303.
3. John Goodchild Pers comm 2/09/2015.
4. Stevenson (1979), p. 177.
5. Andrews (2003), pp. 155–6.
6. John Goodchild pers com. Shore MSS.
7. Stevenson (1989), p. 67.

8. *Sheffield Register, Yorkshire, Derbyshire, & Nottinghamshire Universal Advertiser* – Friday 11 April 1794.
9. Stevenson (1989), p. 31.
10. Paul L. Dawson (2019), *Westgate Chapel and Radical Politics*. Lecture given at Westgate Chapel 13 September 2019 to mark Heritage Open Days 2019.
11. Barrell and Mee (2006–07), p. xx.
12. Wilberforce (1797).
13. Wakefield (1797), p. 4.
14. Thomas Belsham (1798), *A Review of Mr Wilberforce's Treatise*. London, J. Johnson, pp. 2–3.
15. Ibid., p. 202.

Chapter 18: Abolition!

1. Revd Thomas Johnstone (1801), *Two Sermons, on the Alarm of Scarcity, and on the proper Improvement of the late General Fast, preached at the Chapel in Westgate, Wakefield. Rev. Thomas Johnstone*. London: J. Johnson.
2. https://www.historyofParliamentonline.org/volume/1790-1820/member/fox-hon-charles-james-1749-1806
3. Robert Pemberton Milnes and his wife.
4. Anna Maria Wilehelmina Stirling (1913), *The letter-bag of Lady Elizabeth Spencer-Stanhope, comp. from the Cannon hall papers, 1806-1873*. London: John Lane, pp. 123–4.
5. Wilberforce (1843), Vol. III, pp. 283–4.
6. John Goodchild. Northgate End notes MSS.
7. E. Smith (1967), pp. 61–90.
8. https://www.historyofParliamentonline.org/volume/1790-1820/member/wilberforce-william-1759-1833
9. https://www.historyofParliamentonline.org/volume/1790-1820/member/smith-william-1756-1835
10. https://www.historyofParliamentonline.org/volume/1790-1820/constituencies/yorkshire
11. Sheffield City Archives Fitzwilliam MSS. E. 156/11Thomas Lumb to Browns 31 May 1807.
12. E. Smith (1967), pp. 61–90.
13. *Leeds Intelligencer* – 11 June 1807.
14. https://www.historyofParliamentonline.org/volume/1790-1820/member/milnes-robert-pemberton-1784-1858
15. Nickolls (1788), p. 28.

Chapter 19: Yorkshire Unitarians and the Abolition of Slavery

1. https://www.historyofParliamentonline.org/volume/1790-1820/ member/duncombe-henry-1728-1818
2. https://www.historyofParliamentonline.org/volume/1790-1820/ member/stuart-wortley-james-archibald-1776-1845. He supported the imposition of the 'Gagging Acts' in 1819 following Peterloo.
3. *Leeds Mercury* – Saturday 15 February 1817.
4. *Leeds Intelligencer* – Monday 10 February 1817.
5. https://www.historyofParliamentonline.org/volume/1790-1820/ member/smyth-john-henry-1780-1822. He vehemently opposed the suspension of habeas corpus, 26 February 1817, as 'a great departure from the maxims of our ancestors' and was also a critic of the Seditious Meetings Bill, 2 December 1819.
6. *Leeds Intelligencer* – Monday 17 February 1817.
7. *Leeds Mercury* – Saturday 01 February 1817.
8. Martin and Mary Willans' son, Richard was baptised on 24 July 1792 at Westgate Chapel.
9. *Leeds Mercury* – 4 September 1819.
10. https://www.ucl.ac.uk/lbs/person/view/2146652449
11. *Wakefield and Halifax Journal* – 9 May 1823.
12. https://www.historyofParliamentonline.org/volume/1820-1832/ member/wyvill-marmaduke-1791-1872
13. Sheffield City Archives: Yorkshire Protestant Dissenters Association for the Abolition of Slavery circular, begins: 'At a Meeting of Friends of the Abolition of Negro Slavery, held in Leeds, on Monday, September 28th, 1829' (Leeds, 1829).
14. John Goodchild. Rev. Thomas Johnstone MSS. Poster for slave meeting.
15. John Goodchild. Rev. Thomas Johnstone MSS.
16. John Goodchild. Daniel Gaskell MSS Notes.
17. *Leeds Intelligencer* – 5 July 1832.
18. John Goodchild. Daniel Gaskell MSS Notes.
19. *Yorkshire Gazette* – Saturday 15 June 1833.
20. John Goodchild. Daniel Gaskell MSS Notes.
21. Leeds City Library. Joseph Bakers tracts. Volume 1. 'Why did the Ministers of Leeds Absent themselves?'.
22. Ibid., pp. 15–17.
23. John Goodchild Collection. John Goodwyn Barmby MSS.

Conclusion

1. Wilberforce (1843), Vol. III, p. 173.

Bibliography

Archive Sources

Berkshire County Record Office Hartley MSS.
Leeds City Library. Joseph Bakers tracts. Volume 1. Why did the Ministers of Leeds Absent themselves?
North Yorkshire Record Office. Wyvill Mss.
Sheffield City Archives. Wentworth Woodhouse Muniments, Fitzwilliam Papers.
The National Archives, Kew, London.
West Yorkshire History Centre. John Goodchild Collection.
York City Library. Yorkshire Association Papers.

Digital Sources

Africans in Yorkshire: www.africansinyorkshireproject.com
Ancestry.co.uk
Findmypast.co.uk
History of Parliament: www.historyofParliamentonline.org
Oxford Dictionary of National Biography: www.oxforddnb.com
Trans-Atlantic Slave Trade Database: www.slavevoyages.org
University College London Legacies of British Slave Ownership: www.ucl.ac.uk/lbs/

Printed Sources

Andrews, Stuart (2003), *Unitarian Radicalism. Political Rhetoric, 1770–1814*. New York: Pallgrave MacMillan.
Barrell, John, and Jon Mee (eds) (2006–07), *Trials for Treason and Sedition, 1792–1794* 8 vols. London: Pickering and Chatto.

Cappe, Newcome (1757), *A sermon preached at York to a Congregation of Protestant Dissenters on the 27th November 1757, just upon receiving the account of the King of Prussia's Victory.* York: C. Ward.

———— (1777), *A sermon preached on the Thirteenth day of December, the late Day of National Humiliation.* London: J. Johnson.

———— (1780), *A Sermon Preached on Friday the Fourth of February, MDCCLXXX.* London: J. Johnson.

———— (1781), *A Sermon Preached on Wednesday the 21st of February, MDCCLXXX.* London: J. Johnson.

———— (1784), *A Sermon Preached on Thursday the Twenty-ninth of July 1784.* London: J. Johnson.

Clarkson, Thomas (1788), *An essay on the slavery and commerce of the Human Species. 2nd Edition.* London: J. Phillips.

———— (1808), *The History of the Rise, Progress and Accomplishment of the Abolition of the African Slave Trade by the British Parliament.* Philadelphia: James Parke.

Cookson, J.E. (1982), *The Friends of Peace. Anti-war liberalism in England 1793-1815.* Cambridge: Cambridge University Press.

Cooper, Thomas (1824), *Letter to Robert Hibbert, Jun. Esq., in Reply to His Pamphlet, Entitled, 'Facts Verified Upon Oath, in Contradiction of the Report of the Rev. Thomas Cooper, Concerning the General Condition of the Slaves in Jamaica,' &c. &c: To which are Added, a Letter from Mrs. Cooper to R. Hibbert, Jun. Esq., and an Appendix Containing an Exposure of the Falsehoods and Calumnies of that Gentleman's Affidavit-men.* London.

Davis, David Brion (1999), *The Problem of Slavery in the Age of Revolution, 1770-1823.* Oxford: Oxford University Press.

Dawson, Paul Lindsay (2018), *Westgate Chapel Wakefield.* Wakefield: Paul L. Dawson.

———— (2019), *Westgate Chapel and the Wool Trade.* Wakefield: Paul L. Dawson.

———— (2019b), *Westgate Chapel Monuments.* Wakefield: Paul L. Dawson.

———— (2019c), *Lexington to Waterloo. Yorkshire Unitarianism and National Politics 1770-1830.* Wakefield: Paul L. Dawson.

————, 'Rachel and Mary'. Lecture delivered on International Women's Day, March 2020.

Day, Thomas (1784), *Fragment of an original letter on the slavery of Negroes.* London: John Stockdale.

Ditchfield, G.M. (2007), *The Letters of Theophilus Lindsey (1723-1808)* 2 vols. Woodbridge: Church of England Record Society.

Drescher, Seymour (1987), *Capitalism and Slavery*. Oxford: Oxford University Press.

Dresser, Madge (2001), *Slavery Obscured: the social history of the slave trade in an English provincial port*. London: Bloomsbury.

Enfield, William (1788), *A sermon on the centennial commemoration of the Revolution*. London: J. Johnson.

Epstein, James (2007), 'Politics of Colonial Sensation: The Trial of Thomas Picton and the Cause of Louisa Calderon', *American Historical Review* 112 (3).

Haggerty, Sheryllynne (2012), *'Merely for Money'?: Business Culture in the British Atlantic, 1750-1815*. Liverpool: Liverpool University Press.

Hall, Catherine, Nicholas Draper, Keith McClelland, Katie Donnington and Rachel Lang (2014), *Legacies of British Slave Ownership*. Cambridge: Cambridge University Press.

Harris, Michael and Alan J. Lee (1986), *The Press in English Society from the Seventeenth to Nineteenth Centuries*. Fairleigh Dickinson University Press.

Horgan, Kate (2016), *The Politics of Songs in Eighteenth Century Britain 1723–1795*. London: Routledge

Hughes, John (1906), *Liverpool Banks and Bankers. 1760-1837*. Liverpool: H. Young & Sons.

Hunt, E.M. (1977), 'The Anti-Slave Trade agitation in Manchester', *Transactions of the Lancashire and Cheshire Antiquarian Society* Vol. 79.

Jones, Clyve (2003), *Peers, Politics and Power: House of Lords, 1603–1911*. Bloomsbury Academic.

Kippis, Andrew (1788), *A sermon preached before the society for commemorating the Glorious Revolution*. London: J. Johnson.

Maw, Peter (2010), 'Yorkshire and Lancashire ascendant: England's textile exports to New York and Philadelphia, 1750-1805', *The Economic History Review*, 63(3), new series, pp. 734–68.

Minchinton, Walter E., Celia Mary King and Peter B. Waite (1984), *Virginia Slave-trade Statistics, 1698-1775*. Richmond: Virginia State Library.

Munkhouse, Richard (1799), *A Sermon, Preached in the Church of St. John Baptist, Wakefield, on Thursday November 29th 1798*. London: F. and C. Rivington.

Nickolls, Robert Boucher (1788), *Letter to the Treasurer of the society instituted for the purpose of effecting the abolition of the slave trade*. London: James Phillips.

Nicols, John (1831), *Illustrations of the Literary History of the Eighteenth Century*. London: J.B. Nichols and Son.

Oldfield, J.R. (1998), *Popular Politics and British Anti-Slavery*. London: Routledge.

Pick, William (1785), *An Authentic Historical Racing Calendar*. York: W. Blanchard.

Priestley, Joseph (1791), *Letters to the Right Honourable Edmund Burke: Occasioned by His Reflections on the Revolution in France*. Birmingham: Thomas Pearson.

Ramsay, James (1784), *An Essay on the Treatment and Conversion of African Slaves in the British Sugar Colonies*. London: James Phillips.

Rawley, James A. and Stephen D. Bhrednt (2005), *The Trans-Atlantic Slave Trade*. Lincoln: University of Nebraska Press.

Richardson, David Suzanne Schwarz and Anthony Tibbles (2010), *Liverpool and Trans-Atlantic Slavery*. Liverpool: Liverpool University Press.

David Seckers (ed.) (2008), 'The Diary of Hannah Lightbody, 1786–1790', *Enlightenment and Dissent. Special Supplement*, Vol. 24.

Seed, John (1985), 'Gentlemen Dissenters: The Social and Political Meanings of Rational Dissent in the 1770s and 1780s', *The Historical Journal*, 282.

Sharp, Granville (1769), 'Representation of the Injustice and Dangerous Tendency of Tolerating Slavery'. London: George Cruickshank.

——————— (1773), *An essay on slavery: proving from Scripture its inconsistency with humanity and religion; in answer to a late publication, entitled, 'The African trade for Negro slaves shewn to be consistent with principles of humanity, and with the laws of revealed religion.' By Granville Sharp, Esq. With an introductory preface, containing the sentiments of the monthly reviewers on that publication; and the opinion of several eminent writers on the subject. To which is added, an elegy on the miserable state of an African slave, by the celebrated an ingenious William Shenstone, Esq.* London: Isaac Collins.

Smail, John (2001), *Woollen Manufacturing in Yorkshire*. Yorkshire Archaeological Society: Boydell Press

Smith, Adam (1761), *Theory of Moral Sentiments* Second Edition. London: A. Millar.

—————— (1776), *The Wealth of Nations*. London: W. Strahan and T. Cadell.

Smith, E. (1967), 'The Yorkshire Elections of 1806 and 1807', *Northern History – A review of the history of the North of England*, Vol. 2.

Stange, Douglas Charles (1984), *British Unitarians against American Slavery 1833-1865*. London: Associated University Presses.

Stevenson, John (1979), *Popular Disturbances in England 1700-1832*. London: Routledge.

—————— (1989), *Artisans & Democrats: Sheffield in the French Revolution, 1789–97*. Sheffield History Pamphlets.

Surtees Society, *Register of the Freemen of the City of York from the City Records*, vol. I, no. 96 (1897), and vol. II, no. 102 (1900).

Taylor, Lesley and Shirley Levon (2014), *The Two Esthers: Letters from Mrs Robert Milnes of Sheffield and Wakefield to Esther Milnes of Chesterfield 1771-1773*. Taylor Levon Press.

Thom, David A (1854), *Liverpool Churches and Chapels; their destruction, removal or alteration*. Liverpool: Edward Howell.

Turner, William (1777), *The whole service as performed in the congregation of Protestant dissenters, at Wakefield, on Friday, December 13, 1776: Being the day appointed for a general fast. Printed at the request of the congregation. By William Turner*. Wakefield, Thomas Waller.

—————— (1792), *Sermons on various subjects published at the request of the congregation of Protestant Dissenters in Wakefield*. London. J. Johnson.

Vaughan, Benjamin (1793), *Letters, on a subject of the Concert of Princes, and the dismemberment of Poland and France. (First published in the Morning Chronicle between July 20, 1792 and June 25, 1793, by a calm observer [Benjamin Vaughan]*. London, Printed for G.G.J. & J. Robinson.

Wakefield, Gilbert (1792), *Memoirs of the Life of Gilbert Wakefield BA Late fellow of Jesus College*. London: E Hodson.

—————— (1797), *A Letter to William Wilberforce, Esq. On the Subject of his Late Publication*. London: J. Johnson.

Walker, Thomas (1788), *Two Sermons preached in Mill-Hill Chapel, in Leeds*. Leeds: Thomas Wright.

Walvin, James (2011), *The Zong: A massacre, the Law and the End of Slavery*. London: Yale University Press.

Wellbeloved, Charles (1800), *The Principles of Roman Catholics and Unitarians Contrasted: A sermon*. York: T. Wilson.

Wilberforce, Robert Isaac and Samuel Wilberforce (1843), *The Life of William Wilberforce* 5 vols. London: Seeley, Burnside and Seeley.

Wilberforce, William (1797), *A Practical View of the Prevailing Religious System of Professed Christians*. London: T. Cadell and W. Davies.

Williams, John (1833), *Memoirs of the Late Reverend Thomas Belsham*. London: John Williams.

Wilson, Richard George (1971), *Gentlemen Merchants: The Merchant Community in Leeds 1700 – 1830*. Manchester: Manchester University Press.

—————— (1971), 'The Denisons and Milneses: Eighteenth-Century Merchant Landowners', Ward J.T. and R.G. Wilson (eds), *Land and Industry:*

The Landed Estate and the Industrial Revolution. Newton Abbott; David and Charles.

Wood, William, F.L.S. (1794), *A Sermon preached ... on occasion of the death of the Rev. William Turner ... To which are added, Memoirs of Mr. Turner's life and writings.* London: J. Johnson.

Wyvill, Christopher (1794), *Political papers, chiefly respecting the attempt of the county of York* 6 vols. York: W. Blanchard.

Index

A

Atkinson, Law 174, 175, 207

B

Baines, Edward 147, 214, 215, 216
Bakewell, Robert 15, 194, 205, 206,
    209, 223
Barbados 25, 28, 31, 44, 49, 54, 63,
    83, 91, 105, 108, 109, 110, 162,
    176, 208
Barmby, Rev. John Goodwyn 3,
    221, 222
Barnsley 175, 215
Barrett family 26, 27, 40, 52,
    113, 114
Beatson, Rev. John 150, 151
Belsham, Rev. Thomas 139, 140–1,
    172, 186, 200
Belsham, Rev. William 140
Birch family 73, 75, 83, 88
Blundell family 41, 69, 79, 80, 88
Bradford 41, 49, 80, 112, 175
Bright family 74, 88, 143
Brisco family 12, 55, 56, 57, 58, 59,
    60, 61, 77
Bruce, Anne 114, 115
Bullock, Sarah 112
Burke, Edmund 27, 121, 131, 146,
    185, 191, 194, 200, 208, 222,
    227, 228

C

Cadman family 180
Caldwell, Charles 72, 88

Call Lane Chapel, Leeds 46, 101,
    158, 180, 186
Campbell family 57, 58, 112
Cappe, Rev. Newcome 130, 134,
    144, 151, 166, 168, 169
Cartwright, Major John 118, 131,
    132, 133, 134, 136, 146, 176,
    182, 191, 213, 218
Chaloner, Robert 27, 28, 86
Charnock family, xi, 10, 11, 24, 56,
    60, 67, 104, 105
Clarkson, Thomas 17, 19, 22, 133,
    136, 143, 144, 145, 156, 174,
    208, 211, 213, 214, 215, 228
coffee 9, 13, 32, 34, 66, 67, 70, 77,
    84, 94, 114, 142, 225
Cooper, Rev. Thomas 47, 145,
    146, 195
Coore, Foster Lechmere 50, 57, 58
Coulthurst, Rev. Dr Henry William
    34, 176, 177, 207
Cross Street Chapel, Manchester
    195

D

Demerara 29, 41, 63, 64, 66, 78,
    79, 87, 93, 116, 176, 177, 219
Denison family 17, 28, 29, 41, 62,
    72 224,
Digges family 10, 24, 83, 84, 145
Disney, Rev. John 59, 139
Douglass, Frederick 220, 221
Drinkwater, Peter 8, 9, 87
Dunbar, Margaret 118, 119

Duncombe, Charles 29
Duncombe, Henry 134, 154, 155, 211
Dunn, Thomas 79, 93

E
Earle, Hardman 85, 88
Equiano, Olaudah 144, 159, 174,
    175, 181, 182, 195

F
Fawkes, Walter Ramsden 206, 207,
    208, 212, 218
Fitzwilliam, Earl 28, 55, 81, 85, 158,
    167, 172, 208, 209
Fletcher, Thomas 142, 143
Fox, Charles James 137, 140, 144,
    146, 157, 167, 171, 173, 179,
    192, 199, 205, 208
France, Fletcher Yates & Co 142

G
Gales, Joseph 3, 121, 122, 132, 147,
    159, 160, 161, 162, 163, 181,
    182, 196, 197, 198
Gaskell, Benjamin 46, 87, 211, 214
Gaskell, Daniel 46, 86, 214, 218,
    219, 220
Gaskell, James Milnes 87
Gill, Captain William 71
Goore family 41
Gully, John 220

H
Hackney, Captain Alexander 64
Haffey, Henry 83
Haffey, Peter 83
Halifax 7, 11, 25, 26, 34, 39, 42, 43,
    46, 59, 62, 81, 89, 135, 150, 174,
    175, 176, 178, 206, 207, 214
Hammond, Benjamin 43, 44
Hardy, Thomas 146, 192, 195

Hartley, David 129, 136
Heath Academy, the 41, 67, 132
Hey, William 154, 155, 206
Heywood family 8, 10, 24, 41, 51,
    55, 69, 72, 75, 85, 88, 135, 224
Heywood, Arthur 20, 29, 65, 70, 72,
    73, 78, 79, 82, 83, 84, 89
Heywood, Benjamin of Stanley
    Hall, 44, 70, 85, 87, 107, 134,
    224
Heywood, John Pemberton 8, 70,
    87, 88, 168, 224
Heywood, Sergeant Samuel 135
Hibbert family 45, 69, 145
Hibbert, Thomas 33, 84
Higginson, Rev. Edward 221, 223
High Pavement Chapel,
    Nottingham 43, 144
Hodgson family 43
Hodgson, Ellis Leckonby 43, 44, 89
Hollis, Thomas Brand 132, 134
Hurst, Ann 214, 215, 216

I
Ingram family 8, 41, 55
Ingram, Francis senior xi, 41, 51,
    61, 62, 64, 83, 89, 224
Ingram, Francis junior 62
Ingram, William senior 42, 43, 72,
    83
Ingram, William junior 62

J
Jamaica 9, 13, 26, 27, 29, 30, 32, 33,
    34, 35, 36, 37, 39, 40, 41, 42, 45,
    47, 48, 50, 51, 52, 56, 57, 58, 59,
    60, 61, 63, 66, 69, 70, 71, 72, 77,
    78, 80, 84, 86, 105, 109, 111, 112,
    113, 114, 115, 117, 118, 119, 120,
    123, 142, 145, 188, 213, 219
Jebb, Rev. Dr John 132, 133

Jefferson, Thomas 140
Johnstone, Rev. Thomas xii, 3, 54,
    64, 72, 165, 185, 186, 194, 203,
    211, 213, 214, 215, 217, 218,
    219, 223

K
Kingston upon Hull 10, 28, 36, 37,
    67, 102, 103, 115, 122, 129, 136,
    137, 150, 151, 152, 167, 198,
    221, 224
Kingswood Chapel, Birmingham
    195
Kirlew, Ann 114, 115
Kirlew, George 114, 115
Kirlew, Henry 115
Kirlew, Joseph 115

L
Lang, Thomas 164, 165
Lascelles family 25, 55, 134, 206,
    207, 208, 224
Lascelles, Edward 25, 43
Leeds 7, 8, 11, 12, 14, 26, 28, 39, 44,
    45, 46, 47, 53, 56, 60, 66, 67,
    74, 77, 80, 81, 89, 101, 102, 150,
    152, 153, 154, 155, 156, 157,
    158, 159, 164, 166, 174, 178,
    179, 180, 186, 187, 207, 214,
    215, 216, 220, 227
Lewins Mead Chapel, Bristol 74,
    143
Liverpool 8, 10, 11, 13, 17, 20, 29,
    33, 34, 39, 41, 42, 43, 44, 51, 52,
    57, 62, 63, 64, 67, 69, 70, 71, 72,
    73, 74, 75, 76, 77, 78, 79, 80, 83,
    84, 85, 86, 89, 92, 110, 122, 141,
    142, 143, 155, 180, 189, 193,
    195, 207, 210, 224, 227
Lumb, Thomas 86, 147, 206, 209,
    214, 215, 223

M
Malton 1, 55, 91, 158
Manchester 8, 10, 11, 45, 47, 69, 72,
    73, 74, 82, 84, 87, 95, 122, 123,
    134, 139, 145, 146, 147, 155,
    159, 160, 164, 182, 186, 195,
    196, 213, 227
Mill Hill Chapel, Leeds 12, 28, 45,
    46, 47, 81, 135, 144, 156, 166,
    214, 216, 220
Milnes family 9, 11, 12, 46, 54, 56,
    67, 75, 77, 78, 81, 105, 109, 118,
    129, 132, 134, 135, 147, 214,
    215, 225
Milnes, Hannah 69, 84
Milnes, Hannah junior 78, 107, 135
Milnes, James senior 77, 81, 134, 186
Milnes, James junior 82, 85, 132,
    134, 167, 186, 218
Milnes, John (Jack) xii, 3, 57, 77, 79,
    85, 107, 121, 132, 134, 135, 136,
    146, 150, 167, 205, 206, 209,
    214, 223
Milnes, Mary Bridgette, Duchess
    of Galway 82, 105, 106, 108
Milnes, Pemberton (Pem) 46, 70,
    77, 80, 81, 86, 104, 106, 134,
    136, 149, 167, 195
Milnes, Rachel 3, 172
Milnes, Richard, 69, 73, 75, 76, 78,
    81, 82
Milnes, Richard (Dick) Slater 3, 4,
    26, 54, 55, 59, 77, 82, 132, 137,
    167, 168, 169, 170, 171, 172,
    173, 203, 215, 216, 224
Milnes, Sir Robert Shore 50, 54, 78,
    82, 91, 93, 94, 108
Montgomery, Rev. James 182, 198,
    199
Mosely Street Chapel, Manchester
    195

N

Naylor, Rev. Benjamin 182, 198, 199

Naylor, Rev. Dr Martin 79, 147, 211, 215, 217, 219

Newington Green Chapel, London 130, 131, 188

Northgate End Chapel, Halifax 42, 46, 135, 150, 151, 175, 207, 215, 221

O

Oates family 45, 46, 81

Oates, George 46

Oates, George Hibbert 45, 47, 96, 97, 113

Oates, George William 46, 47

Oates, Hibbert 47

Ogden family 43, 69, 71, 73, 75, 76, 79, 88, 135

P

Parke, Thomas 51, 61, 69

Pemberton family 71, 73, 75, 76, 80, 88

Pitt, William 136, 137, 167, 168, 170, 171, 179, 186, 187, 189, 192, 193, 194, 195, 198, 199, 201, 205, 208, 222, 226, 227, 228

Pontefract 7, 29, 43, 62, 93, 108, 170, 209, 220

Prescott, Captain Edward 71, 72

Prescott, Major Robert 72, 77, 86, 94, 107, 108

Price, Rev. Dr Richard 130, 131, 132, 139, 146

Priestley, Rev. Dr Joseph 129, 130, 135, 139, 140, 147, 156, 163, 168, 185, 193, 194

Q

Quakers 136, 153, 169, 170, 172, 180, 181, 227

R

Rathbone, William 143, 195

Reeves, John 191, 192, 194

Rockingham, Charles Watson Wentworth, Marquis of 28, 54, 55, 67, 70, 77, 81, 105, 106, 129, 158, 167

Roscoe, William 143, 195

Rotherham 81, 158, 159

S

Savage family 31, 32, 33

Sawyer, Betsy 119 120

Senhouse, William 162, 163

Sharp, Granville 128, 131, 132, 133, 135, 136, 139, 174

Sheffield 121, 122, 145, 159, 160, 161, 162, 168, 174, 181, 182, 183, 185, 193, 194, 196, 197, 198, 215

Shore family 78, 84, 145, 182, 198

Slater family 88

Slater, Dr Adam 80

Slater, Gill 72, 82, 83

Slater, Jane 80

Slater, Joyce 77, 80, 82, 167

Slater, Thomas 80, 82

Smith, Adam 127, 128, 129

Smith, William 132, 163, 195, 208

Staniforth, Thomas 41, 42, 51, 61, 62, 83, 224

St Giles Church, Pontefract 93, 109, 120, 121

St Saviourgate Chapel, York 134, 166, 168

sugar 9, 10, 12, 14, 15, 20, 56, 176, 180, 225

Swaby, Ruth 120

T

T. & W. Earle, 59, 61, 80, 84, 85
Tarleton family 78, 88
Tarleton, Banastre 81, 143
Tarleton, Edward 77
Tarleton, John 77, 78
Tarleton, Thomas 77, 78
tobacco 9, 10, 12, 13, 20, 24, 25, 42,
    51, 56, 60, 71, 75, 76, 105, 180,
    226
Tierney, George 118
Tierney, James 118
Tierney, Sabena Eleanor 118
Turner, Rev. William senior 3, 77,
    129, 130, 131, 135, 143, 151,
    158, 165, 186, 194, 214, 215,
    223
Turner, Rev. William junior 143,
    171

U

Upper Chapel, Sheffield 121, 122,
    159, 182

V

Vaughan, Benjamin 140, 142, 187,
    188, 203, 208

W

Wadeson, Robert 108, 109
Wakefield xi, xii, 1, 3, 7, 10, 11, 12, 14,
    20, 24, 26, 27, 31, 32, 33, 39, 41,
    42, 43, 46, 47, 53, 54, 56, 59, 60,
    61, 62, 65, 66, 67, 69, 70, 72, 73,
    75, 76, 77, 80, 81, 82, 84, 85, 88,
    89, 93, 94, 101, 104, 105, 106, 107,
    108, 109, 122, 129, 132, 143, 150,
    155, 157, 158, 159, 164, 165, 167,
    177, 185, 186 194, 195, 200, 205,
206, 207, 211, 212, 214, 215, 217,
    218, 219, 220, 221, 223, 224, 225
Wakefield, Rev. Gilbert 144, 188, 189
Walker, Rev. George 43, 122, 144
Walker, Thomas 84, 132, 139, 145,
    195, 196
Westgate Chapel, Wakefield xii, 3,
    46, 56, 64, 65, 66, 70, 77, 79, 81,
    82, 85, 86, 88, 94, 107, 129, 132,
    134, 165, 172, 175, 185, 186,
    194, 203, 212, 214, 215, 216,
    221, 223, 224
Wilberforce, William 26, 127, 129,
    133, 134, 136, 137, 139, 150,
    152, 154, 157, 158, 169, 172,
    173, 174, 175, 177, 179, 182,
    186, 187, 188, 189, 191, 200,
    203, 205, 206, 207, 208, 209,
    219, 224, 228
Wollstonecraft, Mary 131, 146
Wood, Rev. William 156, 157, 158,
    180
Wyvill, Rev. Christopher 55, 132,
    133, 134, 136, 171, 1493, 218
Wyvill, Marmaduke 216

Y

Yates family 29, 44, 142
Yates, Rev. John 141, 142, 143
York, City of 165, 166, 167, 168,
    169, 170, 172, 216, 224, 227
Yorke, Henry Redhead 121, 122,
    196, 197, 198
Yorke, John 58

Z

'Zong Massacre', the 135, 136
Zouch, Henry 81, 134
Zouch, Rev. Thomas 134